The A–Z of
NUTRITIONAL
HEALTH

The A–Z of NUTRITIONAL HEALTH

A guide to the relation between diet and health

ADRIENNE MAYES, PhD

Thorsons
An Imprint of HarperCollins*Publishers*

Thorsons
An Imprint of GraftonBooks
A Division of HarperCollins*Publishers*
77-85 Fulham Palace Road,
Hammersmith, London W6 8JB

This revised paperback published by
Thorsons 1991
First published 1986 as
The Dictionary of Nutritional Health

1 3 5 7 9 10 8 6 4 2

© 1986, 1991 Adrienne Mayes

A CIP catalogue record for this book
is available from the British Library

ISBN 0 7225 2476 5

Typeset by Harper Phototypesetters Ltd.,
Northampton, England
Printed in Great Britain by
Mackays of Chatham, Kent

ACKNOWLEDGEMENT
I wish to thank my husband, Dr Peter Mayes, for his invaluable
constructive criticism and scientific advice.

INTRODUCTION

While everyone appreciates that man must eat in order to live, not everyone realizes the far-reaching effects that eating the wrong sorts of food can have on health.

Food must supply not only energy for growth and movement, protein for muscles, and dietary fibre for roughage, but vitamins and minerals, which are substances required in the diet only in small amounts but vital for health. Some foods, such as fats, alcoholic beverages, confectionery and sugar, are very rich in energy but poor in vitamins, minerals and dietary fibre. However, in the present UK diet, fat and alcohol, two of the less desirable energy sources, together provide about the same amount of energy as the more desirable starchy carbohydrate, high-fibre foods. About half the fat, too, is in the form of saturated, mainly animal, fat.

In recent years it has become appreciated that diets high in fat, particularly saturated animal fat, are associated with increased risk of cardiovascular disease and certain forms of cancer. The incidence of cardiovascular disease in the UK is among the highest in the world, being the cause of death in 40 per cent of men and 38 per cent of women. High blood-pressure, a risk factor for cardiovascular disease, may be linked in some people with a high intake of sodium, which is present in the diet mainly as salt. The risks to health of a high intake of alcohol have long been known. A low intake of dietary fibre is suggested as contributing to the high incidence of many diseases prevalent in Western civilizations including constipation, bowel cancer, coronary heart disease, diverticulitis, piles, gallstones and varicose veins.

The growing realization that the average diet in the UK is not healthy has led health and nutrition authorities to issue proposals for educating consumers, food processors and manufacturers on how to improve the diet. Many of the changes recommended are aimed at reducing the risk of cardiovascular disease.

Broadly the recommendations are to reduce consumption of *all* fat, but

7

particularly of saturated fat, to increase consumption of fibre-rich, starchy carbohydrate foods such as bread, cereals, fruit and vegetables, and to cut down on high alcohol and salt intakes. Such a diet, if varied and composed of a little of many foods and not too much of any one food, when properly prepared from fresh ingredients and consumed in amounts sufficient to supply the appropriate energy intake, will automatically provide enough vitamins and minerals for all except perhaps a small minority who may have special requirements.

Eating habits are formed early in life and are difficult to change, but once the need for change is appreciated and the initial effort made, the new diet usually becomes the normal and preferred diet within a few weeks. The change is made easier if the reasons for it are understood. The present flood of information on nutrition in relation to health provided by the media should help, but to the non-scientist this can be confusing and bewildering and often appears contradictory. This dictionary and guide has been written to provide an explanation of these current ideas and the terminology used, in simple but scientifically accurate terms.

EXPLANATORY NOTES

1 gram (g)   =   1000 milligrams (mg)
1 milligram =   1000 micrograms (μg)
100 grams is approximately 3.5 ounces (oz)
1 kilocalorie (kcal, Cal)   =   approximately 4200 joules (J)
                                  or 4.2 kilojoules (kJ)

Like all dictionaries, this one is for use primarily as a reference book. However, it can also be used by those interested in discovering the connection between nutrition and health. For this purpose it is suggested that the following eight entries are read first: *food groups, energy, carbohydrates, proteins, fats, fibre, vitamins* and *minerals*. This will form a foundation from which to explore further, for example into the connections between dietary fats, blood cholesterol, polyunsaturated fatty acids and coronary heart disease.

The following conventions are used in this book:

1.   The nutrient content given is always of uncooked foods and lean, raw meat and poultry unless otherwise stated. Due regard must therefore be paid to the losses incurred in cooking, etc., in assessing their contribution to the diet.

2.   Distribution of a nutrient in a range of foods is given rather than just rich sources, since it is also useful to know which foods are poor sources. In addition, even moderate sources may make a significant contribution to the daily intake if a large amount of that food is normally eaten.

3.   Where a food is described as providing niacin, the figure given includes the contribution by tryptophan. When described as nicotinic acid, the tryptophan contribution is not included.

4.   When a subject or substance is known by several names, it is described only under its best known one, entries under the other names referring the reader to the main entry.

A

absorption, transfer of nutrients derived from digested foodstuffs from the intestinal lumen into the mucosal epithelium of the intestinal wall. Most are absorbed in the jejunum except for vitamin B_{12}, bile salts, some electrolytes and water, which are absorbed in the ileum. Most water is absorbed in the colon.

Carbohydrates are absorbed as monosaccharides both by an active transport system against the concentration gradient (an energy-requiring process) and by passive diffusion. Fructose is absorbed more slowly than glucose and galactose. After absorption they are transported in the blood of the hepatic-portal vein to the liver.

Lipids are absorbed as fatty acids, monoglycerides, lysophospholipids and cholesterol. In the mucosal cells, triglycerides and phospholipids are reformed and with cholesterol and proteins, form chylomicrons. These pass into the lymph vessels and join the blood in the neck via the thoracic duct. Fatty acids with chains shorter than 10-12 carbons, and free glycerol pass into the blood in the hepatic-portal vein.

Proteins are absorbed mainly as amino acids and di- and tripeptides. The peptides are split into amino acids in the epithelial cells. Amino acids in the naturally occurring L form are absorbed by an active transport system (requiring energy), but the synthetic D form only by slower passive diffusion. After absorption they pass into the hepatic-portal vein. Everybody appears to absorb some molecules of protein whole. This can cause food allergy in some people.

Nucleic acids are absorbed as nucleosides or free purine and pyrimidine bases and ribose or deoxyribose sugars and pass to the liver in the hepatic-portal vein.

---

acacia, gum acacia or gum arabic. Air-dried gummy exudate from *Acacia senegal*. A complex polysaccharide and dietary fibre. Dissolves in water forming a mucilage. Used as a thickener, emulsifier and stabilizer in sweets, etc., and in lozenges and pastilles for its soothing and protecting effect.

acarbose, a bacterial oligosaccharide. Potent enzyme inhibitor, e.g., of pancreatic amylase, sucrase and maltase.

acesulfame potassium, acesulfame K., *see* intense sweetener.

acetic acid, a simple fatty acid. Formed by fermenting ethyl alcohol. Present in vinegar that thereby can be used to preserve or pickle foods. One of the volatile fatty acids formed during colonic fermentation of dietary fibre.

acetoacetic acid and acetone, ketone bodies, *see* ketosis.

acetyl CoA, acetyl derivative of coenzyme A. Common high-energy product formed by the metabolic breakdown of carbohydrates, fats and several amino acids. Its energy is released by oxidation in the Krebs cycle.

acetylcholine, a neurotransmitter derived from choline. Appears to be involved in the pathogenesis of Parkinson's disease and Alzheimer's disease.

achlorhydria, failure to produce hydrochloric acid in the stomach. Seen in the elderly, in pernicious anaemia due to vitamin B_{12} deficiency and in cancer of the stomach.

acids, substances that release hydrogen ions when dissolved in water. The physiologically important ones include hydrochloric acid present in gastric juices, fatty acids, ketone bodies, and amino acids. Acids may be used as food additives to give a sour taste or acidity for technical purposes, e.g., citric acid, or to preserve food, e.g., vinegar.

acne vulgaris, skin disease common in teenagers. Often attributed to excessive consumption of confectionery, though there is no evidence that dietary factors are responsible.

actin, a protein that is linked with myosin (*which see*) in resting muscle.

---

acute, short and may be severe; not long-drawn-out or chronic.

---

adaptogens, anti-stress compounds (ginsenosides) found in ginsengs.

---

additives, chemicals added during the processing of foods to help preserve them, to assist in their manufacture, and to improve their appearance and palatability. With the exception of flavourings, only additives permitted by law may be added to foods. (For a list of the names and serial numbers of permitted additives, *see* serial numbers of additives.)

Additives are used as acids, anti-caking agents, anti-foaming agents, antioxidants, bleaching agents, colours, emulsifiers, flavour enhancers, flavourings, flour improvers, humectants, preservatives, sequestrants, stabilizers, sweeteners, thickeners.

Micronutrients — though not really additives, being normal food components — are sometimes added to restore those lost in food processing (e.g., vitamin C added to dehydrated potato powder; thiamin, niacin and iron added to white flour) or added to enrich a food (e.g., vitamins A and D added to margarine; calcium added to white flour).

---

adenine, a purine found in RNA, DNA, ATP, NAD, NADP and flavoproteins.

---

adenosine triphosphate, *see* ATP.

---

adenosylcobalamin, coenzyme form of vitamin B_{12}.

---

adipocyte, fat storage cell.

---

adipose tissue, body fat deposits. Cells (adipocytes) contain a single large droplet of triglycerides. Acts as energy store constantly being turned over; as body insulation; and as protective cushioning for body organs. Contains 80-85 per cent fat, 2 per cent protein and 10 per cent water. A healthy man contains 8-15kg and a woman 10-20kg.

adolescent nutrition,   is mainly concerned with increased food energy requirement during the adolescent growth spurt. Those with food fads may be at risk of nutrient deficiencies, and a vitamin D supplement may be advisable during winter. Age of greatest susceptibility to anorexia nervosa. Menstruating girls may require an iron supplement.

adrenaline,   a catecholamine (*which see*). Raises: (1) blood-pressure; (2) blood glucose levels (nervous system fuel) by stimulating liver glycogen breakdown and gluconeogenesis, and decreasing insulin release and glucose uptake by the muscles; (3) blood free fatty acids (muscle fuel) by stimulating triglyceride breakdown in adipose tissue. These effects make it and the other catecholamines major elements in the 'fight or flight' response to acute stress.

aerobic,   takes place in the presence of oxygen, e.g. the oxidation of fat in the tissues for the release of its energy.

aflatoxin,   toxin produced by moulds (fungi), e.g., *Aspergillus flavus*, growing on nuts, peanuts and grains stored in warm, damp conditions. Causes liver diseases, including cancer.

agar,   also known as agar-agar, Macassar gum, vegetable gelatin, and Bengal/Japan/Ceylon/Chinese isinglass. Extract of red seaweeds especially *Gelidium* and *Gracilaria*. A polysaccharide of galactose. A dietary fibre, slightly soluble in cold water, soluble in hot water, swelling and forming a stiff jelly on cooling. Used as a substitute for gelatin, as a thickening agent in foods (confectionery, dairy products), in meat canning, as a stabilizer for emulsions, and as a disintegrating agent and binder for tablets. A cathartic that in large amounts, can cause flatulence, distension and intestinal obstruction.

alanine,   name commonly used for alpha-alanine, a non-essential amino acid found in most proteins. Key role in transamination, the transport of amino groups to the liver for excretion as urea; and in gluconeogenesis.
   Beta-alanine is a constituent of coenzyme A and pantothenic acid.

albumin, albumen, major protein of plasma. Soluble, globular, digestible. Synthesized in the liver. Chiefly responsible for maintaining intravascular colloid osmotic pressure. Consequently a major effect of low albumin concentrations (hypoalbuminaemia), seen in liver and kidney diseases and in protein deficiency (e.g., kwashiorkor), is oedema of the soft tissues. Also acts as carrier for bilirubin, fatty acids, trace elements and many drugs.

---

alcohol, formed by the fermentation of sugar and is known chemically as ethanol or ethyl alcohol. It is intermediate between carbohydrate and fat in energy content and spares them isocalorically. It is readily absorbed from the stomach and intestines into the blood, from which it is removed only by the liver at a fixed rate, varying greatly between individuals. The liver oxidizes it to acetaldehyde, which is converted to acetyl CoA and used for energy production, fatty acid synthesis, etc.

Blood clearance About two double whiskys or nearly two pints of beer provide 30g alcohol, which raises the alcohol level in the blood of a 65kg man or 55kg woman to about 75mg or 95mg/dl respectively. This is sufficient to impair judgement and possibly produce signs of intoxication and takes, on average, over four hours to clear from the blood. Neither exercise, caffeine, nor any other substance tested, apart from fructose, has been found to speed this up. Most people are drunk with blood levels of 150mg/dl or more. Chronic high levels of alcohol ingestion frequently lead to addiction and to liver diseases and cirrhosis of the liver.

Approximate alcohol content of beverages: as g per 100ml or 3½ fl oz: beers, 3; wines, 10; fortified wines, 15; spirits, 30.

'Unit of alcohol' A standard glass of sherry or fortified wine, a standard goblet of table wine, half a pint of beer or cider, a quarter pint of strong lager, a single measure of spirits — each provide one unit of alcohol.

Recommendations On average, alcohol contributes 6 per cent of total energy intake, double that of the 1950s. Epidemiological evidence shows that there is a level of intake above which there is increased risk of addiction. The Royal College of Psychiatrists' report recommends that intake of alcohol should not exceed 21 units per week for men and 14 for women. There should be one or two alcohol-free days a week. The recommendations for women are lower because for a given intake of alcohol, levels in the blood are higher in women than in men, even allowing for their smaller size, and women are more susceptible to alcoholic liver disease. Women's greater susceptibility may be because the level of the alcohol oxidizing enzyme, alcohol dehydrogenase, in the lining of the stomach of women is lower than in men, allowing a greater proportion of imbibed alcohol to reach the liver.

Epidemiological evidence on the effect of alcohol on mortality indicates that intake of a little alcohol is more beneficial than none. Consequently the NACNE report recommends that heavier drinkers, rather than all drinkers, reduce consumption, and that alcohol's contribution to total energy intake should be reduced to 5 per cent within five years, and within 15 years should not exceed 4 per cent (i.e., 20g alcohol daily or less than one pint of beer).

Nutritional value Alcoholic beverages provide only 'empty calories' since (apart from some wines, which may contain considerable amounts of iron, such as Médoc (1.3mg per 100ml) and some cheap wines (up to 3.0mg per 100ml), they contain few micronutrients.

Food intake is often reduced in heavy drinkers and alcoholics who may become malnourished and exhibit deficiencies of one or more nutrients, particularly protein, thiamin, niacin, vitamin B_6, folic acid, vitamins A, C and D, magnesium, potassium and zinc.

Hangovers Associated with alcohol are cogeners — higher alcohols, fusel oil, etc. — present in much larger amounts in some drinks than others, and responsible for much of the discomfort of a hangover. Most distressing are those after brandy, followed by red wine, rum, whisky, white wine and gin, whereas after vodka or pure alcohol only tiredness and thirst are experienced. French wines contain variable amounts of histamine (0.1mg/l in champagne to 30mg/l in some burgundies) that may contribute to after-effects of cheap wine.

Associated diseases Alcoholism (addiction); liver diseases and cirrhosis of the liver; diseases of malnutrition due to inadequate food intakes, impaired absorption and/or metabolism. Risk factor for certain cancers (oral cavity, pharynx, oesophagus, larynx). Intake levels correlate positively with blood-pressure. Ingestion during pregnancy may cause fatal malformations and reduced birth weight.

---

ale, *see* beer.

---

aleurone layer, *see* flours, wheat.

---

alfalfa, legume with grass-like taste grown for forage. Rich in protein, calcium, trace minerals, carotene, vitamins E and K, all the water-soluble vitamins, and vitamin D if sun-cured. Small amounts of its dried, ground leaves are used in food supplements. *See also* sprouting of seeds.

algae, simple, mainly aquatic plants. Many are seaweeds, e.g., kelp. Some are cultivated as food sources, e.g., Spirulina, Chlorella, Dunaliella.

alginates, salts of alginic acid, a polysaccharide of mannuronic and guluronic acids obtained from brown seaweeds (e.g., kelp). A dietary fibre. Used as thickening agents and stabilizers in foods, especially salad dressings, dairy products (e.g., whipped cream), as a foam stabilizer in beer, and as binders and disintegrants in tablets.

alimentary canal, continuous tube extending from mouth to anus concerned with processing foodstuffs into forms suitable for absorption into the body, and elimination of waste materials. Comprises oral cavity, oesophagus, stomach, small and large intestines.

allantoin, end-product of purine metabolism in mammals other than man and the higher apes. Formed from uric acid by uricase.

allergen, an antigen involved in an allergic reaction.

allergy, *see* immune system; food allergy.

almonds, nuts providing (per 100g): energy, 565kcal; (g) protein, 16.9; fat, 53.5; total dietary fibre, 14.3; (mg) potassium, 860; iron, 4.2; vitamin E, 20.0. Oleic acid (monounsaturate) forms 71 per cent of total fatty acids.

alpha-amino acids, amino acids in which the acid and amino groups are attached to the same carbon atom, e.g., those occurring in proteins.

alpha-linolenic acid, a polyunsaturated fatty acid of the omega 3 family with 18 carbons and three unsaturated bonds (C18:3 n-3). Probably an essential fatty acid.
  Distribution in foods (as percentage of total fatty acids): linseed oil, over 50; rape-seed oil (high and low erucic acid varieties), 10.5 and 10.0; soya bean oil, 7; corn oil, 1.6; butter, cream and milk, 1.

aluminium,   does not appear to be an essential element for man. A 70kg man contains about 61mg. Europeans and Americans consume between 2 and 160mg daily from naturally occurring sources in foods especially vegetables, from food additives and from foil, cook-ware and containers. Tea may supply 2 to 3mg daily, but its absorption is probably prevented by the tannins and fluoride present. Antacid medicines contribute more. Although most is excreted in the faeces, there is concern that high intakes may be a health hazard in that aluminium may increase the permeability of the brain to undesirable substances and perhaps be concerned in the aetiology of senile dementia (Alzheimer's disease).

---

amenorrhoea,   absence of menstrual blood flow. May be primary when menstruation has never taken place, or secondary when it ceases after having become established. Seen in many female athletes.

---

amino acid, limiting,   is the most deficient essential amino acid in a protein relative to the composition of standard egg or milk protein, which are of high biological value. Tryptophan and lysine are limiting amino acids in maize, lysine in wheat and sulphur amino acids in beef, vegetables and soya beans.

Two proteins, each with a different limiting amino acid consumed simultaneously, make up for the other's deficiency. Such complementary proteins of plant origin form the basis of vegetarian and vegan diets.

---

amino acid score,   another term for chemical score (*which see*).

---

amino acids,   organic molecules containing both an acid group (usually -COOH) and an amino group ($-NH_2$). In most, both groups are attached to the same carbon atom (alpha-amino acids) and these include the 20 present in proteins as well as important biological intermediates like dopa and ornithine, and hormones like thyroxine. Biologically important amino acids in which the groups are attached to different carbon atoms include taurine, beta-alanine and gamma-aminobutyric acid.

Amino acids linked by peptide bonds form peptides. When ten or more are linked they are called polypeptides. Very large polypeptides are proteins.

Of the 20 amino acids occurring in proteins, eight are nutritionally essential, the rest being nutritionally non-essential. The naturally occurring isomer of amino acids in proteins is the L- form, e.g., L-alpha-alanine. (*See also* proteins.)

amino acids, acidic,   amino acids with a side chain also containing an acidic group, e.g., aspartic and glutamic acids.

---

amino acids, basic,   amino acids with a side chain also containing a basic group, e.g., arginine, lysine and histidine.

---

amino acids, branched chain,   amino acids with a branched side chain, e.g., valine, leucine and isoleucine.

---

amino acids, essential,   are the eight required for growth and body maintenance that have to be supplied as such in the diet because the body cannot make them. They are therefore nutritionally essential and are isoleucine, leucine, lysine, methionine, phenylalanine, threonine, tryptophan and valine. Histidine is essential for children and possibly for adults. The amounts required to maintain nitrogen balance in adults and children are shown in Table 1.

Table 1: Estimated requirements of essential amino acids (mg/kg/day)

Amino acid	Infants	Boys (10-12 yrs)	Adults
histidine	28	?	8-12
isoleucine	70	30	10
leucine	161	45	14
lysine	103	60	12
methionine + cystine	58	27	13
phenylalanine + tyrosine	125	27	14
threonine	87	35	7
tryptophan	17	4	3.5
valine	93	33	10

(FAO/WHO, 1983)

Cystine and tyrosine are included because they spare methionine and phenylalanine respectively to some extent.

---

amino acids, glucogenic,   those that, after losing their amino group, usually by transamination, give rise to metabolic intermediates which form glucose. They are alanine, arginine, aspartic acid, cysteine, glutamic acid, glycine, histidine, hydroxyproline, methionine, proline, serine, threonine, and valine. Some, e.g., phenylalanine and tyrosine, are both glucogenic and ketogenic.

---

amino acids, glycogenic,   glucogenic amino acids.

---

amino acids, ketogenic,   those that, after losing their amino group, usually by transamination, give rise to ketone bodies. Only one, leucine, is solely ketogenic, others, e.g., phenylalanine and tyrosine, being both ketogenic and glucogenic.

---

amino acids, large neutral,   have comparatively large but neutral molecules and share a common transport mechanism through the blood-brain barrier and so compete for entry into the brain. They are leucine, isoleucine, phenylalanine, tyrosine, tryptophan and valine.

---

amino acids, non-essential,   are the 12 present in body proteins that the body can synthesize itself and so are not required in the diet. They are therefore nutritionally non-essential, though vital to body proteins and metabolism. They are alanine, aspartic acid, arginine, cysteine, glutamic acid, glycine, histidine, hydroxyproline, proline, serine and tyrosine. Cysteine can spare methionine, and tyrosine can spare phenylalanine in their roles as essential amino acids. Histidine is essential for children and possibly for adults.

---

amino acids, sulphur,   cysteine, cystine, methionine and taurine.

---

aminopeptidases,   enzymes concerned with digestion of polypeptides. Present in intestinal digestive juices.

---

amygdalin,   *see* laetrile.

---

amylases,   starch- and glycogen-digesting enzymes forming oligosaccharides, maltotriose and maltose. Of salivary and pancreatic amylases present in saliva and pancreatic juices respectively, only the latter is physiologically important, the former quickly becoming inactivated by stomach acid.

---

amylopectin, the main and more easily digested constituent of starch (*which see*).

---

amylose, the minor and less easily digested constituent of starch (*which see*).

---

anabolism, that part of metabolism concerned with building up tissues.

---

anaemias, disorders caused by a defect in the number and/or quality of the red blood cells leading to deficient oxygen-carrying capacity of the blood (e.g., low haemoglobin levels). May be caused by a deficiency in one or more of the nutrients required in red blood cell formation or by deficiency of vitamin A or by haemorrhage or by increased destruction of red blood cells (haemolysis).

Symptoms may include pallor, easy fatigue, breathlessness on exertion, giddiness, palpitation and loss of appetite.

Hypochromic anaemia is characterized by decreased haemoglobin in red blood cells.

Haemolytic anaemia is characterized by excessive destruction of red blood cells, e.g., in favism.

Iron-deficiency anaemia is the commonest type of hypochromic and nutritional anaemia. Due to insufficiency of iron because of inadequate intake, impaired absorption, excessive blood loss, or increased requirements (e.g., pregnancy).

Macrocytic anaemia is seen in vitamin B_{12} and folic acid deficiencies. Characterized by reduced numbers of abnormally large, malformed red blood cells.

Nutritional anaemia is caused by insufficient intake of nutrient(s) required in red blood cell formation, most commonly iron, folic acid or vitamin B_{12}, but also protein, vitamins C, E and B_6 and copper.

Pernicious anaemia is macrocytic anaemia caused by failure to absorb vitamin B_{12}, often due to absence of intrinsic factor.

Sports anaemia — *see* athletes.

anaerobic, takes place in the absence of oxygen, e.g., fermentation of dietary fibre in the large intestine.

anaphylaxis, an allergic reaction in response to challenge by antigen such as a particular food protein to which the subject has become sensitive. Symptoms may be gastrointestinal (vomiting; diarrhoea, e.g., reaction to gluten) and/or general (eczema; oedema; urticaria; asthma, e.g., reaction to eggs, strawberries, shellfish).

aneurin(e), *see* thiamin.

angina pectoris, pain in the chest that may radiate to the arm, brought on by a spasm or narrowing of the coronary arteries causing myocardial ischaemia. Attack often induced by exercise or stress.

anion, negatively charged ion.

anorexia, loss or deficiency of appetite for food.

anorexia nervosa, a psychiatric disease arising from the refusal to eat, often leading to severe emaciation through semi-starvation. Patients, usually middle-class, intelligent adolescent or young women, are morbidly afraid of becoming fat. Characteristically they subsist on a 1000 kcal daily diet of fruit, vegetables, cheese or yogurt and black coffee. May alternate with bulimia nervosa (*which see*).

anthropometric measurements, body measurements, e.g., height, weight, fat and muscle content.

antibody, an immunoglobulin protein produced by white blood cells in response to invasion of the body by a foreign substance (antigen), which forms an antibody-antigen complex. *See* immune system.

anti-caking agents, additives used in foods to help them flow freely, e.g., icing sugar.

---

anti-foaming agents, additives used in food processing to prevent excessive frothing on boiling or boiling over in food processing.

---

antigen, a substance foreign to the body that causes the immune system to produce an antibody forming an antigen/antibody complex. *See* immune system.

---

anti-grey-hair factor, para-aminobenzoic acid (*which see*).

---

anti-haemorrhagic vitamin, *see* vitamin K.

---

anti-infective vitamin, *see* vitamin A.

---

anti-neuritic vitamin, *see* thiamin.

---

antinutrients, substances in food that inhibit proper utilization of its nutrients by interfering with their digestion and/or absorption. Include enzyme inhibitors, phytates, lectins, tannins, saponins, etc.

---

antioxidants, prevent or retard the oxidation of fats and oils that leads to rancidity. Vitamins E and C are antioxidants permitted to be added to any food. Others like gallic acid or butylated hydroxyanisole (BHA) or butylated hydroxytoluene (BHT) are permitted only in certain foods, such as the fats used for making cakes. *See* additives.

Vitamins C and E, beta-carotene and the enzymes glutathione peroxidase and superoxide dismutase are among substances in the body that have protective antioxidant functions, including preventing the formation of, or scavenging, free radicals (*which see*), highly reactive molecules that, in excess, can cause cell damage.

anti-pernicious anaemia vitamin, *see* vitamin B_{12}.

---

anti-rachitic vitamin, *see* vitamin D.

---

anti-sterility vitamin, *see* vitamin E.

---

antivitamins, substances that prevent the absorption of vitamins or destroy them in the gut, e.g., thiaminase, an enzyme in raw fish which destroys thiamin and may cause a deficiency in animals (e.g., cats) fed too much. No such effect of thiaminase has been seen in man.

---

apatite, the chief mineral of tooth enamel, a crystalline form of calcium phosphate.

---

apoenzyme, the protein part of an enzyme that is inactive without its coenzyme or prosthetic group.

---

apoproteins, proteins that combine with lipids, forming lipoproteins, the form in which lipids (cholesterol and fat) are transported in the blood.

---

appetite, desire for food. Evoked by hunger and the taste and smell of certain foods. Its control by the brain may be a balance between hunger and satiety signals or simply the presence or absence of a satiety signal. Mechanisms producing signals may include: blood glucose, free fatty acid and amino acid levels; brain levels of certain amino acids (e.g., glycine) and their neurotransmitter derivatives (e.g., noradrenalin, serotonin, histamine and GABA); distention of gastrointestinal tract by food; hunger contractions by empty stomach; secretion of gastrointestinal and other hormones in response to food in the gut that may inhibit further intake; environmental temperature, cold stimulating and heat depressing; and in the longer term, energy output and level of energy (adipose tissue) stores. Net effect of regulation in normal adult is to adjust energy intake to output and so maintain body weight constant.

apthous ulcer, *see* ulcer, apthous.

---

araban, a polymer of arabinose, a pentose. Constituent of pectin.

---

arabinose, pentose monosaccharide. Found in gum arabic (from acacia) and in plum and cherry gums.

---

arachidonic acid, a polyunsaturated fatty acid of the omega 6 family, with 20 carbons and four unsaturated bonds (C20:4 n-6). Can be formed in the human body and in most animals from dietary linoleic acid, but is an essential fatty acid for some animals like the cat, which cannot carry out the conversion. Vital role as immediate precursor of prostanoids (Series 2) and leukotrienes (Series 4) (*see* Figure 2, page 79), and structurally as constituent of cell membranes. Seldom found in vegetable oils.

Distribution in foods (as percentage of total fatty acids): liver, 5.1–14.3; kidney, 2.6–7.1; cod, 3.9; beef, 1.0; eggs, 0.8.

---

arginine, a non-essential basic amino acid. May be partly essential in children. Participates in the urea cycle (*which see*).

---

arrhythmia, of the heart, describes any deviation from the normal rhythm.

---

arrowroot, starchy root or tuber of *Maranta arundinacea* grown in West Indies. Almost pure starch, being virtually devoid of protein (0.2g per 100g), vitamins or minerals.

---

arsenic, may be an essential element for man, but its biological role is unknown. Highly toxic substance, particularly in its inorganic forms compared with the naturally occurring organic forms. Total daily UK dietary intake averages 89μg, two-thirds from fish and shellfish in which it occurs in the organic form. Less than 30μg of the daily intake is in the inorganic form. FAO/WHO recommended tolerable daily intake for inorganic arsenic is 2μg/kg body weight.

arteriosclerosis, 'hardening' of the arteries. Degenerative change associated with ageing and usually with some degree of atherosclerosis (*which see*).

---

arthritis, rheumatoid, a disease principally affecting the synovial membrane lining the socket of the joints which becomes inflamed and thickened. Muscular stiffness is followed by pain and swelling of many joints. Appears to be an auto-immune disease as a characteristic antibody is present in the plasma. Some cases have been suggested as being caused by food allergies. During the active stage of the disease, the patient usually suffers fever, malaise and anorexia and is frequently anaemic. Marked clinical improvement is often associated with improved nutrition. *See also* osteoarthritis.

---

ascorbic acid, *see* vitamin C.

---

asparagine, the amide of aspartic acid. In plants acts as a store of ammonia for use in amino-acid synthesis during growth.

---

aspartame, a permitted intense sweetener (*which see*) without a bitter aftertaste. A synthetic dipeptide of aspartic acid and the methyl ester of phenylalanine. Unsuitable for use by sufferers from phenylketonuria.

---

aspartic acid, a non-essential acidic amino acid.

Aspergillus, mould. *A. flavus* grows on nuts and grains producing aflatoxin B_1, a toxin that can cause liver cancer. *A. parasiticus* grows on cereals, potatoes and onions producing aflatoxin.

---

assimilation, the process by which digested foodstuffs are absorbed and utilized by the tissues for the production of energy and for growth and repair.

---

ataxia, inability to co-ordinate movement, e.g., in multiple sclerosis and vitamin B_{12} deficiency.

atheroma, soft plaque found in artery walls of sufferers from athero-sclerosis.

---

atherosclerosis thickenings or plaques in artery walls composed of lipids (e.g., cholesteryl esters and cholesterol), complex carbohydrates, blood and blood products, fibrous tissue and calcium deposits. Commences in most adolescents with formation of fatty streaks that develop into raised lesions or plaques. Soft plaques, or, atheroma, unlike hard or fibrous plaques, do not contain much fibrous tissue. Plaques narrow the lumen of the artery. Their roughened surface may cause platelet aggregation and formation of a blood clot that can become incorporated into the plaque or completely block the vessel. Advanced plaques may be calcified.

---

athletes, in training have increased requirements for energy foods, protein, thiamin and possibly riboflavin and vitamins C and E. Since about 12 per cent of the energy in a mixed diet is from protein, increased food intake sufficient to supply the higher energy needs simultaneously provides the extra protein required. However, many in training choose protein and carbohydrate supplements to avoid the bulk of high-energy but low-fat foods.

For endurance sports, higher muscle glycogen levels are induced by high carbohydrate diets after depletion by exercising tc exhaustion. Pre-exercise glucose ingestion may actually hasten fatigue onset, but dilute (5 per cent) glucose drinks during prolonged exercise may delay hypoglycaemia and fatigue. The efficacy of bee pollen, wheatgerm oil and ginseng supplements, traditionally used to increase energy output, is unproven. There is some evidence to suggest that a supplement of carnitine (2g) may improve physical endurance, possibly by increasing lipid turnover and hence conserving muscle glycogen.

Iron deficiency and sports anaemia leading, in women, to secondary amenorrhoea, are common though their cause is uncertain — increased destruction of red blood cells and gastro-intestinal bleeding being two suggested mechanisms. An iron supplement may be indicated.

---

atom, the smallest particle of an element that can exist alone or in combination with one or more atoms of the same or another element.

---

atomic weight, of an element relates its weight (or mass) to that of the reference element, carbon, which is 12. (*See* Table 14, page 294 for atomic weights.)

ATP,   adenosine triphosphate. The most important immediate source of energy for cell metabolism. Contains high energy phosphate bonds. Formed from adenosine diphosphate (ADP) and inorganic phosphate using energy derived from oxidation of fuels such as glucose and free fatty acids.

---

attention deficit disorder,   hyperactivity and disturbed behaviour in children, in some of whom it appears to be attributable to sensitivity to certain food additives (e.g., azo-dye colours, benzoate preservatives), natural food constituents such as salicylates, or to food allergies. *See* Feingold diet.

---

avidin,   protein in egg white that, until denatured by cooking, combines with biotin preventing its absorption.

---

avocado pear,   unusual among fruits in that it has a high fat content and is therefore a source of energy. Fat mainly monounsaturated. Provides (per 100g: energy, 223 kcal; (g) fat, 22.2; protein, 4.2; carbohydrate, 1.8; (mg) potassium, 400; vitamin B_6, 0.42.

B

B complex vitamins,   a group of water soluble vitamins often found associated together in foodstuffs such as liver, wholegrain cereals, pulses, green vegetables and dairy products. The richest sources are dried brewer's yeast and yeast extract, but these are usually consumed only in supplements or in nutritionally insignificant quantities. The vitamins comprise thiamin, riboflavin, niacin, vitamin B_6 and B_{12}, pantothenic and folic acids and biotin. They form coenzymes or prosthetic groups for many vital metabolic reactions that make them essential for life, growth, heart function and health of the skin, nervous and digestive systems. A dietary deficiency of one is likely to be accompanied by a dietary deficiency of them all. A high intake of one may cause a relative deficiency of the others. Moderate dietary excesses are excreted harmlessly in the urine.

Associated with these vitamins in foods are substances such as choline, inositol, para-aminobenzoic acid and orotic acid, frequently called B complex factors, that are not vitamins for man.

B$_{15}$, *see* pangamic acid.

B$_{17}$, *see* laetrile.

Bacillus cereus, a bacterium that produces toxic food poisoning by releasing toxins (exotoxins) into food before it is eaten. An aerobe that produces spores often found in cereals, especially rice, cornflour and spices. Spores survive light cooking and multiply rapidly unless refrigerated. Foods commonly affected are rice, cornflour and meat products. Main symptoms, which appear in 2-15 hours and last 6-24 hours, are vomiting, abdominal pains and diarrhoea.

---

bacteria, single-celled microscopic organisms found almost everywhere. May be harmful to man, e.g., causing food poisoning, or helpful, e.g., carrying out fermentation of undigested foodstuffs in the colon.

---

baking, *see* dry heat cooking.

---

balance, a person is nutritionally in balance as regards energy, protein, vitamins and minerals, if dietary intake equals output or excretion. A person is in positive balance if intake exceeds output and in negative balance if output exceeds intake. *See* nitrogen balance.

---

banana, a fruit that, because of its high carbohydrate content compared with most fruits, can act as an energy source.

Provides (per 100g): energy, 79 kcal; (g) carbohydrate, 19; protein, 1.1; fat, 0.3; water, 70.7; (mg) vitamin B$_6$, 0.5. *See* dyspepsia.

---

basal metabolic rate (BMR), is the energy required when lying completely at rest for the activity of the internal organs and to maintain body temperature. It is expressed as energy expenditure per square metre of body surface (calculated from weight and height). Expressed in this way BMR is greater for men than women, but expressed per kg lean tissue the sex difference disappears because women are fatter than men. The BMR is high in actively growing young children, falls rapidly to age 12, and then declines slowly throughout life. The BMR of people in cold climates is usually about 10 per cent higher than of those in the tropics.

base, chemically, a substance that combines with an acid to form a salt.

beans, pulses. Include:
aduki, small sweet red bean used in puddings and savoury foods.
broad, ripe seed of *Vicia faba*. Contains toxins that cause favism in certain people.
butter, seed of *Phaseolus lunatus*.
French, unripe seed of *Phaseolus vulgaris*, the *kidney bean*, eaten in the green pod.
haricot, ripe seed of *Phaseolus vulgaris*, the *kidney bean*. Used for making baked beans. The pulse most likely to cause flatulence.
locust, seed of *Ceratonia siliqua*.
mung, green gram. Used for their sprouts.
runner, seed of *Phaseolus multiflorus*. Always eaten unripe in the green pod.
scarlet runner, seed of *Phaseolus coccineus*. Always eaten sliced in the green pod.

beef, ox, bull or cow meat. Lean beef provides (per 100g): energy, 123 kcal; (g) water, 74.0; protein, 20.3; fat, 4.6; (mg) iron, 2.1; zinc, 4.3; thiamin. 0.07; riboflavin, 0.24; niacin, 9.5; vitamin B_6, 0.32; (μg) vitamin B_{12}, 2.0.

beer, ale or stout, alcoholic beverages, the best being brewed from malted barley, but also by fermenting maize, millets or rice with wild yeasts. Barley is sprouted, activating the enzyme diastase that begins the splitting of starch in the grains. This activity is stopped by heating (malting). The dried malt is ground and mixed with water to produce the mash. The fluid from the mash is called the wort, and it is boiled to kill enzyme activity. Hops are added during boiling (or synthetic chemicals identical to those present in hops) to give the bitter flavour. The cooled wort is then fermented with yeast, British-type ales at between 15-20°C with *Saccharomyces cerevisiae*, the yeast rising to the top, and lagers at lower temperatures with *S. carlsbergensis*, the yeast sinking to the bottom. Clearing agents (gelatin, isinglass or tannin) are generally added.

Most provide (per 100g): energy, 30–60 kcal; (g) alcohol, 3.7; and small amounts of nicotinic acid and riboflavin. A pint of ordinary beer provides 17g alcohol and 170 kcal.

---

beriberi, thiamin deficiency disease. Formerly widespread among the polished rice-eating people of the East where occasional outbreaks still occur. Also seen world-wide in those with high alcohol intakes and those on carbohydrate-rich/thiamin-poor diets. Three forms that may occur singly or two or three together: wet beriberi, characterized by oedema often associated with high-output heart failure; dry beriberi, characterized by a polyneuropathy affecting the peripheral nerves; Wernicke-Korsakoff syndrome, affecting the brain.

---

beta-alanine, an amino acid constituent of coenzyme A and pantothenic acid. Differs from alanine (alpha-alanine) and other amino acids found in proteins in that its acid and amino groups are attached to adjacent instead of to the same carbon atom.

---

beta-carotene, *see* carotenoids.

---

beta-hydroxybutyric acid, a ketone body, *see* ketosis.

---

beta-sitosterol, a phytosterol that is poorly absorbed. Because it interferes with the absorption of cholesterol, it has been used to lower blood cholesterol levels.

---

betaine, a methyl donor and lipotropic factor that helps prevent certain types of fatty liver. An intermediate in the conversion of choline to glycine. Found particularly in beetroot.

---

bezoar, a hard ball of undigested food formed in the oesophagus, stomach or intestines that can cause an obstruction.

bile, gall. A bitter, alkaline, greenish-yellow fluid secreted by the liver, stored in the gall-bladder and delivered into the duodenum via the bile duct. Contains water, bicarbonate, mucin, lecithin, cholesterol, bile salts and pigments. It emulsifies fats, enabling them and the fat-soluble vitamins to be digested and absorbed; helps neutralize acid chyme; and acts as the excretory route of cholesterol from the body.

---

bile acids, cholic and chenodeoxycholic acid. Synthesized in the liver from cholesterol and then conjugated (joined) with the amino acids glycine or taurine, forming the primary bile acids that are secreted into the bile.

---

bile acids, primary, glycocholic, taurocholic, glycochenodeoxycholic and taurochenodeoxycholic acids. Compounds formed in the liver by conjugating (joining) bile acids with glycine or taurine. Secreted into the bile.

---

bile acids, secondary, formed by action of intestinal bacterial enzymes on primary bile acids, deconjugating and deoxygenating them. Deoxycholic acid is formed from glyco- and tauro-cholic acids, and lithocholic acid from glyco- and tauro-chenodeoxycholic acids.

---

bile duct, carries bile from the gall-bladder to the duodenum.

---

bile pigments, bilirubin and biliverdin formed in the liver from haemoglobin and excreted in bile.

---

bile salts, sodium and potassium salts of bile acids. They help neutralize acid chyme, emulsify lipids, enabling them to be digested, and form water-soluble particles with the products of lipid digestion (mixed micelles) so they can be carried to the intestinal absorbing surface through the aqueous medium of the lumen contents.

---

bilirubin, a bile pigment — breakdown product of haemoglobin normally excreted in the bile. In jaundice its concentration in the blood rises, causing yellow coloration of skin, whites of eyes and urine.

biliverdin, green bile pigment formed by oxidation of bilirubin.

---

bioavailable, available for use by the body, e.g., iron in meat is more bioavailable than is iron in vegetables.

---

bioflavonoids, formerly incorrectly called vitamin P. Water-soluble flavone derivatives. Include hesperidin and rutin. Found with vitamin C in foods such as citrus fruits, green peppers, buckwheat. Probably enhance absorption of vitamin C. May increase resistance of capillaries and reduce their permeability to red blood cells. A normal diet provides about 1g daily.

---

biological value (BV), of a protein is the percentage of the absorbed protein retained in the body. Unlike net protein utilization (NPU), it does not take digestibility into account, but as 90–95 per cent of protein in a normal UK diet is digested, values for BV and NPU are often similar. Chemical scores, which are based on the amino acid content of the protein, match BVs fairly well.

Example BVs: the proteins of eggs and human milk, 100; cheese, meat and fish; 75; soya bean flour, 70; bread, 50; maize, 36; gelatin, 0.

---

biotin, water-soluble vitamin and member of B complex. Also known as vitamin H and coenzyme R.

Functions as coenzyme for many carboxylase enzymes (introduce carbon dioxide into a molecule) that take part in carbohydrate, protein and fat metabolism. Essential for growth and for maintenance of healthy nervous tissue, skin, hair, bone marrow and sex organs.

Deficiency leads to no specific disease in adults but to seborrhoeic dermatitis in babies. Deficiency unlikely in adults as it is synthesized extensively by intestinal bacteria. Can be induced by feeding raw egg white that contains the protein, avidin, which combines with biotin, preventing its absorption.

Requirement EC RDA is 150μg while the USA estimated safe and adequate daily intake is 30-100μg. Daily supply in UK in 1986 (not allowing for 10 per cent wastage and excluding out-of-home meals) averaged 35μg (37.5μg with contributions from alcoholic drinks and confectionery), derived mainly from (per cent): eggs, 31; milk and products, 23; and cereals, 17 (bread, 10). Most of the requirement is met from intestinal bacterial synthesis.

Toxicity Apparently none.

Stability Stable to heat and light. Most losses due to leaching into cooking water — between 10 and 30 per cent being lost in home cooking of meat, fish and vegetables.

Distribution in foods (in µg per 100g): chicken liver, 210; other livers, 27–41; dried brewer's yeast, 80; kidneys, 24–37; eggs, 25; mackerel, 7; cod, 3; meat, trace to 3; milk, 2; vegetables, 0.1–0.6; butter, 0; Wholegrain cereals are a source, except for wheat in which it is unavailable.

---

blackcurrant seed oil, forms 30.5 per cent by weight of the seed and is rich in polyunsaturated fatty acids, linoleic acid forming 47–49 per cent of its total fatty acids, gamma-linolenic acid 15–19 per cent, alpha-linolenic acid 12–14 per cent and stearidonic acid 3–4 per cent.

---

blanching, partial pre-cooking at high temperatures for a short time, often by dipping in very hot water, but also by hot air, steam or microwave. Essential before freezing, dehydrating or canning. Inactivates enzymes, reduces bulk, expels air, cleans, helps remove excess salt from meat and skin from almonds, etc. Nutritional losses include 10–20 per cent of sugars, salts and protein, some thiamin, riboflavin and niacin and up to a third of vitamin C.

---

bleaching agents, some are permitted as additives to whiten flour, e.g., chlorine.

---

blood, red viscous fluid filling heart and blood vessels. A 70kg man contains about 5.6l. Consists of a fluid portion, plasma (55 per cent of total volume) and cells of three types — red, white and platelets. Red normally outnumber white by 500 to 1.

Functions are to carry nutrients and oxygen to the tissues and to transport waste materials to the kidneys, lungs, liver and skin for excretion. Blood cells are formed in the bone marrow. Haemorrhaging is normally prevented by blood clotting.

---

blood cells, red, erythrocytes. Formed in bone marrow. Average life is 120 days. Colour is due to the content of haemoglobin, which contains iron and transports oxygen to the tissues from the lungs and carbon dioxide back.

Normal blood contains an average of 5.4 million per ml. When mature they contain no nucleus.

---

blood cells, white, leukocytes. Formed in bone marrow. Average life a few hours to a few days. Normally 4,000–11,000 per ml blood. Three main types: (a) granulocytes or polymorphonuclear leukocytes (neutrophils, eosinophils and basophils); (b) lymphocytes, and (c) monocytes or macrophages. Functions include phagocytosis (engulfment) and destruction of bacteria (by neutrophils and monocytes) and of antigen-antibody complexes (by eosinophils), and a key role in immunity (lymphocytes).

---

blood corpuscles, red and white blood cells.

---

blood sugar, glucose is the main sugar of the blood. Its concentration in normal human beings is between 80 and 100mg per dl in the post-absorptive state, between 120 and 130mg per dl after a carbohydrate meal and during fasting it falls to around 60–70mg per dl. Its level is strictly controlled by alterations in its uptake and output by the liver and other tissues. Hormones such as insulin lower the level by increasing glucose uptake by the tissues. Adrenalin and glucagon raise it by releasing glucose from glycogen in the liver. Cortisone raises it by decreasing glucose uptake by the tissues. At relatively high levels, glucose spills over into the urine-producing glycosuria. Elevated blood-sugar levels (hyperglycaemia) are found in sufferers from diabetes mellitus in whom the ability to secrete insulin has been lost. Some people suffer from low blood sugar levels (hypoglycaemia). Hypoglycaemia of such severity as to lead to unconsciousness, because glucose is required as fuel by the brain, is seen in diabetics taking too high a dose of insulin for the amount of carbohydrate consumed or exercise taken. *See* glucose.

---

blood-brain barrier, so called because of the very slow transport of some substances from the blood into the brain. Water, carbon dioxide and oxygen cross readily, glucose, ketone bodies, amino acids and fatty acids more slowly, and other substances like proteins, catecholamines, serotonin, etc., hardly at all. Glucose is the brain's normal energy source, but during starvation it adapts to obtaining up to 50 per cent of its energy requirements by oxidizing ketone bodies. Oxidation of fatty acids by the brain is very limited.

blood-pressure, the pressure exerted by the blood on artery walls. Measured in mm of mercury, both when the heart is maximally contracted — the systolic pressure, and when it relaxes — the diastolic pressure. Above normal blood-pressure is known as hypertension.

BMI, *see* body mass index.

BMR, *see* basal metabolic rate.

---

body mass index (BMI), equals weight in kg/height^2 in metres. Also known as Quetelet's index. Figure relates weight to height. The acceptable BMI for men is 22.0 and for women, 20.8. A person is obese if the BMI is above 30 for a man and 28.6 for a woman. (*See* Table 12, page 287.)

---

boiling, cooking by immersing food in boiling water. Results in inevitable loss by leaching into cooking water of some minerals and, more importantly from the nutritional viewpoint, of vitamins. The loss is minimized by using a small volume of water and presenting as small a surface area of the food as possible. Crushing, chopping, slicing and shredding of food not only increase the surface area but set free nutritionally destructive enzymes. Peeling vegetables before cooking increases nutrient loss e.g., of vitamin C from potatoes.

---

borage seed oil, rich in polyunsaturated fatty acids, linoleic acid forming 37 per cent, gamma-linolenic acid 25 to 27 per cent and alpha-linolenic acid 0.1 per cent of its total fatty acids.

---

boron, an essential mineral for plants and possibly, under certain circumstances, for some animals. Preliminary unconfirmed studies suggest that boron may help prevent bone calcium loss in postmenopausal women and assist arthritic patients.

The diet provides 1.5–3mg daily, mainly from plant sources, meat and fish being poor sources. Richest sources (mg per 100g): soya meal, 2.8; prunes, 2.7; raisins, 2.5; almonds, 2.3; rosehips, 1.9; peanuts, 1.8; hazelnuts, 1.6; dates, 0.9; honey, 0.7; wine, up to 0.8.

botulism, severe and often fatal food poisoning caused by the bacterium *Clostridium botulinum.*

---

bovine spongiform encephalopathy (BSE), 'mad cow disease'. A disease of the brain and nervous system of cattle. Causative agent unknown, but the disease develops some time after cattle eat high protein concentrate made with offal from infected animals or sheep with a similar disease ('scrapie'). No evidence that it can be passed to humans or cause the rare forms of human dementia characterized by similar symptoms. Strict precautions are in force in regard the use of brain, etc., in human and animal food supply.

---

bowel, intestines, gut. Small and large bowels correspond to small and large intestines.

---

brain, offal. Calf and lamb brain provides (per 100g): energy, 110 kcal; (g) water, 79.4; protein, 10.3; fat. 7.6; (mg) iron, 1.6; zinc, 1.2; thiamin, 0.07; riboflavin, 0.24; niacin, 5.2; vitamin C, 23.0; vitamin E, 1.2; (μg) vitamin B_{12}, 9.0.

---

bran, husk of grain with some adhering endosperm. High in dietary fibre and vitamin B complex. Cereal dietary fibres are the most effective in increasing faecal weight by attracting and holding water.

Wheat bran is the commonest and the most effective source of dietary fibre for preventing and treating constipation, haemorrhoids and anal fissure. Large particles are more effective than small and raw bran is better than prepared or cooked. Gives softer, bulkier stools, normalizes the transit time, and relieves symptoms. Holds 4.5g water per g material, or more with the large-particled variety. Poorly fermented by colonic bacteria often remaining identifiable after passing through gut. Only about 15 per cent of its cellulose and 60 per cent of its non-cellulosic fibres are fermented, probably at least partly due to its high lignin content. Good food sources include bran and wholewheat breakfast cereals and wholemeal bread.

Provides (per 100g): energy, 188 kcal; (g) total dietary fibre, 45 (10 per cent lignin, 24 per cent cellulose, 66 per cent hemicelluloses); protein, 6.4; fat, 4.2; available carbohydrate, 28.7; (mg) magnesium, 590; zinc, 13.3; thiamin, 0.65; riboflavin, 0.51; niacin, 17.7; pantothenic acid, 2.5; vitamin B_6, 2.5.

Oat bran provides (in g per 100g): protein, 22; available carbohydrate, 43; fat, 7; dietary fibre, 14.

Reported to lower blood cholesterol levels, probably due to its gum content. Rolled oats have a dietary fibre content of about 7 per cent.

Corn bran appears to be unchanged after passing through gut, yet contains less lignin than wheat bran. Its fibre provides (in g per 100g): lignin, 1.1; cellulose, 23.3; hemicelluloses, 75.6.

---

brandy, spirit distilled from champagne grapes. Provides (per 100ml): energy, 220 kcal; (g) alcohol, 32; carbohydrate trace.

---

bread, composed of dough made from flour (usually wheat but can be rye), yeast and water and subsequently baked. Only wheat and rye contain gluten and so can be made into leavened bread. *See* gluten.

White bread is made from 72 per cent extraction flour and is allowed, by law, to contain other ingredients including salt, fats, sugar, milk and milk products, egg, rice and soya flour, wheatgerm, oats, enzyme-active preparations, bleachers and improvers, preservatives, emulsifiers and stabilizers.

Brown bread must contain not less than 0.6 per cent crude fibre (corresponding to an extraction rate of about 85 per cent) and may be coloured by caramel. It is allowed to contain other ingredients as in white bread.

Wholemeal bread must be made from 100 per cent extraction flour, and may contain other ingredients as in brown bread except for certain bleaching and flour-improving agents. If milk and milk products, egg, wheatgerm, rice or oats are used, that fact must be indicated in the name of the bread.

Where a flour improver is used in any bread, the consumer must be informed in the ingredients list or by a notice in the shop.

In soda bread, sodium bicarbonate has been used as a raising agent.

In the UK, bread provides about 15 per cent of the average daily energy intake. Though the consumption of wholemeal and brown bread is increasing, their consumption is still far exceeded by that of white bread. The NACNE report recommends increasing bread consumption by 25–30 per cent as an alternative source of energy to fat and to provide more insoluble dietary fibre.

Nutritive properties are the same as the flour from which it was made but diluted by about one third by water added to make the dough. *See* flours; wheat; Table 3, page 107.

British gum, *see* dextrin.

brown fat,   *see* fat, brown.

---

browning,   of potatoes, apples, etc., exposed to air is due to an enzymic oxidation by phenolases (*which see*); of food on cooking or prolonged storage is due to non-enzymic Maillard reactions (*which see*).

---

brucellosis,   an infection in man produced by *Brucella* bacteria found in the milk of infected goats and cows. Eradication of the disease in cattle has proved difficult. Pasteurization makes contaminated milk, cream and cheese safe. Symptoms include a recurrent fever. Several hundred cases are notified each year, chiefly among stockmen and veterinary surgeons.

Brunner's glands,   in the walls of the duodenum produce intestinal digestive juices.

---

brush border,   the minute projections (microvilli) from the cells lining the intestines into the lumen. *See* intestinal wall.

BSE,   *see* bovine spongiform encephalopathy.

---

buccal cavity,   *see* oral cavity.

---

bulimia nervosa,   compulsive overeating. Binge eating, usually in secret, often accompanied by self-induced vomiting and laxative abuse to control weight. Carbohydrate (sugar) craving. May alternate or follow on from anorexia nervosa (*which see*). In both there is a morbid fear of becoming fat. Mainly affects white women who usually present with it in their twenties. Physical symptoms include fatigue, feeling 'bloated', 'puffy cheeks', irregular or absent menstruation, and toothache. May be a depressive disorder. It was first described in 1980.

---

bulking aids,   are additives that add to the bulk of a food without increasing its energy value, e.g., guar gum.

burning feet syndrome, pains in feet and legs that may be intense, particularly at night. A polyneuropathy seen world-wide, including UK elderly, among those long on poor diets particularly deficient in protein and B complex vitamins.

butter, produced from soured cream by churning. Provides (per 100g): energy, 740 kcal; (g) water, 15.4; protein, 0.4; fat, 82.0; (mg) sodium, salted, 870/unsalted, 7; (μg) vitamin A, 520–970; carotene, 350–650 (both seasonal); vitamin D, 0.63–1.0. Polyunsaturated to saturated fatty acid ratio (P/S) 0.05.

butyric acid, a four carbon fatty acid. One of the volatile fatty acids formed during colonic fermentation of dietary fibre. Contributes to the taste of milk fat and butter.

BV, *see* biological value

C

cadmium, does not appear to be an essential element. It is poorly absorbed from food and water but accumulates slowly in the body throughout life ultimately reaching 20–30mg, highest concentrations being in the kidney. Cadmium poisoning, a known industrial hazard, affects the kidneys. In Japan, rice grown on land irrigated with water polluted by cadmium from a mine is thought to have caused the severe and often fatal form of osteomalacia called Itai-itai. In Shipham, Somerset, where the cadmium content of the soil is very high from the spoils of a disused local zinc mine, moderately elevated dietary intakes and higher serum and urine cadmium levels compared with a nearby uncontaminated area have apparently produced no significant health effects so far. Toxic effects of environmental cadmium may be mitigated by dietary zinc, copper, selenium and calcium. Some reports indicate its concentration in the kidney correlates with the incidence of hypertension.

caffeine, a methylxanthine (*which see*) present in coffee, tea and cola drinks.

---

calcidiol, the form of vitamin D that circulates in the blood.

---

calciferol, plant source vitamin D.

---

calcitonin, thyroid hormone that helps control plasma calcium levels.

---

calcitriol, active hormonal form of vitamin D that promotes calcium absorption.

---

calcium, an adult man contains about 1,200g of this essential mineral, 99 per cent of it in bones and teeth, mainly as phosphate. The bones are constantly being remodelled, 700mg calcium entering and leaving them daily. Lactating mothers lose an average of 250mg daily in their milk.

According to the OPCS Dietary and Nutritional Survey, average daily intakes in 1986–7 were 940mg for men and 730mg for women. Main sources (per cent): milk and milk products, 48; cereal products, 25; and vegetables, 7.

Functions Besides forming the hard substance of the skeleton, the 10g present in soft tissues and body fluids regulates nerve and muscle function, hormonal actions, blood clotting, rennin milk curdling, etc. In the cell, bound as ions to the protein calmodulin, it modulates the activities of a great variety of enzymes.

Absorbed in the first part of the small intestine by means of a protein synthesized in response to active vitamin D. Lactose (milk sugar) increases absorption. Absorption is inhibited by compounds forming insoluble complexes (phytates, oxalates, phosphates), by undigested fats forming insoluble soaps and by uronic acid-rich dietary fibres, unless released by bacterial fermentation in the colon. Normally 70–80 per cent of dietary calcium is lost in the faeces, but this is decreased on low-calcium diets.

High blood phosphate levels reduce active vitamin D formation and so reduce calcium absorption. In animals, a dietary calcium to phosphorus ratio of 2:1 leads to maximal calcium absorption and minimal bone loss. In human beings, the optimum ratio is not known, but the increased intake of phosphate food additives contributes to the low ratio in the diet (currently 1:1.13 in the USA). Whether this contributes to excess bone loss found in postmenopausal osteoporotic women is not yet clear.

The control of plasma calcium balance in the body is complex. The parathyroid hormone keeps plasma calcium levels within narrow limits, a fall increasing secretion of the hormone. This activates calcium release from the bone and production of active vitamin D in the kidney. Active vitamin D increases intestinal absorption and stimulates reabsorption of excreted calcium in the kidney. Plasma calcium levels are also controlled by the thyroid hormone, calcitonin, and by oestrogens that decrease calcium release from bone. Oestrogens also partially inhibit parathyroid hormone responsiveness.

Excreted mainly in the faeces, but also in the urine (160mg daily), and by sloughing of dead cells from the skin (50mg daily) and traces in the sweat. Though high-protein diets increase absorption (by forming amino acid chelates), the benefit is more than outweighed by the increased urinary excretion that follows. High sodium intake also increases urinary calcium loss. On low-calcium diets, faecal loss is reduced.

Deficiency is usually caused by vitamin D deficiency or a metabolic defect, but also by dietary deficiency. Leads to rickets in children and osteomalacia in adults, and may contribute to osteoporosis. Muscles lose tone and become flaccid so infants with rickets are late in sitting, standing and walking, besides having poorly formed bones. Symptoms include tetany, a twitching particularly of the face, hands and feet as a result of overexcitability of the nerves and muscles in the absence of calcium modulation.

The high level of phosphorus compared with calcium in cow's milk may contribute to the neonatal tetany of infants on cow's milk formula.

Requirement UK RDA is 500mg, the EC and USA RDA being 800mg. RDA increased to 1200mg in pregnancy and lactation. Some consider higher intakes would be desirable and some suggest peri- and post-menopausal women should consume 1000–1500mg daily to help prevent loss of bone mass (*see osteoporosis*).

Toxicity Hypercalcaemia (high blood levels) usually as a result of excessive intakes of vitamin D or hyperparathyroidism or other metabolic disorder. Can be fatal in infants. Probably no danger of toxicity from high dietary intake in a healthy person because the homeostatic mechanism strictly controls absorption.

Distribution in foods (in mg per 100g): dairy products (Cheddar cheese, 800; yogurt, 180; milk, 120; cream cheese, 98); tinned sardines, 550; watercress, 220; soya bean flour and dried brewer's yeast, 210; white flour (fortified in UK), 140; winter cabbage, 57; eggs, 52; brown rice, 38; wholemeal flour, 35; fish, 17–32; meat and poultry, 3–24.

calculus, solid deposits or 'stones' formed in body reservoirs and their ducts, e.g. stones in the kidney and bladder, and gallstones.

---

calorie (c), the unit of heat, formerly based on the amount of heat needed to raise the temperature of 1g of water 1°C, but now based on the heat of combustion of benzoic acid (the thermo-chemical calorie) and is 4.184 J, or for practical nutrition purposes, 4.2 J. The unit used in nutrition is the kilocalorie (kcal or C) which is equal to 1,000 c. 1 kcal = 4.2 kJ.

---

calories, 'empty', describes foods such as sugar and alcoholic beverages that provide energy but little or nothing in the way of micronutrients (e.g., vitamins and minerals).

---

calorimeter, bomb, apparatus used for measuring the amount of oxidizable energy present in a food by burning it in oxygen and measuring the heat released. The body will only get this amount of energy if it can oxidize this food completely. Not all the energy in protein, for example, is available to the body, some being excreted in the urine as urea, which the body cannot oxidize.

---

calorimetry, measurement of heat output. Direct calorimetry of man and animals involves placing the subject in an insulated chamber and measuring the heat output from the rise in temperature of water flowing round the chamber walls, a method seldom used nowadays. Instead indirect calorimetry is used, based on the fact that when an organic substance is completely combusted either in the calorimeter or in the body, oxygen is consumed in amounts directly related to the energy liberated as heat. Oxygen consumption is therefore measured, usually by means of a spirometer, an apparatus worn by the subject into which he or she breathes.

The sum of the heat energy output plus mechanical work performed gives an estimate of the energy expenditure involved in performing a task.

Campylobacter enteritis, now the most common cause of food poisoning. Self-limiting infection with few complications. Source is usually undercooked, infected poultry, cross-contamination from handling infected poultry and raw or defectively pasteurized milk.

Canbra, new genetic variety of rape seed yielding an oil, canola oil (*which see*), with a low erucic acid content.

---

cancer, malignant tumours. Eighty per cent of human cancers appear to be more determined by habit, diet and custom than by genetic factors, and are therefore potentially preventable. It is estimated that 30–40 per cent of cancer in men and 60 per cent in women is induced by the diet.

Carcinogenic agents naturally present or added to foods and others that cause cancers of the gastrointestinal tract or related organs include: tobacco — its chewing may cause carcinoma of the buccal cavity and oesophagus; aflatoxins produced by moulds growing on peanuts or grains stored in warm, damp conditions, cause liver cancer in animals and probably in man; nitrosamines formed from nitrites reacting with amines, cause stomach cancer in animals and possibly in man — present in some foods as such or may be derived from nitrites and nitrates added to foods as preservatives or present in soil; hydrazines from mushrooms; safrole from sassafras, mace, nutmeg and black pepper; cycasin from cycad nut.

Epidemiological and laboratory studies show a higher incidence of cancer of the breast, large bowel and prostate in populations eating foods containing large amounts of both saturated and unsaturated fat, and a lower incidence associated with less fat consumption. Population studies suggest that frequent consumption of foods containing vitamin A-producing carotenes or vitamin C (i.e., fruit and vegetables) can reduce susceptibilities to cancers of the bladder, large bowel, skin, lung, stomach and oesophagus. There is a higher incidence of oesophageal and stomach cancers in parts of Japan, China and Iceland where salt-cured and smoked foods are eaten frequently. Such foods may be contaminated by polycyclic aromatic hydrocarbons from the smoke or by nitrosamines, both suspected of causing human cancers. Excessive alcohol drinking, especially combined with smoking, appears to increase the probability of cancers of the mouth, larynx, oesophagus and respiratory tract, and may be linked with colon and rectal cancers.

Based on these epidemiological and laboratory studies, US interim guidelines designed to reduce the risk of developing cancer through diet suggest:

1. Eat less fat — reduce overall fat consumption to about 30 per cent of daily energy intake.
2. Eat more fruit, vegetables and wholegrain cereals.
3. Eat very little salt-cured, salt-pickled and smoked foods.
4. Drink alcohol only in moderation.

Other dietary factors associated with cancer, most of which are taken care of by following the above dietary guidelines, are an increased risk seen with obesity and high meat and cholesterol intakes and a decreased risk with high dietary fibre, cruciferous vegetables (e.g., Brussels sprouts, cabbage), beta-carotene, beta-sitosterol, synthetic antioxidants, vitamin E and selenium intakes.

---

canning, foods are sterilized and then sealed into tins. Their shelf-life is indefinite from the microbiological viewpoint, but there is a decline in organoleptic and nutritional properties during storage due to chemical reactions, some loss also occurring during the canning process. Of the vitamins, A, C and thiamin are particularly vulnerable.

---

canning, aseptic, food is heated to 150–175°C for a few seconds and then tinned under aseptic conditions. Flavour, colour and vitamin retention are superior to conventional canning.

---

canola oil, rape seed oil with low erucic acid content, derived from Canbra, a new genetic variety of the seed. As per cent of total fatty acid content: oleic acid, 55; alpha-linolenic acid, 10; erucic acid, 2.

---

capillaries, tiny blood vessels whose thin walls facilitate rapid exchange of substances between the contained blood and the surrounding tissues.

---

capric acid, a saturated ten carbon fatty acid.

---

caprylic acid, a saturated, eight carbon fatty acid. Possesses antifungal activity against Candida species.
As per cent of total fatty acids: coconut oil, 7; butter, 1.

---

capsaicin, the active principle of hot paprika or chilli peppers. Produces a local anaesthetic effect by depleting nerve fibres of the neurotransmitter, substance P.

---

carbohydrate classification, *see* Figure 1, page 46.

Figure 1. The components and classification of dietary fibre and carbohydrates.

			Components			
			sugars	mono- and disaccharides		
			dextrins	oligosaccharides	available carbohydrate	
			glycogen starch resistant starch			total dietary carbohydrate
dietary fibre* — Southgate method of analysis	dietary fibre* — Englyst method of analysis	non-starch plant polysaccharides	pectins gums mucilages hemicelluloses cellulose	polysaccharides	unavailable carbohydrates	
			lignin			

*see fibre, dietary

---

carbohydrate craving, consumption of excessive amounts of carbohydrate (sugar) food to bring about desirable changes in mood. Tendency may increase premenstrually and during the short winter days (*see* seasonal affective disorder). Seen in some obese people and in bulimia nervosa.

---

carbohydrates, organic compounds of carbon, hydrogen and oxygen in which, with few exceptions, the ratio of hydrogen to oxygen is 2:1 as in water — hence the name 'hydrate of carbon'. Food carbohydrates include starches, glycogen, dextrins, sugars and dietary fibres. Starches, glycogen, dextrins and sugars make up the available carbohydrates, ones that man can digest with his own enzymes and use as energy sources. Dietary fibres are non-available carbohydrates because man himself cannot digest them and they form roughage. *See Figure 1.*

Chemically the sugars are either monosaccharides with six carbons (e.g., glucose, fructose) or five carbons (e.g., ribose), or disaccharides comprising two monosaccharide units joined together (e.g., sucrose or 'sugar', lactose, maltose). Chains of 3–15 monosaccharide units are called oligosaccharides (e.g., dextrins). Complex carbohydrates or polysaccharides are straight or branched chains of many monosaccharide units that may be all the same or different. They include the starches and glycogen and dietary fibres, such as cellulose and the gums.

Digestion and fate Dietary fibres are not digested by man himself and are either fermented by bacteria in the colon or pass out unchanged in the stool. Available carbohydrates are digested mainly in the small intestine to disaccharides in the lumen and to monosaccharides as they are being absorbed. They are used for the production of energy by being oxidized to carbon dioxide and water, which are waste products, or stored as glycogen or converted to fat and stored.

Requirements Available carbohydrates simply provide energy that can also be obtained from dietary fats and proteins, parts of which can be converted to glucose, the energy source essential for the brain and red blood cells, so carbohydrates would appear to be non-essential in the diet. However, about 45 per cent of the UK total energy supply (including alcohol) is obtained from carbohydrates and nutritionists recommend that this should be increased to 50 per cent. Most should be derived from complex carbohydrates, which are cheap and accompanied by micronutrients and dietary fibre.

In the total absence of dietary carbohydrate, ketosis occurs due to incomplete oxidation of fats, and there is excessive breakdown of muscle protein and significant loss of salt and water. To prevent these effects, a minimum daily intake of 100g of carbohydrate is recommended.

Food sources Sugars such as glucose and fructose are found in fruits and honey, lactose in milk and maltose in beer. Sucrose, cane or beet, is extracted and used in cooking and food processing as a sweetener. Nutritionists discourage the use of sugars as they provide calories without accompanying nutrients, i.e., 'empty calories', as well as being cariogenic.

Complex carbohydrates such as starches are found in wheat, rice, pulses and potatoes. Glycogen is present in meat and liver. Such foods, particularly if not over-refined, also provide other nutrients and dietary fibres.

---

carbohydrates, available, carbohydrates that can be digested by man's own enzymes. Comprise the sugars (mono- and disaccharides), dextrins, starches from plant sources and glycogen from animal sources.

---

carbohydrates, unavailable, carbohydrates that cannot be digested by man's own enzymes. Formerly an alternative name for dietary fibre. However, some definitions of dietary fibre include lignin, which is not a carbohydrate. Until recently, it was considered to comprise all plant polysaccharides other than starch, but now it is realized that some forms of starch are resistant to digestion and so it also includes resistant starch. (*See* Figure 1, page 46.)

---

carboxypeptidase, enzyme concerned with protein digestion. Present in pancreatic digestive juices.

carcinogenic, cancer producing.

---

carcinoma, a tumour arising in epithelial tissue.

---

cardiovascular disease, comprises coronary heart disease plus cerebrovascular disease.

The Committee on Medical Aspects of Food Policy (COMA) Report on Diet in Relation to Heart Disease (1984) made dietary recommendations aimed to reduce the incidence of cardiovascular disease, particularly coronary heart disease. These included a reduction in the contribution of fat to the diet from 42 per cent of the energy intake (excluding alcohol) to 35 per cent, with saturated fat forming no more than 15 per cent of the total energy consumed, thereby increasing the polyunsaturated to saturated fat ratio (P/S) from 0.23 to 0.45. Sugar intakes should not be increased, excessive alcohol intakes avoided and ways of reducing salt intake that might contribute to hypertension, should be considered. The reduced energy intake was to be compensated for by an increased intake of fibre-rich, complex carbohydrate foods such as bread, cereals, fruits and vegetables. About 40 per cent of the recommended decreases in fat and saturated fat could be achieved by avoiding cream, switching to semi-skimmed milk and low-fat cheeses. About 80 per cent would be achieved if skimmed milk was used.

Among the expected biochemical effects of those measures was a reduction in blood cholesterol levels, a risk factor for cardiovascular disease. The OPCS Dietary and Nutritional Survey 1986–7 revealed that fat still contributes 40 per cent of food calories (i.e., excluding alcohol), but that the P/S ratio averaged 0.40 for men and 0.38 for women. Over 85 per cent of the respondents consumed more than the amount of fat recommended by COMA. Only about one-third had blood cholesterol levels in the desirable range (less than 5.2 mmol/l).

Both in the USA and UK deaths from cardiovascular disease have been falling in recent years though prevalence of the disease in middle age may actually have increased. Some people have suggested the fall in death rate may be due to improvements in the diet and it has also been attributed to a decline in risk factors such as smoking and elevated serum cholesterol levels, as well as to improved medical treatment.

It is still generally agreed that while polyunsaturated fat in the diet should increase compared to saturated fat, which should be reduced, it should still not form more than 10 per cent of food energy intake. Some suggest the ratio of omega 6 to omega 3 polyunsaturated fatty acids should be approximately 3:1. Disadvantages of a very high intake of omega 6 polyunsaturates (above

12 per cent of energy as linoleic acid) are that it lowers HDL ('good') cholesterol levels, suppresses the immune system, is associated with an increase in gallstones, and suppresses the metabolism of omega 3 polyunsaturates.

Recent studies indicate that replacing saturated fat with monounsaturated fat has an equivalent LDL ('bad') cholesterol lowering effect to polyunsaturated fat, and, unlike a high carbohydrate or high polyunsaturated fat diet, it does not lower HDL cholesterol levels.

Epidemiological evidence suggests consumption of omega 3 polyunsaturates (notably eicosapentaenoic acid, or, EPA and docosahexaenoic acid, or, DHA) is associated with decreased risk of cardiovascular diseases. Consumption of fish oils (rich in EPA and DHA) lowers plasma triglycerides (fat) and VLDL cholesterol levels, slightly raises HDL cholesterol levels, but does not lower and sometimes slightly raises, LDL cholesterol levels, unless very large amounts are consumed. Fish oil appears to inhibit atherosclerosis in pigs and primates independently of its effect on plasma cholesterol and in human beings it increases bleeding time and reduces thrombotic tendency, but scarcely affects platelet aggregation. Several studies show it lowers blood-pressure. Consuming oily fish twice a week, though supplying only 3g EPA, appears to reduce total mortality. However, very high intakes of fish oil (over 20g daily) increase the requirement for vitamin E, and may impair diabetic control and make asthma worse.

The Mediterranean diet, which is associated with a low incidence of cardiovascular mortality, besides being rich in monounsaturated fat (olive oil) and complex carbohydrates, includes garlic (*which see*). Increasing evidence suggests that at least a clove a day of high-quality garlic may be protective because of its blood cholesterol and triglyceride lowering properties and anti-thrombotic activity.

A daily intake of about one unit of alcohol (*see* alcohol) appears to have a greater protective effect than none. However, a higher intake increases the risk of coronary heart disease, hypertension and alcoholism.

A large intake of soluble dietary fibre, e.g., as rolled oats (60g or more daily), may lower blood cholesterol levels.

Salt, and hence sodium, intake is unnecessarily high and may influence hypertension, a risk factor for cardiovascular disease. However, only a very low sodium diet will reduce hypertension to any extent and then only in salt-sensitive people.

To be really effective, a healthy diet must be part of a healthy lifestyle with no smoking, adequate exercise and no excessive stress.

---

caries, dental,   decay of the enamel of the teeth. Prevalent in developed societies with a high sugar intake. Usual cause of tooth loss up to age 45;

thereafter periodontal disease takes over. Extent expressed by the DMF index. Produced by bacteria, particularly *Streptococcus mutans*, which reside on and between the teeth. They ferment sugars ingested as food and drink forming lactic acid, which at concentrations sufficient to produce a pH of 5 or lower, dissolves calcium phosphate in the tooth enamel. Some bacteria, including *S. mutans*, also produce dental plaque that protects them and potentiates their cariogenicity.

The most cariogenic sugars appear to be sucrose, followed closely by glucose and fructose, and then by maltose and lactose, and lastly by galactose. The sugar alcohols and other bulk sweeteners are much less cariogenic than sucrose, some even promoting remineralization. Intense sweeteners are non-cariogenic, and saccharin appears to inhibit caries, and thaumatin may aid remineralization. Acid-containing foods such as fruit juices and chewable ascorbic acid tablets are also cariogenic.

Complete tooth loss affects nutrition particularly in the elderly. Their consumption of meat, fresh fruit and vegetables and total energy is reduced, resulting in lower haemoglobin and vitamin C levels, increased gastro-intestinal irritation and increased mortality from choking. However, no striking differences in digestion or nutritional status have been noted.

Caries can be prevented or considerably reduced by largely excluding food and drink containing sugars and acids from the diet, particularly between meals, and by good oral hygiene; and in the young only, by fluoride in the drinking water or topically applied, which decreases the acid solubility of the enamel. Other dietary components that inhibit decay include cocoa, milk, calcium phosphate, peanuts and oat hulls.

---

cariogenic, dental caries producing, e.g., sucrose.

---

carnitine, stimulates the oxidation of long chain fatty acids, of pyruvate, and of branched chain amino acids. Synthesized from lysine in muscle and kidney. Additional carnitine is obtained by non-vegetarians from meat and dairy products. Widely distributed in body, particularly in muscles.

The amount of carnitine in muscles is not thought to be a limiting factor in energy supply. Whether moderate exercise reduces muscle content is disputed. However, there is some evidence to suggest a carnitine supplement (2g) may improve physical endurance in those undergoing intense physical exercise, possibly by increasing lipid turnover and hence conserving muscle glycogen.

There is no evidence that carnitine supplementation helps slimming by burning up excess fat in the tissues, unless the obese person is suffering from a metabolic carnitine deficiency, which is comparatively rare. Vegetarians generally derive sufficient from body synthesis.

---

carob,   a substitute for cocoa that, unlike cocoa, does not contain methyl-xanthine stimulants such as theobromine. Suitable for those with a food intolerance to cocoa products. Naturally sweeter than cocoa. Produced by grinding the de-seeded fruit pod of *Ceratonia siliqua*.

Carob provides (per 100g): energy, 380 kcal; (g) protein, 3.8; fat, 0.2; (mg) calcium, 290; sodium, 10; potassium 800.

---

carob gum,   locust bean gum. *See* galactomannan.

---

carotenes,   *see* carotenoids.

---

carotenoids,   red and yellow pigments found in many animals and plants. Some (e.g., the carotenes, mainly beta-carotene and also cryptoxanthin and beta-zeacarotene) can give rise to vitamin A (retinol) in the body and are sometimes called pro-vitamin A, but others (e.g., canthaxanthin, lycopene) cannot. The conversion to vitamin A takes place mainly in the intestinal mucosa but also in the liver and other tissues. Alpha-, beta- and gamma-carotene are red carotenoids found in green leafy vegetables, yellow vegetables, and fruits.

Carotene is poorly absorbed from foods (about one third) and the efficiency of conversion from beta-carotene, the most potent vitamin A precursor, is about one-half and from other pro-vitamin A carotenoids, about one-quarter. Therefore in calculating the contribution of carotenoids to the vitamin A content of a food, the following relationship is used:

1 retinol equivalent = $1\mu g$ retinol or $6\mu g$ beta-carotene or $12\mu g$ other pro-vitamin A carotenoids.

Carotenoids are transported in the serum associated with lipoproteins. Their level in the blood is primarily regulated by the amount in the food. They are stored in body fat.

Function as vitamin A precursors and antioxidants. Carotenoids quench (inactivate) singlet oxygen, a reactive oxygen species formed by photo-sensitized reaction, dispersing the reactivity as heat or being oxidized to form inactive derivatives. Carotenoids can also quench free radicals, highly reactive species that can cause damage in the body.

In laboratory studies, beta-carotene has been shown to protect against the mutagenic effect of light in bacteria; to protect cells against chemical carcinogens by preventing damage to the nucleus; to protect against chemically induced colon cancer in animals; and to prolong the time before ultraviolet light causes skin cancer in animals.

Because of its ability to protect against photosensitized damage, supplementation with beta-carotene is used to reduce the symptoms of people with erythroporetic photoporphyria, who are light sensitive and whose skin is harmed by sunlight.

Initial epidemiological surveys indicated an inverse relationship between diets rich in retinol and several types of cancer, but subsequent studies suggest the link is to the carotenoid content of the diet. Carotenoids may act by slowing down the promotional phase of carcinogenesis and so do not appear to depend on their prior conversion to vitamin A.

There is epidemiological evidence linking beta-carotene with the prevention of lung cancer, higher intakes reducing the risk in former smokers and higher blood levels reducing the risk in smokers. Currently many human intervention studies are testing the chemopreventive action of beta-carotene for colon, oesophageal, lung and skin cancers. The daily supplemental dose is usually 15mg.

Toxicity High intakes do not lead to vitamin A toxicity, the body converting only what it needs, and the only adverse effect appears to be that they may cause reversible skin yellowing.

---

carrageen moss, seaweed found on west coast of Scotland, South Wales and Ireland. Contains less than 1 per cent fat, an appreciable amount of protein, and a high content of minerals.

---

carrageenan, also known as carrageen, carrageenin, carageenan and Irish moss. Extract of red seaweeds, chiefly *Chondrus crispus* and *Gigartina stellata*. A polysaccharide of galactose sugar and dietary fibre soluble in hot water forming viscous solution. Gelling, emulsifying and stabilizing agent and viscosity builder in foods (jams, jellies, instant milk puddings, processed cheese) and non-foods (e.g., toothpaste). When degraded can cause liver damage, stomach ulcers, colonic irritation and immunological effects.

---

carrier, a person with a symptomless bacterial infection that he or she can transmit to others. Particularly dangerous if a food handler.

carrots, root vegetable. Rich in carotenes (12 000μg carotene per 100g).

---

casein, insoluble protein derived from the soluble milk protein, caseinogen.

---

caseinogen, principal protein of milk. Protein quality high. The enzyme rennin in the stomach of babies clots milk by converting soluble caseinogen to insoluble casein.

---

cassava, also known as manioc, yuca and tapioca. A starchy root or tuber of *Manihot esculenta* and the principal food of many in the tropics. Its very low protein content (1g per 100g) is the reason that kwashiorkor is common in many countries dependent on it. Roots grated and dried in sun to prevent enzymic release of hydrogen cyanide from compound present in outer parts of root. Prevalence of neuropathies in cassava-dependent communities may be attributable to residual cyanide.

---

catabolism, that part of metabolism concerned with the breakdown of substances in the tissues.

---

catalyst, initiates or speeds up a chemical reaction but remains unchanged after performing its task many times. Enzymes act as catalysts for the many chemical reactions that take place in the metabolic processes of animals and plants.

---

cataract, opaqueness of the eye lens that may lead to impaired sight or blindness. Biochemical alteration of the lens proteins is thought to be involved. Nutritional factors suggested as participating include severe dehydration due to cholera-like diarrhoea with or without heat stroke; and a high consumption of milk by lactose (milk sugar) digesters.

---

catechol oxidase, *see* phenolase.

---

catecholamines, comprise dopamine, noradrenaline and adrenaline, and are derived from phenylalanine and tyrosine in neurons and the adrenal medulla. They act as neurotransmitters and neural hormones, and raise blood-pressure (pressor amines). *See* adrenaline.

---

cathartic, causes evacuation of the bowels.

---

cation, positively charged ion.

---

cellulose, polysaccharide found in plant cell walls. Composed of glucose molecules so linked that it cannot be digested by the enzymes of man and other animals. An important insoluble dietary fibre that holds water and may reduce abnormally high pressures in the bowel, but may also affect trace mineral excretion. About 50 per cent of cellulose is fermented in man's colon by bacterial enzymes, and bacteria in the rumen of cattle, sheep, etc., can digest cellulose (*see* fibre, dietary).

---

cephalin, phosphatidylethanolamine. *See* phospholipid.

Ceratonia siliqua, leguminous evergreen tree growing mainly in the Mediterranean area. Carob gum or locust bean gum is obtained from its seeds and carob from the de-seeded pods.

---

cereal grains, the seeds of domesticated grasses. The chief single energy source of most of the world's population, e.g., they supply 70 per cent of the energy intake in much of Asia and Africa and 29 per cent in the UK. They include wheat, rice, maize, millets, barley, oats and rye. Wheat is the most important crop in the world. The cereal of choice in temperate or dry climates is wheat and in most damp, tropical ones, rice. Maize is hardy, easily cultivated and relatively immune from predatory birds. Millet grows in hot climates on poor soil with limited water supply. Barley is grown mainly for brewing and cattle fodder. Oats, a hardy crop, were once the staple food of the Scots, but are now grown mainly as cattle fodder. Rye grows in poor soils in cold climates. Corn is the term used for the most familiar local cereal and may mean wheat in England, oats in Scotland, and maize in the USA.

All can be ground into flour for cakes or porridge, but only wheat and rye contain enough gluten that enables them to be baked into bread. They provide energy and protein (7.5–13.0g per 100g), usually of good quality. Their limiting amino acid is lysine, except for maize where it is tryptophan. They are devoid of vitamin C and practically devoid of vitamin A activity. As whole grains, most provide adequate amounts of B vitamins. They contain appreciable amounts of calcium and iron, but also phytic acid and dietary fibre, which interfere with mineral absorption.

---

cerebrosides, glycolipids containing galactose. Found in brain, the myelin of nerve fibres and other tissues.

---

cerebrovascular disease, *see* stroke.

---

ceruloplasmin, a copper-containing enzyme required for iron absorption.

---

cervonic acid, *see* docosahexaenoic acid.

---

cetoleic acid, a mono-unsaturated fatty acid of the omega 11 family with 22 carbons (C22:1 n-11). Found mainly in fish. May be oxidized only slowly by man.

Distribution in foods (as percentage of total fatty acids): herring, 17.4; mackerel, 9.9; cod, 0.8.

---

cheese, produced by clotting of fresh or soured milk with rennet. The clot of protein traps the milk fat, is removed from the whey, salted and ripened in cheese bags during which bacterial fermentation takes place, the particular bacteria and moulds responsible giving the cheese its characteristic texture and flavour. Most is made from cow's milk, but Roquefort comes from ewe's and Norwegian from goat's milk.

Most provide 23–35 per cent protein of high biological value. The fat content usually varies from 23–40 per cent, Edam-type being 22.9 per cent, Stilton 40 per cent and Cheddar 33.5 per cent. Cottage cheese contains 13.6 per cent protein and 4.0 per cent fat (or 0.4 per cent if made without added cream). Cream cheese contains 3.1 per cent protein and 47.7 per cent fat. Their energy values (kcal per 100g) vary: cottage cheese, 96; Camembert, 300; Edam, 304; Cheddar, 406; cream cheese, 439; Stilton, 462.

All contain large amounts of sodium. Cottage and cream cheeses contain 450 and 300mg per 100g respectively and the rest 610–1420mg per 100g, Stilton, Camembert and Danish blue types being the highest. Cheeses are rich sources of calcium, vitamin A (except cottage cheese), and riboflavin.

---

cheilosis, zone of red, denuded skin at line of closure of lips. Frequently seen in sufferers from pellagra and angular stomatitis. Also appears during periods of drought and lack of fresh foods. Condition overlaps with chapped lips seen in healthy people exposed to cold winds or excessive sunlight.

---

chelated compounds, are those formed between amino acids, dextrans or chelating agents like the additive EDTA (Serial No. 385) and di- or tri-basic minerals such as calcium, zinc, manganese, iron, etc. Amino acid chelates are formed during normal digestion and facilitate mineral absorption and retention in the body.

---

chemical score, or amino acid score, a chemical grading of the nutritional quality of a protein obtained by comparing its essential amino acid content (usually just the limiting one) with that of a reference protein, usually egg. Examples: egg, 100; milk, 95; beef, 93; soya beans, 74; rice, 67; wheat, 53; maize, 49. Chemical scores match biological values, which measure retention of absorbed protein in the body, fairly well.

---

chestnuts, nuts of the sweet chestnut tree providing (per 100g): energy, 170 kcal; (g) protein, 2.0; fat, 2.7; water, 51.7; total dietary fibre, 6.8; (mg) potassium, 500.

---

chicken, poultry meat. Usually eaten with skin, which has a high fat content.

The meat/meat plus skin provide (per 100g): energy, 121/230 kcal; (g) water, 74.5/64.4; protein, 20.5/17.6; fat, 4.3/17.7; (mg) iron, 0.7/0.7; zinc, 1.1/1.0; thiamin, 0.10/0.08; riboflavin, 0.16/0.14; niacin, 11.6/9.9; vitamin B_6, 0.42/0.30; (μg) vitamin B_{12}, traces.

---

chief cells, found in stomach walls. Secrete gastric juices, which contain hydrochloric acid and digestive enzymes (*see* digestion).

Chinese restaurant syndrome, symptoms experienced by some after eating Chinese food. Attributed to its high content of monosodium glutamate, but this may not be entirely responsible. Symptoms that develop after half-an-hour and last two to three hours include headache, nausea, sweating, weakness, abdominal pain, face flushing and watery eyes.

---

chloride, an electrolyte (negatively charged — anion) taken into body largely as sodium chloride (common salt). An essential non-metallic mineral.

Functions With sodium, it is concerned with the electrolyte and acid-base balance of extra-cellular fluids like blood plasma. It forms hydrochloric acid, which is responsible for the high acidity of the gastric juices.

Excretion into the urine, sweat and gut mostly follows that of sodium, but may be lost in urine associated with ammonia and in vomit as hydrochloric acid.

Deficiency may occur in infants fed salt-free formulas. Can occur secondary to vomiting, diuretic therapy and renal disease.

Requirement No RDA but the USA estimated minimum daily adult requirement is 750mg.

Distribution in foods (in g per 100g): common salt, 60.7; Camembert and Danish blue-type cheeses, 2.32–2.39; tinned ham, 1.67; kipper, 1.52; Cheddar cheese, 1.06; white bread, 0.89; wholemeal bread, 0.86; yogurt and celery, 0.18; eggs and watercress, 0.16; cod, 0.11; milk, 0.10; herring and potatoes; 0.08; carrots; 0.07; tomatoes, lettuce and honeydew melon; 0.05; winter cabbage; 0.03.

---

chlorophyll, the green pigment present in all green plants that enables them to use the sun's energy to synthesize carbohydrates from carbon dioxide and water (photosynthesis).

---

chocolate, derived from cocoa nibs obtained by roasting and dehusking the fermented dried seed (bean) of the cocoa plant, *Theobroma cacao*. Sugar is added and, for milk chocolate, dried or condensed milk. Used for confectionery and for coating biscuits, etc.

Plain/milk chocolate provides (per 100g): energy, 525/529 kcal; (g) protein, 4.7/8.4; fat, 29.2/30.3; carbohydrate, 64.8/59.4; (mg) sodium, 11/120; potassium, 300/420; calcium, 38/220; iron, 2.4/1.6.

cholecalciferol,   *see* vitamin D.

---

cholecystokinin,   pancreozymin. Hormone that stimulates gall-bladder contraction and pancreatic enzyme secretion as well as stimulating both insulin and glucagon release from the pancreas. Secreted by the upper intestinal mucosa in response to various stimuli, e.g., acid, amino acids, fatty acids. Also found in brain, suggesting a neurotransmitter function.

---

cholesterol,   a sterol found in all animal tissues and so in all foods of animal origin, though eggs are the only common food rich in it. Virtually absent from foods of plant origin.

The adult body contains about 150g (2g per kg body weight). The average Western diet provides around 500mg each day, of which about half is absorbed. Adults synthesize daily two to four times the amount of cholesterol absorbed from the food. About 0.5g cholesterol is excreted by the liver daily into the bile, either as such or after oxidation to bile acids, and removed from the body in the faeces.

Cholesterol, like all lipids, is carried in the blood as lipoproteins, mainly as cholesteryl esters with fatty acids. Though cholesterol metabolism is subject to feedback control in that increased dietary intake tends to decrease its synthesis in the body and increase its breakdown, decreasing dietary intake does decrease blood cholesterol levels. Some sterols other than cholesterol (e.g., sitosterol in plants and molusc sterols) tend to inhibit its absorption. (For the effects of saturated and polyunsaturated fatty acids on blood cholesterol levels and the relevance of the levels to coronary heart disease, and the meaning of 'good' and 'bad' cholesterol, *see* fats.)

Average cholesterol content of some foods (mg per 100g): herring oil, 760; cod liver oil, 570; salmon oil, 485; eggs, 450; liver, 330; squid, 280; butter, 230; shrimp, 157; crab, 71; Cheddar cheese, 70; chicken breast, 69; beef, 65; margarine, 0–50 (depending on proportion of animal fat included); oyster, 47; clam, 36; mussel, 36; milk, 14; vegetable oil, 0.

---

cholesteryl esters,   compounds of cholesterol with acids, e.g., fatty acids.

---

cholesteryl hydrolase,   enzyme concerned with digestion of cholesteryl esters. Present in pancreatic digestive juices.

choline, a member of the B complex but not a vitamin since it can be synthesized by man. Best absorbed as phosphatidylcholine (lecithin), of which it is the active constituent. Functions as a source of methyl groups, structurally in membrane phospholipids, in fat transport and prevention of fatty livers (a lipotropic factor) and as a precursor of the neurotransmitter acetylcholine.

Good food sources include liver, lecithin granules, heart, egg yolk, beef steak and wheatgerm.

---

chromium, an essential mineral present in all living matter. Only the trivalent form is active. Total adult body content is 5–10mg. Food sources, mainly grains and cereal products, appear adequate. Use of stainless steel cookware contributes significantly to dietary intake. Mean daily intakes from food in the UK (1976–78) were between 80 and 107µg.

Functions probably as a potentiator of insulin action in the regulation of glucose uptake by the tissues. An organic compound, the glucose tolerance factor (GTF), which contains trivalent chromium bound to nicotinic acid and amino acids, is much more active than inorganic chromium.

Chromium may also have a role in lipid metabolism.

Absorption By a pathway apparently shared with zinc, is about 1 per cent of inorganic trivalent chromium, but more of organically bound chromium in food. Actual absorption of about 1µg daily appears to maintain balance. Transported to the tissues bound to the protein transferrin.

Excretion Very little excreted and that via the kidneys.

Deficiency Dietary deficiency on its own appears unlikely. The glucose tolerance (ability to utilize dietary glucose) of people with protein-energy malnutrition is improved by a chromium supplement.

Requirement No RDA but the USA estimated safe and adequate daily intake is 50–200µg.

Toxicity Like all minerals excess intake is harmful. Hexavalent chromium (chromate) is much more toxic than trivalent chromium.

Food sources Fairly evenly distributed in food groups, highest concentrations being in fish (particularly shellfish), meat, fruit and unrefined sugars; brewer's yeast is a good source of GTF.

---

chronic, lasting, long-drawn-out; not acute.

---

chylomicrons, a lipoprotein composed almost entirely of triglycerides. Formed by the small intestines following the absorption of fat from food. *See* fats.

chyme,   acid, creamy-yellow, thick fluid formed in the stomach from partially digested food.

---

chymotrypsin,   enzyme concerned with protein digestion. Present in pancreatic digestive juices.

---

cider,   an alcoholic drink made by fermenting apple juice. Dry/sweet/ vintage cider provides (per 100ml): energy 36/42/101 kcal; (g) alcohol, 3.8/3.7/10.5; carbohydrate, 2.6/4.3/7.3.

---

cirrhosis,   hardening of an organ, usually the liver. Degenerative changes in liver cells as a result of viruses, bacteria or toxic substances like alcohol, lead to fibrosis. The fibrous tissue is interspersed with orange nodules of regenerating liver cells. In spite of the liver's regenerating capacity, the fibrous tissue eventually contracts and may obstruct the blood or bile flow.

---

cis **fatty acids,**   *see* fatty acids, *cis*.

---

citric acid cycle,   also known as the Krebs cycle after its discoverer. It is a series of oxidative reactions that lead to the release of energy from the common high energy product, acetyl-CoA, formed by the metabolic breakdown of carbohydrates, fats and several amino acids.

---

citrulline,   an amino acid component of the urea cycle (*which see*).

Clostridium botulinum,   a bacterium that produces toxic food poisoning called botulism, which is rare and fatal in about 65 per cent of cases. The exotoxin it releases into food before it is eaten is the most virulent poison known, 1g being sufficient to kill 100,000 people. A spore forming anaerobe. Occurs in soil and vegetables grown thereon, in fish and intestines of pigs. Spores are extremely heat-resistant and may survive in non-acid tinned food (above pH 4.5) that has not been adequately heat-treated. Nitrite preservatives prevent anaerobic growth and hence botulism. Foods commonly affected are inadequately processed tinned meat, vegetables and fish. Main symptoms, which appear in 24–72 hours and lead to death within a week or a slow recovery, are double vision, headache, constipation and paralysis.

Clostridium welchii, (or *perfringens*), a bacterium that causes intestinal food poisoning by producing toxins only when multiplying in the intestinal tract but not in the food itself before it is eaten. Responsible for about 20 per cent of infections in the UK. Spores found in soil, in human and animal intestines and in excreta. Spores are fairly heat-resistant up to 110°C. The bacterium itself is an anaerobe that grows rapidly up to 50°C, is killed above 60°C, but does not grow below 10°C. Foods commonly affected are gravy, stews, pre-cooked meat. Main symptoms, which appear in 8–22 hours and last 12–24 hours, are abdominal pain and diarrhoea.

---

coagulation, of a protein is the process that makes it insoluble. It is irreversible and destroys any pharmacological properties but not the nutritional value. Effected by heat, strong acids and alkalis, etc., which alter the arrangement and cross-linking of the polypeptide chains, allowing them to aggregate and precipitate or coagulate. Coagulation occurs when an egg is cooked or wheat dough baked into bread.

---

cobalamin, *see* vitamin B_{12}.

---

cobalt, an adult 70kg man contains about 1.5mg of this mineral, essential in the diet only as a component of vitamin B_{12}. The vitamin is synthesized in the rumen of cattle and sheep by bacteria that can utilize elemental cobalt, so food sources of the vitamin are meat and liver.

Functions Of cobalt itself, none are known.

Absorption of elemental cobalt takes place readily in the intestines where it shares a transport mechanism with iron.

Excretion of elemental cobalt is primarily in the urine.

Deficiency None except as regards vitamin B_{12}.

Requirement None except as regards vitamin B_{12}.

Toxicity Low, but cobalt added to beer in the 1960s to improve its head caused severe cardiomyopathy and mortality among heavy beer drinkers consuming up to 18mg daily.

Distribution in foods *see* vitamin B_{12}.

---

cocoa, derived from the fermented, dried seed (bean) of the cocoa plant, *Theobroma cacao*. These are roasted and dehusked, and the split beans are called cocoa nibs from which the cocoa and chocolate are obtained. Used for beverages and flavouring. Appears to inhibit dental caries. Contains the methylxanthines, theobromine and some caffeine (65.5 and 5.3mg per serving respectively), and tannins.

Cocoa powder provides (per 100g): energy, 312 kcal; (g) protein, 18.5; fat, 21.7; (mg) calcium, 130; sodium, 950; potassium, 1,500.

---

coconut, a stone fruit or loupe of the *Cocos nucifera* palm tree. Not botanically a nut. The milk has little nutritive value. The dried white flesh, or copra, is rich in fat that is extracted as coconut oil used for cooking and soap making. Residual cake is used for cattle food. Copra is a good food eaten as such or fried. Desiccated coconut is used by confectioners and cake makers for its flavour.

Fresh flesh provides (per 100g): energy, 351 kcal; (g) protein, 3.2; fat, 36.0; total dietary fibre, 13.6; (mg) potassium, 440. Desiccated contains nearly double these amounts.

---

coconut oil, unusual among plant oils particularly, but also among fats, in that most of its fatty acids are saturated. Most saturated fats are solid at room temperature. Coconut oil is liquid because a high proportion of its saturated fatty acids are short chain and liquid at room temperature. As per cent of total fatty acids: saturated, 90 (lauric, 48; myristic, 16; palmitic, 9; capric, 7; caprylic, 7); the monounsaturate oleic, 6.6; the polyunsaturate, linoleic, 1.8.

---

cod-liver oil, rich in vitamins A and D and in unsaturated fatty acids, including the polyunsaturate eicosapentaenoic acid (EPA), which forms about 8 per cent of its total fatty acids, and docosahexaeonoic acid (DHA) about 9 per cent.

Codex Alimentarius, part of the FAO/WHO Commission on Foods Standards concerned to simplify and integrate food standards for international adoption.

---

coeliac disease, or gluten enteropathy, arises in individuals sensitive to gluten, the chief protein of wheat, gluten-like proteins present in rye and in small amounts in barley and oats. Sufferers develop lesions of the small intestine leading to diarrhoea and malabsorption of fat (causing steatorrhoea, failure of children to thrive, weight loss in adults), of iron folate and vitamin B_{12} (that may lead to anaemia), of vitamin D (that may lead to rickets or osteomalacia) and of vitamin K (that may lead to haemorrhage). Symptoms, which usually appear before the age of three, but may present at any age, are relieved if gluten is excluded absolutely from the diet, usually for life. The lesions are probably due to a local immunity reaction to gliadin, a component of gluten. Prevalence of the disease in the UK is about 1 in 2,000, and shows a familial tendency.

coenzyme, the non-protein part of an enzyme (usually formed from a B vitamin) that loosely associates with the protein apoenzyme to form the active or holoenzyme (e.g., pyridoxal phosphate, biotin, thiamin pyrophosphate).

coenzyme A, acts as donor and acceptor of acyl groups, e.g., acetyl, in many reactions concerned with carbohydrate and fat metabolism. Main constituent is pantothenic acid.

coenzyme Q, ubiquinone. Key component of respiratory chain that is concerned with tissue oxidation of food for the release of its energy. Structure similar to vitamins E and K.

coffee, a beverage produced by infusing roasted and ground beans that are seeds of the coffee tree, which grows in the tropics. Accounts for 16 per cent of the liquid intake, other than water, in the UK. Contains the methylxanthine caffeine. The caffeine content of a 6 fl oz cup of brewed coffee is 100–150mg, of instant coffee, 60-80mg, and of decaffeinated coffee, 3–5mg. Undecaffeinated, in moderate amounts it is a mild cerebral stimulant and diuretic and, in excessive amounts a cause of anxiety symptoms, gastrointestinal discomfort and insomnia. Contains polyphenols that inhibit non-haem iron absorption.

Coffee drinking has been linked with the incidence of pancreatic, ovarian and bladder cancers, with cardiac arrhythmias and cardiovascular disease, and as producing teratogenic effects, but as yet there is no proof that moderate coffee drinking is harmful.

A cup of coffee provides about 0.6mg nicotinic acid, 16mg magnesium, and is a source of potassium.

collagen, commonest animal protein and chief component of connective tissue. A fibrous glycoprotein. Present in skin, tendon, bones, teeth, blood vessels, muscles. Resists digestion but boiling in water produces the soluble protein, gelatin. Rich in proline and hydroxyproline. Requires vitamin C for its formation.

---

colon, greater portion of the large intestine, extending from the ileum to the rectum. Comprises ascending, transverse and descending colon. Main site of absorption of water causing contents to become more solid. Contents subject to fermentation by bacteria.

---

colostrum, first breast milk. *See* milk.

---

colours, are added to foods to make them attractive. Over 30 are permitted in the UK and these include synthetic organic dyes as well as products of natural origin such as chlorophyll, caramel, carotenoids, beetroot red and the natural substances paprika, saffron, turmeric and sandalwood. *See* additives.

MAFF proposes to restrict amounts of colours used in a wide range of foods and to prohibit or restrict certain colours currently permitted in foods. Proposals include the removal of crocin and santalin (the colouring principles of saffron and sandalwood, respectively) from the list of permitted colours. The use of other natural source colours (solvent-extracted annatto, canthaxanthin and the paprika extracts, capsanthin and capsorubin) are being re-examined. Closely specified standards for caramel colours and their use are recommended.

COMA report, in this book refers to the report of the Committee on Medical Aspects of Food Policy on Diet in Relation to Cardiovascular Disease. *See* cardiovascular disease.

Committee on the Toxicity of Chemicals in Food, Consumer Products and the Environment, advises at the request of the government, on the toxic risk to man of the use of chemicals including any that are proposed to be used as food additives.

---

complementary value, or supplementary value, of proteins. The ability to make good each other's limiting amino acid when combined.

compound, consists of elements chemically united in fixed proportions to form a new substance with new properties.

---

confectionery, includes toffees (sugar, syrup and a little fat), boiled sweets (often 50 per cent sucrose and 40 per cent glucose) and chocolate (cocoa, other fats and sucrose). Cocoa appears to inhibit the cariogenic properties of confectionery to some extent.

---

conjugate, joining of a molecule with another molecule of a different kind, e.g., haemoglobin, which is a conjugate of a protein, globin, with the iron-containing pigment, haem.

---

constipation, delay in passage of faeces. In healthy people defecation may occur daily or only once or twice a week. Constipation is present only if delay causes discomfort and indigestion. Common causes are small faecal bulk and persistent neglect of the call to defecate. A high intake of dietary fibre, particularly of coarse bran, usually prevents or cures constipation, but if persistent a doctor should be consulted.

---

contraceptive pill, usage appears to increase the dietary requirement for vitamin B_6. Blood levels of vitamin A are raised in users.

---

cook-chilled, describes food for sale already cooked and then chilled to increase shelf-life. Keeps fresh for the time indicated on the label provided it is stored at the proper refrigerator temperature all the time. Directions regarding usage and reheating should be followed carefully to avoid the risk of food poisoning caused by contamination with *Listeria* (*which see*).

---

copper, the adult body contains about 100mg of this essential mineral, the highest concentrations being in the liver, brain and kidney.

Daily UK household supply in 1986 (not allowing for 10 per cent wastage and out-of-home meals) averaged 1.25mg (1.51 with contributions from alcoholic drinks and confectionery) derived mainly from (per cent): cereals, 32 (bread, 18); meat and meat products, 26; vegetables, 17 (potatoes, 8).

Functions as a component of many enzyme systems (oxidases), one of which, ceruloplasmin, is required for iron absorption. Metabolism closely linked with that of iron. Required for red blood cell formation.

Absorption requires complexing with a substance present in the saliva and gastric juices because it readily forms insoluble salts in the alkaline intestinal fluids. About 30 per cent is absorbed. High intakes of zinc reduce copper absorption. Transported in the blood, bound to protein and taken up by the liver, where it is either excreted in the bile or converted to oxidase enzymes.

Excreted via the bile and is not reabsorbed. Copper homeostasis is maintained by this means.

Deficiency Dietary deficiency unlikely in UK. May occur in premature infants because their copper reserves are low and their milk and cereal diet is naturally low in copper. Presents as chronic diarrhoea and leads to anaemia. Seen also in protein-energy malnutrition. Effects of severe deficiency include defective synthesis of body proteins, reduced defence against infections, and degenerative changes in the nervous system.

Menke's disease (kinky or steely hair syndrome) is a rare inherited inability to absorb copper that, if untreated, leads to mental retardation, failure to keratinize hair, which becomes kinky, and death.

Requirement No RDA but USA estimated safe and adequate daily intake is 1.5–3.0mg.

Toxicity rarely seen. Manifestations include blue-green diarrhoeal stools and saliva, breakdown of red blood cells and abnormalities of kidney function.

In the rare, inherited Wilson's disease, there is failure to form ceruloplasmin and copper accumulates mainly in the liver and brain. Dementia and liver failure occur.

Distribution in foods (in mg per 100g): oysters, 7.6; ox, pig, lamb, calf liver, 2.5, 2.7, 8.7, 11.0 respectively; lentils, 0.58; parsley, 0.52; walnuts, 0.31; wholemeal bread and peanuts, 0.27; peas, 0.23; mackerel, 0.19; lean meats, 0.14–0.17; white bread and potato, 0.15; watercress, 0.14; eggs and tomatoes, 0.10; winter cabbage and cod, 0.06; milk, 0.02.

---

copra, dried white flesh of coconut.

---

coprophagy, feeding on own faeces. Enables animals like rabbits that practise this to make use of B vitamins synthesized by colonic bacteria.

---

coprosterol, also known as coprostanol. A sterol found in faeces. Derived from cholesterol by bacterial action in the colon.

Cori cycle,   or lactic acid cycle, describes the cycle of events that follow when glucose in muscles is broken down to provide energy in the absence of oxygen. The lactic acid formed passes into the bloodstream to the liver where it is converted to glucose, which is transported back to the muscles. Named after its discoverer.

---

corn sugar gum,   *see* xantham gum.

---

corn oil,   or maize oil. Rich in polyunsaturated fatty acids, linoleic acid forming 50 per cent of its total fatty acids and alpha-linolenic acid 1.6 per cent.

---

corn syrup,   glucose syrup derived from corn. Often used as a sweetener in food products. Consists mainly of glucose with maltose, dextrins and water and is cariogenic.

---

coronary heart disease,   or ischaemic heart disease are synonymous terms for a group of syndromes arising from failure of the coronary arteries to supply sufficient blood to the myocardium or heart muscle. In most cases associated with atherosclerosis of the coronary arteries. Includes myocardial infarction, angina pectoris, and sudden death with infarctions. The most important risk factors for the disease, which are all controllable at least to some extent, are raised blood cholesterol levels (*see* fats), high blood-pressure and smoking — in that order. Other risk factors, some controllable, some not, include ageing, maleness, family history of the disease, lack of physical exercise, obesity, diabetes mellitus, gout, other abnormalities of serum lipids including triglyceride (fat) levels, use of some types of contraceptive pill, stress and personality type A (competitive, aggressive, driving, perfectionist). For its dietary prevention, *see* cardiovascular disease.

---

coronary thrombosis,   blockage of a coronary artery by a blood clot, or, thrombus.

---

covalent compounds,   are formed when constituent atoms share electrons. Carbohydrates, proteins and fats are typical examples.

cream, contains all the fat and usually one third to a half of the protein and lactose of milk.

Double/whipping/single cream provides (per 100g): energy, 447/332/212 kcal; (g) protein, 1.5/1.9/2.4; fat, 48.2/35.0/21.2; (mg) calcium, 50/63/79; (μg) vitamin A: summer, 450/325/200; winter, 330/240/145; carotene: summer, 280/205/125; winter, 160/115/70.

---

creatine, an amino acid derived in the body from glycine. Not a constituent of proteins. Forms creatine phosphate, which contains a high-energy phosphate bond and so acts as an energy store in the muscles. (*See* athletes.)

---

creatinine, anhydride of creatine. Its 24-hour urinary excretion is proportional to an individual's muscle mass.

---

cretinism, is due to a congenital thyroid deficiency and results in a dull-looking child, underdeveloped both mentally and physically.

Crohn's disease, or chronic regional enteritis. A chronic inflammatory disease affecting any part of the gastrointestinal tract from mouth to anus, but typically the terminal ileum and ascending colon. Characterized by abdominal pain, diarrhoea, weight loss and malabsorption syndrome. Cause unknown.

---

cyanocobalamin, *see* vitamin B_{12}.

---

cyclamate, an intense sweetener (*which see*) permitted for use in the EC. Thirty times as sweet as the same weight of sucrose.

---

cyclo-oxygenase, enzyme that catalyses the conversion of 20 carbon polyunsaturated fatty acids to prostanoids, hormone-like substances that control many body functions. Inhibited by aspirin and indomethacin.

---

cysteine, a non-essential sulphur amino acid that can, in part, spare essential methionine. Precursor of taurine and utilized in synthesis of coenzyme A.

cystine, a non-essential, sulphur amino acid formed by linking two cysteine molecules by their sulphur atoms. Often forms bridge between polypeptide chains in proteins, e.g., insulin. Forms about 12 per cent of hair and insulin proteins.

cytosine, a pyrimidine found in RNA and DNA. *See* nucleic acids.

D

dahls, pulses widely cultivated in India. Include Bengal gram (*Cicer arietinum*), black gram (*Vigna mungo*), green gram (*V. radiatus*) and red gram or pidgeon pea (*Cajanus cajan*). Khesari dahl (*Lathyrus sativus*) is very resistant to drought but, if eaten to excess, causes lathyrism (*which see*).

dehydroascorbic acid, oxidized form of ascorbic acid. Has full vitamin C activity.

demulcent, substances that sooth and protect the alimentary canal, e.g., acacia.

denaturation, of a protein is a change to its structure caused by gentle heat, mild acid (e.g., vinegar), dilute alcohol (e.g., wine), etc. It makes the protein less soluble. Enzyme or hormonal activity (if any) is lost. More drastic treatment (e.g., strong heat) causes coagulation.

deoxyribonuclease, enzyme concerned with digestion of deoxyribonucleic acids (DNA). Present in pancreatic digestive juices.

deoxyribonucleic acid (DNA), or desoxyribonucleic acid, a nucleic acid (*which see*). Carrier of genetic information.

---

deoxyribose, or desoxyribose. Pentose (5 carbon) monosaccharide having one less oxygen atom than ribose. Found in DNA. Made in the body. Dietary deoxyribose is not an important energy source.

---

dermatitis herpetiformis, skin disease usually found in sufferers from coeliac disease.

---

desaturase enzymes, remove hydrogen from fatty acids forming unsaturated (double) bonds. Delta-6 and delta-5 desaturases catalyse the first and second dehydrogenations in the conversion pathways of linoleic and alpha-linolenic acids to the starting materials for prostanoid and leukotriene synthesis. Saturated and *trans* fatty acids, alcohol and, possibly, age reduce the activity, particularly of the delta-6 enzyme in animals. *See* Figure 2, page 79.

---

desoxyribonucleic acid, *see* deoxyribonucleic acid (DNA).

---

detergents, failure to rinse or wipe dry detergent-washed dishes could result in adults consuming 75mg detergent daily, and bottle-fed babies 250mg. Whether these intakes cause deleterious changes in the human alimentary canal is not known. Such changes were seen in rats given proportionately higher intakes for several months.

---

dextran, glucose polysaccharides produced by bacteria growing on a glucose substrate. Forms chelates.

---

dextrin, also known as British gum. An oligosaccharide being partially digested starch. Used as easily digestible carbohydrate for sick patients.

---

dextrose, *see* glucose.

DHSS, Department of Health and Social Security, now split into the Department of Health and the Department of Social Security.

---

diabetes mellitus, a syndrome characterized by a raised blood glucose level (hyperglycaemia) due to deficiency or diminished effectiveness of the pancreatic hormone, insulin. Also affects metabolism of fat and protein. Glucose spills over into the urine (glycosuria) leading to polyuria and loss of weight. An acute and dangerous possible complication is ketoacidosis resulting from incomplete oxidation of fatty acids, yielding ketone bodies, which are strong acids whose neutralization upsets the body's acid-base balance. Long-term complications include an increased risk of athero-sclerotic disease and certain obstetrical difficulties, and specific changes in eyes, feet, nerves and kidneys. It is the commonest hormonal disorder. About 1 per cent of the population in the UK have diagnosed diabetes and about 1 per cent are estimated to be undiscovered diabetics. There are two types:
1. *Insulin dependent* — also known as Type I or juvenile-onset type. Usually appears before age 40 in normal or below normal weight people. Symptoms are severe and, without insulin, fatal ketoacidosis may occur.
2. *Non-insulin dependent* — also known as Type II, adult or maturity-onset type, and the more common. Appears in middle-age or later, frequently in obese people, in whom the hyperglycaemia can often be controlled just by diet, or by diet and a hypoglycaemic drug. Less prone to develop ketoacidosis, but as equally subject to long-term complications as the insulin-dependent type.

Current dietary treatment advocates that complex carbohydrate/high dietary fibre foods (e.g., pulses, various cereals and vegetables, wholemeal bread) provide 50 per cent of the energy intake; usually prohibits readily absorbable carbohydrates such as sucrose and glucose, but allows fructose, which does not require insulin for its uptake by the liver; and permits sugar alcohols as sweeteners, but in moderate amounts since they are as fattening as carbohydrates. Fat intake should be low with the aim of reducing the risk of atherosclerotic diseases. Energy intake must aim to reduce the weight of the obese, making their hyperglycaemia easier to control.

Law Since 1986, regulations closely control the composition and labelling of foods claimed as suitable or specially made for diabetics, to take account of these objectives.

---

diarrhoea, is the frequent passage of loose or watery stools, and may be acute or chronic. It is a symptom, not a disease. Causes include neuro-muscular overactivity consequent to emotional states; irritation or inflammation of the bowel mucosa by bacterial, viral, protozoal, chemical or physical agents (e.g., in food poisoning); Crohn's disease; ulcerative colitis; gastroenteritis; malabsorptive disorders; excessive use of laxatives.

Replacement of lost fluids to prevent dehydration is important. Achieved by adding commercially available mixtures of glucose and electrolytes to water to make a drink isotonic with the blood and so easily absorbable.

---

diet, (a) the habitual food; (b) a prescribed course of food, e.g., low calorie for slimmers, gluten-free for coeliacs.

---

diet, balanced, supplies the energy, protein, dietary fibre, vitamins, minerals including trace elements, essential fatty acids and essential amino acids in amounts and forms that maintain good health. Present opinion is that good health is more likely to be maintained if most of the energy is supplied in the form of complex carbohydrate/high dietary fibre foods such as whole cereals, vegetables and fruits, while that obtained from fat, particularly saturated fat as found in dairy products (other than skimmed milk), meat and meat products, is kept low. The other requirements of a balanced diet will automatically be supplied by following these principles.

---

dietetics, the interpretation and application of the scientific principles of nutrition to feeding in health and disease.

---

digestibility, of a foodstuff is the proportion of the foodstuff consumed that is absorbed into the bloodstream, usually 90–95 per cent. Apparent digestibility is the difference between intake and output in the faeces. True digestibility makes allowance for faecal contents not derived from the foodstuff, such as shed lining cells from the intestines, bacteria, etc.

---

digestion, the process by which food is rendered absorbable so that it can be used by the body for energy, growth and repair. Food is made up of carbohydrates, proteins and fats, large molecules that have to be broken down (digested) into small ones by enzymes in digestive juices so they can be absorbed, as well as vitamins, minerals including trace elements, water and dietary fibre or roughage. About 8 litres of digestive juices containing 50g of protein (enzymes) are formed daily.

Digestion commences in the oral cavity as the food is chewed and mixed with saliva, which contains the enzyme amylase that begins the breakdown of starch, the chief dietary carbohydrate, to maltose. Lingual lipase, secreted at the back of the tongue, commences digestion of fat and continues it in the stomach. After swallowing, the food passes down the oesophagus into the stomach.

The secretion of the digestive juices in the stomach and later from the pancreas and in the intestines, is governed by nerve impulses, by the presence of the food itself and by hormones, such as gastrin, cholecystokinin and secretin. The gastric juices contain acid that stops further action by the salivary amylase, but allows the enzyme pepsin in the juices to begin the breakdown of proteins to peptones. Mucus secreted by the stomach lining stops the stomach being damaged by the acid. Gastrin production ceases when the acidity reaches a certain point. Digestion in the stomach results in a thick, creamy acid liquid called chyme.

Chyme passes into the first part of the small intestine, the duodenum, where it meets bile from the liver, which more than neutralizes the acid in the chyme, creating an alkaline environment. Mucus secretions again protect the walls of the intestines. Pancreatic juices continue digestion with the enzyme pancreatic amylase completing the breakdown of starch to maltose, trypsin converting peptones to peptides and lipase acting on fats that have been emulsified into small droplets by the bile, breaking them down into monoglycerides, glycerol and fatty acids.

Intestinal juices produce peptidases that break down peptides into amino acids and other enzymes which break down the remaining carbohydrates.

The digested food, together with vitamins and minerals, are then absorbed into the cells lining the intestine. The lining of the small intestine is thrown into folds and covered with minute projections called villi, providing an absorbing surface of over 300 sq m. From the cells, fatty substances pass into the lymphatic system that enters the bloodstream in the neck and the rest pass directly into the blood in the hepatic portal vein and are carried straight to the liver for processing or distribution to the tissues.

Residual waste matter, which is composed mainly of dietary fibre, passes into the first part of the large intestine, the colon, where much of the water is absorbed and fermentation of the residue by 'friendly' bacteria takes place. Bacteria makes up 65–75 per cent of the semi-solid faeces that pass through the second part of the large intestine, the rectum, and are expelled from the body through the anus.

---

diglycerides, lipids that are esters of the alcohol, glycerol, with two fatty acids.

dihomo-gamma linolenic acid (DGLA), a polyunsaturated fatty acid of the omega 6 family, with 20 carbons and three unsaturated bonds (C20:3 n-6). Derived in the body from linoleic acid. Vital role as immediate precursor of arachidonic acid and of prostanoids (Series 1) and leukotrienes (Series 3). *See* Figure 2, page 79.

---

dipeptidases, enzymes concerned with digestion of polypeptides. Present in intestinal digestive juices.

---

disaccharides, sweet, soluble sugars that yield on hydrolysis two mono-saccharides which may be both the same (e.g., maltose) or different (e.g., sucrose).

---

disease, is defined in the Medicines Act 1968 as including any injury, ailment or adverse condition whether of mind or body.

---

dishcloths, particularly when soiled, allow the survival and transfer of microorganisms (e.g., *Salmonella* species, *Staphylococcus aureus*) to hands, surfaces, etc. Drying reduces the number of organisms on the surfaces but is less effective for dishcloths, even clean ones, because they take longer to dry. Chemical disinfection of dishcloths (e.g., with bleach) substantially reduces contamination, though this may be unreliable for heavily con-taminated cloths. Detergent washing alone is insufficient to decontaminate cloths and drying afterwards at room temperature leads to regrowth of survivors. The use of disposable dishcloths is safest.

---

disseminated or multiple sclerosis, variably progressive disease of the nervous system in which patchy, degenerative changes occur in nerve sheaths followed by sclerosis. Symptoms usually appear in young adults and include limb weakness, parasthesia, ataxia, and loss of bladder control. Affects about 1 in 2,000 in the UK. Cause unknown, but may include a trace element deficiency and some trials indicate a high dietary intake of polyunsaturated fatty acids reduces the number and duration of relapses.

---

diuretic, an agent that increases the flow of urine, e.g., the methyl-xanthines present in tea and coffee.

diverticulosis, blind pouches present in the oesophagus, stomach or small and large intestines, but most frequently in the colon. When inflamed the condition is called diverticulitis. Up to about 30 per cent of people over the age of 60 in the USA and UK have diverticulosis, but only 5–10 per cent of these develop diverticulitis. A diet high in dietary fibre, particularly wheat bran, is beneficial in preventing and relieving the disease.

DMF index, standard way of expressing extent of dental caries. Stands for number of teeth that are decayed, missing or filled. In UK average DMF at age 12 is 5–7.

DNA, deoxy- or desoxy-ribonucleic acid. A nucleic acid containing deoxyribose. Carrier of genetic information.

DoH, Department of Health.

docosahexaenoic acid (DHA), or, cervonic acid, a polyunsaturated fatty acid of the omega 3 family with 22 carbons and six unsaturated bonds (C22:6 n-3). Found particularly in brain, nervous tissue, testes and the retina of the eye. Derived in the body from alpha-linolenic acid. Present particularly in fish oils. Can be converted by the body into 20 carbon, five double bond, eicosapentaenoic acid (EPA) (*which see*).

Distribution in foods (as percentage of total fatty acids): cod, 33.4; haddock, 24.5; halibut, 15.0; mackerel, 12.6; plaice, 10.3; lamb's brain, 9.5; herring, 6.5; turkey, 5.0; livers, 1.2–4.8; chicken, 1.0; (in g per 100g food): mackerel, 1.85; herring, 1.08; halibut, 0.25; cod, 0.16; haddock and turkey, 0.10; livers, chicken, 0.04, ox, 0.32; chicken meat/meat and skin 0.04/0.17.

dopa, intermediate in formation of catecholamines and melanin from tyrosine.

dopamine, a catecholamine (*which see*). Metabolic intermediate between tyrosine and adrenaline. Appears to be involved in the pathogenesis of schizophrenia and Parkinson's disease.

double bonds, describes the unsaturated bonds between atoms found for example in unsaturated and polyunsaturated fatty acids.

---

dry heat cooking, comprises roasting, grilling, baking and toasting. It uses a higher temperature than boiling or steaming and so loss of heat sensitive nutrients, such as thiamin and vitamin C, is greater. Minerals are not destroyed by heat but they may be lost, together with water soluble vitamins such as niacin, by leaching into the drippings from the food unless these are utilized, e.g., in making gravy.

Fats are stable to moderate heat but decompose at high temperatures, with formation of acrid-smelling acrolein. Dry heat converts starch to pyrodextrins, which contribute to the brown colour of breadcrust and toast. Sucrose is caramelized. Proteins are sensitive to heat but their nutritive value is only affected at high temperatures, such as in roasting, when the availability of some amino acids (lysine, aspartic acid and glutamic acid) is reduced. Protein and carbohydrate occurring together in a food may react, undergoing non-enzymic browning (Maillard reaction). This results in loss of nutritional value, particularly of lysine and methionine, but produces desirable changes in flavours, colours and smell, e.g., in bread during baking and toasting, in nuts and coffee beans during roasting.

---

drying, of food to preserve it has little effect on its protein quality if the temperature is kept below 100°C. Vitamin C is the most vulnerable nutrient, its loss increasing with the length of drying time.

---

duck, poultry meat. Usually eaten with its skin, which has a high fat content.

The meat/meat plus skin and fat provide (per 100g): energy, 122/430; (g) water, 75.0/43.9; protein, 19.7/11.3; fat, 4.8/42.7; (mg) iron, 2.4/2.4; zinc, 1.9/1.3.

---

duodenum, first part of the small intestine. Receives bile and pancreatic juices whose alkalinity helps neutralize the acidity of chyme from the stomach. Brunner's glands in the walls secrete intestinal digestive juices.

---

dyspepsia, indigestion. Any gastrointestinal symptom associated with taking food, e.g., nausea, heartburn, discomfort or distension. May be psychological in origin or due to food intolerance (both described as 'functional') or a symptom of disorder in the digestive tract (e.g., an ulcer) or associated structures (e.g., gall-bladder, pancreas, etc.) or of general disease, e.g., heart failure. Bananas have been advocated in the treatment of gastric ulcers and a preliminary trial found banana powder taken four times daily relieved non-ulcer indigestion.

dysphagia, difficulty in swallowing.

E

E numbers, are food additive serial numbers that begin with an E to show that they have been agreed for use throughout the EC. Eventually all serial numbers are expected to be EC agreed. *See* serial numbers.

EDTA, ethylenediamine tetra-acetic acid. Forms stable complexes with some metals, so acts as sequestering or chelating agent. Used in measuring dietary fibre.

EC, European Community.

EFA, *see* essential fatty acid.

eggs, mainly those of hens. Highly nutritious food apart from their high cholesterol content (about 250mg in an average 60g egg) which, if too many are eaten, may raise blood cholesterol levels. An average egg provides 6g fat and 6g protein. Egg protein has the highest biological value for human adults of all food proteins. An egg contains about 30mg calcium, and, in a bound form unavailable to man, 1.5mg iron. The yolk is a fair source of vitamin A, though the carotenoid yolk colouring is not a vitamin A precursor. Provides significant amounts of B vitamins, but little or no vitamin C. Eggs from free-range hens contain more folate and vitamin B_{12} than those from battery hens. The avidin in the white, unless cooked, binds with biotin in egg yolk preventing its absorption.

Eggs should be stored in the refrigerator and, to avoid the risk of food poisoning by *Salmonellae* (*which see*) with which some may be contaminated, they should not be eaten raw and should be cooked thoroughly until yolks and whites are solid. This applies particularly when for consumption by vulnerable groups such as the elderly, infants, the sick, and pregnant women. Cracked eggs should not be used.

The whole/white/yolk of an egg provides (per 100g): energy, 147/36/339 kcal; (g) water, 74.8/88.3/51.0; protein, 12.3/9.0/16.1; fat, 10.9/0/30.5; (mg) sodium, 140/190/50; potassium, 140/150/120; calcium, 52/2/130; iron, 2.0/0.1/6.1; zinc, 1.5/0.03/3.6; thiamin, 0.09/0/0.30; riboflavin, 0.47/0.43/ 0.54; niacin, 3.68/2.73/4.75; vitamin E, 1.6/0/4.6; (μg) vitamin A, 140/0/400; vitamin D, 1.75/0/5.0; vitamin B_{12}, 1.7*/0.1/4.9; total folate, 25*/1/52; biotin, 25/0/60. (*Value for battery hens. Whole deep litter/free-range eggs provide (μg per 100g): vitamin B_{12}, 2.6/2.9; folic acid, 32/39.)

---

eicosanoids, comprise the prostanoids and leukotrienes, 20 ('eicosa') carbon, hormone-like substances derived from dihomo-gamma-linolenic acid (DGLA), arachidonic and eicosapentaenoic (EPA) acids. These acids are 20 carbon, polyunsaturated fatty acids usually derived by desaturation and chain elongation within the body of essential fatty acids obtained from the food, mainly plant sources. These processes are catalysed by desaturase and elongase enzymes. Arachidonic acid and EPA are also obtained from animal and fatty fish-food sources respectively. One of the intermediates in DGLA synthesis in the body, gamma-linolenic acid (GLA), is present in certain plant oils (e.g., blackcurrant, borage and evening primrose), providing an additional dietary source. Blackcurrant oil also contains stearidonic acid, an intermediate in the body's synthesis of EPA. These food sources may be particularly useful if the desaturases are inefficient. *See* Eicosanoid Derivation Figure 2, page 79.

---

eicosapentaenoic acid (EPA), also known as timnodonic acid. A polyunsaturated fatty acid of the omega 3 family with 20 carbons and five unsaturated bonds (C20:5 n-3). Formed in the body from alpha-linolenic acid. Vital role as immediate precursor of prostanoids (Series 3) and leukotrienes (Series 5) (*See* Figure 2, page 79) and structurally as constituent of cell membranes. Oils of fish and marine animals from temperate waters are rich in EPA.

Figure 2: Eicosanoid derivation from essential fatty acids and food polyunsaturated fatty acids

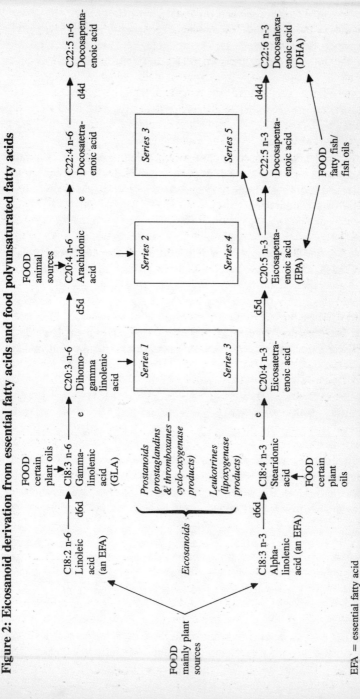

EFA = essential fatty acid
d6d, d5d and d4d = delta-6, delta-5, and delta-4-desaturase enzymes respectively
e = elongase enzyme

Distribution in foods as percentage of total fatty acids: cod, 17.2; haddock, 12.0; halibut, 10.3; mackerel, 7.3; herring, 7.0; turkey, 1.5; lamb's brain, 0.7; as g per 100g food: herring, 1.17; mackerel, 1.07; halibut, 0.17; cod, 0.08; haddock, 0.05; turkey meat/meat and skin, 0.03/0.10.

---

elaidic acid, *trans*-isomer of oleic acid. *See* fatty acids.

---

elastin, an insoluble, fibrous, connective tissue glycoprotein. Naturally elastic due to presence of loops in its polypeptide chains, which can stretch out and recoil. With age, elastic properties diminish. Present in arteries, lung and skin tissues and tendons.

---

elderly, as the level of physical activity declines, energy requirements fall, but the need for vitamins and minerals remains virtually unchanged. Consequently the proportion of energy-rich fatty foods should be decreased and those with high nutrient density increased, e.g., milk, eggs, fish, fruit, vegetables. Digestive and absorptive ability may be reduced. Obesity is probably the commonest nutritional disorder, at least in women. The elderly who do not eat a balanced diet should take a multi-vitamin and mineral supplement.

---

electron, smallest particle of negative electricity.

---

electrovalent compounds, are formed between ions of opposite electrical charge (cations and anions). They include salts such as common salt or sodium chloride in which sodium is the positively charged cation and chloride the negatively charged anion.

---

element, any substance that cannot be decomposed chemically. Alone and in combination they constitute all matter. There are about 103 known elements.

---

elements, trace, elements required in the diet in amounts of less than 100mg daily. Also known as trace minerals. Include metals, e.g., copper, and non-metals, e.g., selenium. *See* minerals, essential.

emollient, describes substances that have a softening and soothing effect, e.g., ispaghula.

EMS, *see* eosinophilia myalgia syndrome.

---

emulsifiers and stabilizers, are substances that are respectively capable of making and stabilizing an emulsion which is a uniform dispersion of two or more substances like oil and water, which do not mix. Apart from foods themselves, only permitted emulsifiers like lecithin and glyceryl monostearate and stabilizers such as the vegetable gums are allowed in foods. They are used in the manufacture of cakes, ice-cream and salad creams, etc. *See* additives.

---

emulsion, a uniform dispersion of two or more immiscible substances such as water and oil. Emulsifying agents such as bile or lecithin, which act because they are partly soluble in both substances, help to keep the substances from separating and, in the case of foods, a stabilizer like the vegetable gums is often added to maintain the emulsion. *See* additives.

---

endocrine, secreting internally. Describes glands that produce secretions or hormones which pass directly into the bloodstream, e.g., gastric mucosa produces gastrin; pancreas produces insulin and glucagon.

---

endogenous, formed by the body, e.g., cholesterol in the body is made up of that formed by the body itself, endogenous, and that absorbed from the food, exogenous.

---

endorphins, opioid peptides released by the pituitary gland. May be concerned in the body's control of pain and may account for placebo effects.

---

endosperm, *see* flours, wheat.

---

endotoxins, poisons produced within the bacterial cell and released only when they die. Endotoxic bacteria (e.g., *Salmonellae*) cause infective food poisoning, symptoms appearing at least 12 hours after consumption of contaminated food when enough bacteria have died to build up sufficient endotoxins. Symptoms are fever, headache, diarrhoea and vomiting. Heat sufficient to kill the bacteria destroys the endotoxins. Endotoxins do not stimulate antitoxin formation by the immune system; instead the bacteria themselves are attacked by antibodies.

---

energy, capacity for work. Exists in various forms including solar, chemical, mechanical, light, heat and electrical, which are quantitatively interchangeable. Green plants, unlike animals, make use of solar energy, which they convert to chemical energy by synthesizing complex organic molecules (carbohydrates, proteins and fats) from simple inorganic ones and carbon dioxide (*see* photosynthesis). Animals are directly or indirectly dependent on plants for their energy source, which they consume in these chemical forms and use to perform mechanical work, to maintain body tissues and temperatures and for growth.

Of the total energy in food as measured in a bomb calorimeter, some is lost in the faeces and is unavailable. Of the available energy some is not completely released by oxidation in the body (e.g., urea from dietary protein) and is lost in the urine and some is lost through thermogenesis. The remainder, described as net energy, is used by the body for mechanical work, etc.

Efficiency of utilization If dietary carbohydrate is not oxidized directly and is stored as glycogen, 5 per cent of its energy content is lost in the process and if stored as fat, 28 per cent is lost. The energy cost of protein synthesis and degradation is about 24 per cent of the available energy in amino acids. The cost of storage and remobilization of fat is about 7 per cent of its energy content.

At best, man can convert only 25 per cent of the chemical energy in food into mechanical work, a rate comparable to an internal combustion engine, the rest being dissipated as heat.

Units of energy used in nutrition are the kilojoule (kJ) and megajoule (MJ). One MJ is equal to 1,000 kJ. Energy is also expressed quantitatively as heat, the unit of heat used in nutrition being the kilocalorie (kcal or C). 4.2 kJ = 1 kcal for practical purposes.

Energy value of food is calculated using the following conversion factors: (per g) carbohydrate (expressed as monosaccharide), 16 kJ (3.75 kcal); protein, 17 kJ (4 kcal); fat, 37 kJ (9 kcal); alcohol, 29 kJ (7 kcal). Following implementation of EC directives the conversion factor per g carbohydrate will become 17 kJ (4 kcal).

Energy requirements are proportional to the intensity of muscular work, light physical activity (e.g., vacuum cleaning) using 2.5–4.9 kcal per min, moderate work (e.g., gardening) 5.0–7.4, heavy work (e.g., coal-mining) 7.5–9.9 and very heavy work (e.g., steel-furnace worker) more than 10.

Requirements are also proportional to lean body weight, and are therefore higher per kg of total body weight in men than in women who are fatter. Requirements are increased by pregnancy and lactation. They decrease with age and are less in hot climates. Per kg of body weight they are greatest during the first year of life, thereafter falling slowly as the rate of growth per unit of body weight falls with age.

An individual's daily energy requirement is made up of energy expended in sleeping (500 kcal), at work (950–1800 kcal depending on degree of physical activity) and in non-occupational activities (700–1650 kcal).

UK RDAs are therefore based on age, sex and occupational activity. For example, for a man aged 18–34 in a sedentary, moderately active or very active occupation the RDAs are 2,510, 2,900 and 3,350 kcal respectively, whereas for a woman over 75 leading a sedentary life, the RDA is 1,680 kcal. RDAs for other population groups are given in Table 5, pages 224-225.

NACNE recommendations regarding desirable food energy sources are given under NACNE.

Humans in developing countries subject to seasonal marginal energy intakes, have low basal and sleeping energy expenditure and high work efficiency that enables them to cope. Energy expenditure in slimmers decreases with reduced energy intake making weight loss more difficult. Energy requirements of the slimmed obese are lower than before weight loss and lower than lean people of the same weight.

Distribution in food (kcal per 100g): vegetable oil, 899; butter, 740; margarine, 730; peanut butter (smooth), 623; almonds, 565; chocolate (plain), 525; double cream, 447; Cheddar cheese, 406; sugar, 394; polished rice, 361; honey, 288; white bread, 233; chicken meat and skin, 230; mackerel, 223; wholemeal bread, 216; single cream, 212; wheat bran, 188; meats, 123–162; eggs, 147; chicken meat, 121; cottage cheese, 96; potatoes, 87; cod, 76; peas, 67; milk (whole), 65; yogurt, 52; parsnips, 49; milk (skimmed), 33; winter cabbage, 22; mushrooms, 13; lettuce, 12.

Law From 1986, energy claims for a food must be capable of fulfilment and the food must be labelled with its energy content.

---

energy dense,   describes foods with a high energy value per g of food. The lower the moisture content, the higher the fat content and the lower the dietary fibre content, the more energy dense is the food. Pure oil is the most energy-dense food possible.

energy release, from carbohydrates, fats and, to a lesser extent, proteins, uses oxygen and produces energy-rich adenosine triphosphate (ATP), a readily available energy store, plus the waste products carbon dioxide and water. All three foodstuffs are converted by separate oxidative processes to energy rich acetyl CoA, which is then oxidized in the citric acid cycle producing a hydrogen-rich coenzyme (NADH) and prosthetic group ($FADH_2$). These enter the respiratory chain, a series of oxidative steps leading to the production of ATP. Because fat contains a higher proportion of hydrogen than either carbohydrate or protein, it produces more of the hydrogen-rich compounds and so, gram for gram, yields more ATP or energy than either carbohydrates or proteins and is consequently more 'fattening' than either of them.

---

enrichment, addition of nutrients to a food beyond the levels originally present. When the additions are legally imposed, the term fortification is used.

---

enterohepatic circulation, recycling of substances between the liver and intestines, e.g., bile salts. Bile salts formed in the liver from cholesterol pass into the duodenum in the bile where they emulsify lipids and form water-soluble emulsified droplets with the products of lipid digestion (mixed micelles). These diffuse to the absorbing surface of the jejunum where the digested lipids are deposited and absorbed, the bile salts remaining in the lumen. Intestinal bacteria convert some of the primary bile salts to secondary bile salts, and 99 per cent of both are then absorbed into the blood from the ileum and returned to the liver for reuse in the bile. The cycle is repeated 6–10 times daily and is so efficient that only about 500mg bile salts daily from the recycling pool of 3–5g escape reabsorption and are eliminated in the stool. This 500mg represents the major pathway for elimination of cholesterol from the body.

---

enterotoxins, exotoxins that affect the intestines (enteron) causing vomiting, abdominal pain and diarrhoea. They are poisons released from bacteria as they grow and multiply in food. *See* food poisoning.

---

enzyme activation tests, used for diagnosis of deficiency states of some vitamins that act as coenzymes or prosthetic groups. Suitable enzymes exist *in vivo* as a mixture of holoenzyme (active) and apoenzyme (protein —

inactive without its vitamin coenzyme). The change in activity when the extra vitamin is added is determined. An increase in activity of more than 20 per cent indicates deficiency of the vitamin. Thiamin, riboflavin and vitamin B_6 deficiencies can be diagnosed using the red blood cell enzymes transketolase, glutathione reductase and aspartate or alanine aminotransferase respectively.

---

enzyme activators, small molecules or ions that increase the activity of an enzyme, e.g., minerals such as calcium, magnesium, copper, molybdenum and zinc and hydrogen ion.

---

enzyme inhibitors, may be competitive or non-competitive, reversible or non-reversible. Competitive inhibitors may combine with the enzyme preventing its combination with the normal substrate that they often chemically resemble. Products of some metabolic reactions inhibit further activity of the enzyme producing them.

---

enzyme repression, a reduction in synthesis of the apoenzyme (protein). May be caused by an excessive build up of the end-products of the reaction or by a hormonal effect.

---

enzymes, protein catalysts produced by the living cell that are responsible for most metabolic reactions. In some, the active or holoenzyme consists of a protein part (apoenzyme) and either a coenzyme or prosthetic group, both small, non-protein molecules usually formed from a B vitamin. Coenzymes readily dissociate from their protein (e.g., pyridoxal phosphate, biotin, thiamin pyrophosphate). Prosthetic groups are tightly bound to their protein (e.g., flavin mononucleotide and flavin adenine dinucleotide). Being proteins, enzymes are inactivated by heat and coagulation.

---

eosinophilia myalgia syndrome (EMS), a rare blood disease that causes crippling muscle pain, skin rashes, high fever and sometimes death. Recent cases have arisen in some people taking the amino acid, tryptophan, as a supplement. Although its cause is attributed to a contaminant introduced during manufacture by a company in Japan, and not to the tryptophan itself, the use of free tryptophan in supplements or for food fortification, has been banned except under doctor's prescriptions, until the contaminant has been identified.

epidemiological, scientific study of the distribution of diseases.

---

epinephrine, *see* adrenaline.

---

epithelium, surface layer of cells covering the skin and mucous surfaces and lining body cavities and intestines.

---

ergocalciferol, *see* vitamin D.

---

ergosterol, a phytosterol found in yeasts and fungi. On irradiation with ultraviolet light it forms ergocalciferol (vitamin D_2).

---

erucic acid, a monounsaturated, 22 carbon fatty acid of the omega 9 family (C22:1 n-9). Principal fatty acid of rape-seed oil. When large amounts are fed to animals, changes occur in the heart because the acid is only slowly oxidized. Canbra, a new genetic variety of rape-seed, contains only 2 per cent erucic acid. Since 1977, no oil or fat or food containing an oil or fat with more than 5 per cent of its fatty acids as erucic acid may be sold.

---

erythorascorbic acid, *see* isoascorbic acid.

---

erythrocytes, *see* blood cells, red.

Eskimos, in Greenland eat large quantities of marine animals whose high content of omega 3-rich fish oils are thought to be responsible for their low incidence of coronary heart disease and tendency to bleed. *See* prostanoids.

---

essential amino acids, *see* amino acids, essential.

---

essential fatty acids (EFA), *see* fatty acids, essential.

essential oils, *see* oils, essential.

---

esters, compounds formed between acids and alcohols, e.g., fats.

---

ethanol, alcohol formed by fermentation of sugar. Ethyl alcohol. *See* alcohol.

---

ethnic and religious groups, some practise dietary restrictions, e.g., Hindus, Jews, Muslims, Orientals (*see* macrobiotics), Rastafarians, Seventh-day Adventists (*which see*) and Sikhs. See Table 16, page 295.

---

ethyl alcohol, ethanol. *See* alcohol.

---

eucaryotes, organisms whose cells have a nucleus, e.g., most plants and animals.

---

evening primrose oil, forms 17 per cent by weight of the seed and is rich in polyunsaturated fatty acids, linoleic acid forming about 72 per cent of its fatty acids and gamma-linolenic acid 8 to 10 per cent.

---

excipients, additives used in forming tablets and capsules. They bind the pharmacologically active ingredients together (e.g., calcium sulphate).

---

exocrine, secreting externally. Describes glands that produce secretions which leave the gland via a duct, e.g., salivary glands, pancreas (pancreatic digestive juices).

---

exogenous, supplied from outside the body, e.g., cholesterol in the body is made up of that absorbed from the food, exogenous, and that synthesized by the body itself, endogenous.

---

exotoxins, poisons released from bacterial cells as they grow and multiply in food before it is eaten. Exotoxic bacteria (e.g., *Staphylococci, Bacillus* *cereus*) cause toxic food poisoning, symptoms normally appearing in much less than 12 hours after consumption of contaminated food. Symptoms are vomiting, abdominal pains and diarrhoea. Heat sufficient to kill bacteria may not inactivate exotoxins, which require an hour at 60°C or a half hour at 100°C (boiling water). Exotoxins stimulate the immune system to form antitoxins specific to themselves. Botulism is also caused by an exotoxic bacterium, *Clostridium botulinum* (*which see*).

---

extracellular,   outside the cell.

---

extrusion cooking,   food is subjected to gradually increasing temperature and pressure for very short periods so its water content becomes super-heated steam and is then extruded through apertures. The consequent reduction in pressure causes the super-heated steam to evaporate; the material expands and the protein gel in the presence of starch confers a texture on the product. Used in preparation of textured soya-bean products, etc. Destroys toxins. Causes some loss of vitamins and of lysine in protein and greater loss of amino acids added for fortification purposes.

F

FAC,   *see* Food Advisory Committee.

---

factory farming,   labour-saving intensive farming systems for livestock production, aimed at maximum turnover of capital in shortest possible time and the production of standardized food for the mass market.

FAD and FADH$_2$,   oxidized and reduced forms of flavin adenine dinucleotide (*which see*).

faecal-oral diseases, infections spread by flies or human hand of harmful bacteria or viruses excreted in the faeces and urine to food. Include dysenteries and acute gastroenteritis caused by the virus *Escherichia coli.*

faeces, waste matter excreted from the bowel. Evacuated faeces form the stool. Usual output on Western diets is 80–160g (wet weight) daily, compared with about 225g from vegetarians and 470g from Ugandan villagers consuming very high-fibre diets. Consists of bacteria that form 55 per cent of the dry weight or 65–75 per cent of the wet weight of the stool, unfermented dietary fibre, undigested food residues, bile salts, cast-off intestinal mucosal cells, mucus, substances secreted into the intestinal lumen, water, etc. Odour mainly due to skatole and indole, putrefaction products of tryptophan.

familial, runs in families, e.g., coeliac disease, cardiovascular disease, atopic allergy.

FAO, Food and Agriculture Organization of the United Nations.

fat, brown, specialized fat stores responsible for 'dietary-induced thermogenesis' in which glucose and fatty acids from food are oxidized, with release of their energy as heat rather than trapped in ATP. Its activity may account for how some people can 'eat and not get fat'. It is reduced or absent in obese people.

fats, the common term for lipids in food, are organic substances that are insoluble in water but soluble in organic solvents like ether, chloroform and benzene.

In the present UK diet, about 42 per cent of the total energy intake (or 38 per cent if alcohol is included) is provided by fat. Total fat in the diet is made up of visible fat like butter, margarines, vegetable oils and fat accompanying meats and invisible fat closely associated with other constituents as in lean meat.

Only certain polyunsaturated fatty acids (PUFA) are essential components of the diet, because all other lipids can be made in the body from carbohydrates and proteins.

Chemically, lipids are a diverse group of esters or potential esters of fatty acids. Esters are compounds between alcohols (e.g., glycerol, cholesterol) and acids. A fatty acid consists of carbon atoms with hydrogen atoms attached, arranged in a chain that ends in a carboxylic acid group (-COOH). The chain length varies and it may be saturated, unsaturated or polyunsaturated depending on whether the bonds between the carbons are fully saturated with hydrogen or not. Generally the fatty acids of foods of animal origin (except, e.g., fish oils) are more saturated than those of plant origin (except, e.g., coconut and palm oils).

Lipids may be divided into simple lipids like the fats (solid triglycerides, e.g., butter), oils (liquid triglycerides) and waxes; complex lipids such as the phospholipids, glycolipids and lipoproteins that contain additional groups besides fatty acids and alcohols; and lipids derived from both the above by hydrolysis such as the fatty acids, steroids, and sterols like cholesterol.

Functions Structural, e.g., phospholipids in cell membranes. Energy source — fatty acids and their partial oxidation products, ketone bodies, are used as an energy source by many tissues. Energy reserve — fatty acids are stored as triglycerides in adipose tissue. Hormonal — the sex and adrenal cortex hormones are steroids. Prostanoids and leukotrienes, important hormone-like substances, are derived from particular PUFA. Vitamin D and bile acids are steroids.

Digestion is commenced in the buccal cavity and continued in the stomach by lingual lipase that splits off a single fatty acid from triglycerides. Most takes place in the duodenum after dispersal of the lipids into small droplets or micelles through the emulsifying action of bile salts, etc. Enzymes in the pancreatic juices split off one or more fatty acids from triglycerides, phospholipids and cholesteryl esters. The digested lipids pass through the intestinal absorbing surface from the micelles leaving the bile salts behind. In the cells, triglycerides and phospholipids are re-formed, much of the cholesterol is re-esterified, and these lipids are combined with proteins to form chylomicrons (a lipoprotein) that pass into the lymph entering the bloodstream in the neck. Fatty acids with chains shorter than 10–12 carbons and glycerol pass directly into the hepatic-portal vein blood going to the liver.

Adults can digest and absorb at least 95 per cent of the fat intake. Fat in the stools, steatorrhoea, is a symptom of failure in secretion of bile salts or pancreatic juice or of malabsorption syndrome.

Transport and fate Lipids are insoluble in water and so for transport in the blood are combined with proteins (apoproteins) forming lipoproteins that mix with blood. These are chylomicrons and the very low density-, intermediate density-, low density- and high density-lipoproteins (VLDL, IDL, LDL and HDL respectively). They differ in density, particle size and composition. Those formed from digested lipids that pass into the lymph are chylomicrons in which about 88 per cent of the lipid content is triglycerides. Chylomicrons lose much of their triglycerides to the peripheral tissues as thcy pass through thcm in capillarics. Thcy thcn transfcr somc of thcir proteins, etc., to HDL and eventually become chylomicron remnants that are taken up by the liver.

VLDL are formed in the liver from triglycerides synthesized from glucose after a glucose meal or from fatty acids mobilized from adipose tissue between meals and during starvation. VLDL contain about 56 per cent triglycerides, the rest being phospholipids and cholesterol. They transport triglycerides and cholesterol out of the liver to peripheral tissues where they deposit much of their triglycerides. They then transfer some of their proteins, etc., to HDL eventually becoming IDL and then LDL. The predominant lipid in LDL is cholesterol and this is deposited in peripheral tissues and in the liver, which takes up the LDL.

HDL are synthesized by the liver and intestines. About 45 per cent of their lipids are phospholipids and 35–40 per cent cholesterol. The main lipid in newly formed HDL is phospholipid and it picks up cholesterol from the peripheral tissues forming HDL_3, which picks up more cholesterol and also phospholipids and protein from chylomicrons and VLDL, forming HDL_2, which is broken down in the liver. HDL therefore transports cholesterol from peripheral tissues to the liver.

Toxicity None of the dietary lipids are toxic in the short term. In the long term, a high intake of fat appears to be concerned in the development of many diseases of Western civilization such as cardiovascular disease, certain cancers (e.g., breast, colon), gallstones. Total cholesterol levels in the blood correlate positively with the incidence of coronary heart disease. The correlation is stronger when only LDL levels are considered. In contrast, HDL cholesterol levels (HDL_2 particularly) correlate negatively with the incidence of coronary heart disease. Consequently LDL cholesterol is popularly known as 'bad' cholesterol as it reflects cholesterol being taken to peripheral tissues (e.g., blood vessels) and deposited (e.g., in plaques), whereas HDL cholesterol is 'good' since it reflects cholesterol scavenged from peripheral tissues being carried to the liver for excretion.

LDL particles may have to be modified (e.g., by oxidation) before they become atherogenic and it has been postulated that antioxidants such as vitamin E or carotenoids may inhibit this oxidation.

A high intake of saturated fats tends to raise LDL cholesterol levels whereas replacing saturates with PUFA lowers them. PUFA may lower serum cholesterol by removing the blocking effect of saturated fat on the receptors that take up LDL. The ratio of PUFA/saturated fat (P/S) in the diet is therefore important.

The OPCS Dietary and Nutritional Survey 1986-7 revealed that only about one third of respondents had serum cholesterol levels in the desirable range of less than 5.2mmol/l. Total serum cholesterol levels of 7.8mmol/l or more were found in 8 per cent of women and 6 per cent of men.

For dietary recommendations intended to reduce the incidence of coronary heart disease, *see* cardiovascular disease.

Requirements   Fat is the most energy-dense food and so a convenient and palatable source of energy, though theoretically carbohydrates and proteins could replace it as an energy source. However, unless the diet contains at least 20 per cent of the energy as fat, it is difficult to prepare acceptable meals.

In order to maintain health, at least 1–2 per cent of the energy content of the diet must be provided by certain PUFA known as essential fatty acids. (*See* fatty acids, essential.)

Distribution of lipids in foods (in g per 100g): vegetable oils, 99.9; butter, 82.0; margarines, 81.0; almonds, 53.5; double cream, 48.2; Cheddar cheese, 33.5; avocado pear, 23.5; single cream, 21.2; chicken meat plus skin, 17.7; mackerel, 16.3; eggs, 10.9; livers, 6.3–10.3; lean meats, 4.6–8.8; chicken meat, 4.3; cottage cheese, 4.0; whole milk, 3.8; wholemeal bread, 2.7; white bread, 1.7; yogurt (low-fat), rice and lentils, 1.0; cod, 0.7; peas, 0.4; old potatoes and skimmed milk, 0.1; winter cabbage, watercress, oranges and plums, trace.

Law   From 1986, a claim relating to PUFA in food may only be made if at least 35 per cent by weight of the food is fat and at least 45 per cent of its fatty acids are PUFA and not more than 25 per cent are saturated. The food must be stated to be low in saturated fatty acids and the quantities of PUFA and saturated fat must be given.

Low cholesterol claims may only be made for a food if it contains not more than 0.005 per cent cholesterol and if a PUFA claim can be made, and is made, for the food.

No suggestion is allowed that the food is beneficial to health because of its PUFA or low cholesterol content.

---

fats, polyunsaturated,   fat in the food, usually of plant origin, in which the fatty acids are predominantly polyunsaturated. Exceptions include fish oils and coconut and palm oils.

---

fats, saturated,   fat in the food, generally of animal origin, in which the fatty acids are predominantly saturated. Exceptions include fish oils and coconut and palm oils.

---

fatty acid formulas,   expressed as number of carbon atoms followed by the number of double or unsaturated bonds and the fatty acid family.

Formulas of nutritionally and biologically important acids are given in Table 2.

Table 2: Formulae of nutritionally and biologically important fatty acids

Saturated	*Short-hand formula of acid**
acetic	C2:0
propionic	C3:0
butyric	C4:0
caprylic	C8:0
capric	C10:0
lauric	C12:0
myristic	C14:0
palmitic	C16:0
stearic	C18:0
Monounsaturated	
palmitoleic	C16:1 n-9
oleic	C18:1 n-9
elaidic	tC18:1 n-9 *trans* isomer of oleic
erucic	C22:1 n-9
cetoleic	C22:1 n-11
Polyunsaturated	
Two double bonds	
linoleic	C18:2 n-6
linoelaidic	ttC18:2 n-6 *trans* isomer of linoleic
Three double bonds	
alpha-linolenic	C18:3 n-3
gamma-linolenic (GLA)	C18:3 n-6
dihomo-gamma-linolenic (DGLA)	C20:3 n-6
mead	C20:3 n-9
Four double bonds	
stearidonic	C18:4 n-3
arachidonic	C20:4 n-6
Five double bonds	
eicosapentaenoic (EPA) or timnodonic	C20:5 n-3
docosapentaenoic or clupanodonic	C22:5 n-3

Six double bonds
docosahexaenoic (DHA) or Cervonic   C22: n-3

* The short-hand formula of a fatty acid consists of the number of carbon atoms followed by the number of double (unsaturated) bonds and the fatty acid family. (All unsaturated bonds are in *cis* form unless *trans*, indicated by t/tt)

---

fatty acid oxidation,   proceeds in steps with production of acetyl CoA, which enters the citric acid cycle for complete oxidation to carbon dioxide and water with a high energy yield. Some acetyl CoA units in the liver combine, forming ketone bodies used by the tissues for energy. During starvation ketone body production increases, leading to ketosis.

---

fatty acids,   organic acids and lipids found free or combined as esters of alcohols such as glycerol and cholesterol. Important energy sources for tissues other than red blood cells and the brain. As phospholipids they have a structural function in cell membranes. Some give rise to important hormone-like substances, prostanoids and leukotrienes.

Chemically   Consist of a chain of from two to 26 carbon atoms (usually an even number) to which are attached hydrogen atoms, the carbon at one end being a carboxylic acid group (-COOH). Over 40 are found in nature. The bonds between the carbons may be single, forming a saturated (fully hydrogenated) acid, or there may be one or more unsaturated bonds forming a monounsaturated or polyunsaturated acid respectively. Unsaturated bonds are also known as double bonds. Fatty acids in fats of food of animal origin are predominantly saturated (saturated fats) while those from plant sources are usually predominantly polyunsaturated (polyunsaturated fats). Exceptions include fish oils, which are predominantly polyunsaturated, olive and canola oils, which are predominantly monounsaturated, and coconut and palm oils, which are predominantly saturated.

Cis *and* trans *unsaturated bonds*   In nature most unsaturated bonds are in the *cis* form, i.e., both hydrogen atoms are on the same side of the bond. This makes the molecule flexible and allows it to bend. Their presence in oils and in cell membranes increases liquidity or fluidity. When oils are chemically 'hardened' in the food industry (as in the preparations of many margarines; *see* hydrogenation, catalytic), unsaturated bonds may move along the chain and/or change into the *trans* form where the hydrogen atoms are on opposite sides of the bond and this makes the molecule rigid and unable to bend, like a saturated fatty acid. Their presence solidifies fats and reduces the fluidity of cell membranes. Unsaturated fatty acids with one or more of their double bonds in the *trans* form are thought to be metabolized like saturated fatty acids.

In metabolically important PUFA, the *cis* bonds are interrupted by a methylene group ($-CH_2-$)

$$H \quad H \quad H$$
$$| \quad\quad | \quad\quad |$$
$$- C - C - C -$$
$$| \quad\quad | \quad\quad |$$
$$H \quad H \quad H$$

saturated or single bonds

$$H \quad H \quad\quad\quad H \quad H$$
$$| \quad\quad | \quad\quad\quad\quad | \quad\quad |$$
$$- C = C - CH_2 - C = C -$$

cis, cis methylene interrupted
unsaturated or double bonds

$$H \quad\quad\quad\quad\quad H$$
$$| \quad\quad\quad\quad\quad\quad |$$
$$- C = C - CH_2 - C = C -$$
$$| \quad\quad\quad\quad\quad\quad |$$
$$H \quad\quad\quad\quad\quad H$$

trans, trans methylene interrupted
unsaturated or double bonds

$$H \quad H \quad\quad\quad H$$
$$| \quad\quad | \quad\quad\quad\quad |$$
$$- C = C - CH_2 - C = C -$$
$$\quad\quad\quad\quad\quad\quad\quad\quad |$$
$$\quad\quad\quad\quad\quad\quad\quad\quad H$$

cis, trans methylene interrupted
unsaturated or double bonds

Fatty acid families The position of the unsaturated bonds in the chain separates fatty acids into families. Metabolically important are the omega 3 (or n-3), the omega 6 (or n-6) and (to a lesser extent) the omega 9 (or n-9) families. The number in the name refers to the position of the unsaturated bond furthest away from the carboxylic acid group, being on the third, sixth or ninth carbon atom respectively from the other or omega end of the molecule. The body cannot insert unsaturated bonds between that bond and the omega end of the molecule, nor can it interconvert the families.

Short-hand formula of a fatty acid consists of the number of its carbon atoms and unsaturated bonds and its family, e.g., arachidonic acid C20:4 n-6, eicosapentaenoic acid (EPA) C20:5 n-3. *See* fatty acid formulas *and* Table 2.

Essential fatty acids (EFA) Linoleic acid (C18:2 n-6) certainly, and probably alpha-linolenic acid (C18:3 n-3) are nutritionally essential since they must be present in the diet because they cannot be synthesized by the body and are required for growth and health. *See* fatty acids, essential.

Prostanoids and leukotrienes are synthesized from the 20 carbon PUFA, dihomo-gamma-linolenic, arachidonic and EPA. *See* eicosanoids.

Dietary intake of fatty acids A high dietary intake of saturated fatty acids leads to high levels of blood cholesterol and triglycerides, risk factors for coronary heart disease. Reducing saturated fat intake and increasing intakes of PUFA lower these levels. At present, saturated fatty acids form about 17 per cent of food energy and PUFA about 6.6 per cent according to the OPCS nutrition survey 1986-7. The COMA target was that not more than 15 per cent of food energy should come from saturated plus *trans* fatty acids. Longer term aims are to reduce saturated fat intake to 10 per cent of food energy, i.e., one-third of total fat intake. Some nutritionists suggest the ratio of omega 6 to omega 3 PUFA in the diet should be 3:1.

---

fatty acids, *cis*,   unsaturated fatty acids in which the double bonds are in the *cis* configuration, the predominant form in nature, e.g., as in linoleic acid. *See* fatty acids. Only *cis* polyunsaturated fatty acids can give rise to prostanoids and leukotrienes (*which see*), hormone-like substances that control many body functions.

---

fatty acids, derived essential,   polyunsaturated fatty acids derived in the body from nutritionally essential fatty acids and that have vital roles as intermediates in the body's production of prostanoids and leukotrienes.

---

fatty acids, essential (EFA),   are nutritionally essential because they cannot be made by the body and are required for growth and health. Linoleic acid certainly and alpha-linolenic acid probably are essential, at least partly because they give rise to 20 carbon polyunsaturated fatty acids from which prostanoids and leukotrienes are derived. They and their derivatives also have a structural role in cell membranes. Arachidonic acid is an EFA in some animals such as the cat, but in man it can be derived from linoleic acid.

During EFA deficiency, members of the omega 9 fatty-acid family take over some of the structural functions of the EFAs but they cannot form prostanoids or leukotrienes. The concentration of mead acid (*which see*) (C20:3 n-9; three double bonds — a triene) increases and a rise in the ratio of triene to tetraene (arachidonic acid — 4 double bonds) in serum is diagnostic of EFA deficiency. EFAs must form at least 1–2 per cent of the total energy intake (corresponding to 2–5g linoleic acid) and considerably more during pregnancy and lactation. Vegetable-seed oils are particularly rich in EFAs, e.g., safflower-seed and linseed oils.

The symptoms of EFA deficiency are scaly dermatitis, hair loss and poor wound healing. These can be cured by linoleic acid but not by alpha-linolenic acid. Diets high in saturated and *trans* fatty acids aggravate EFA deficiency in animals, possibly by inhibiting desaturase enzymes.

fatty acids, monounsaturated, contain one unsaturated or double bond, e.g., oleic acid. At present, nearly half the dietary fatty acids are monounsaturated. Monounsaturated fats (e.g., olive oil) when replacing saturated fat in the diet, lower LDL ('bad') cholesterol levels, though not as markedly as do polyunsaturated fats, but unlike the latter that either have no effect on HDL ('good') cholesterol level or, at high intakes, tend to lower it, monounsaturates tend to raise it. Monounsaturates do not affect blood triglyceride (fat) levels.

---

fatty acids, polyunsaturated, contain two or more unsaturated or double bonds. Include the essential fatty acids linoleic and alpha-linolenic, and others such as arachidonic and eicosapentaenoic with important metabolic functions. With some exceptions (e.g., fish oils, coconut and palm oils), fats of plant origin (seed oils) contain a higher proportion of polyunsaturates (PUFA) than those of animal origin. When they replace animal fats in the diet, they tend to lower blood cholesterol levels and hence reduce a risk factor for coronary heart disease. While PUFA of plant origin (omega 6 family — *see* fatty acids) lower LDL ('bad') cholesterol levels, those from fish (omega 3 family) do not, except with high intakes, and may even raise them. Large intakes of fish oil PUFA, unlike plant oil ones, lower blood triglyceride (fat) levels and hence reduce another risk factor for coronary heart disease. Both omega 3 and 6 PUFA give rise to prostanoids and leukotrienes, hormone-like substances that control many body processes.

---

fatty acids, saturated, contain no unsaturated bonds, all bonds being single, e.g., palmitic acid. Fats of animal origin (dairy products and meat) contain a higher proportion than those of plant origin, with some exceptions such as fish oils and coconut and palm oils. High intakes raise blood cholesterol and triglyceride (fat) levels, risk factors for coronary heart disease. While saturated fatty acids with 12 to 16 carbons raise plasma total and LDL ('bad') cholesterol levels, stearic acid which has 18 carbons does not, possibly because it is rapidly converted to the monounsaturate oleic acid (*see* fatty acids, monounsaturated) and nor do the medium chain length saturates with eight or ten carbon atoms.

---

fatty acids, short chain, *see* fatty acids, volatile.

fatty acids, *trans*, unsaturated acids, in which one or more of the double bonds are in the *trans* configuration, e.g., as in elaidic acid, instead of the *cis* form that predominates in nature (*see* fatty acids). This makes the molecule rigid with a structure similar to that of a saturated fatty acid. The presence of elaidic acid solidifies fats. Formed during the processing of natural oils, e.g., in the preparation of some margarines.

The body cannot use *trans* fatty acids for synthesis of prostanoids and leukotrienes, hormone-like substances that control many body functions, but they only appear to affect their synthesis in the body if the diet is deficient in linoleic acid. *Trans* fatty acids appear to raise LDL ('bad') cholesterol levels in the blood and decrease HDL ('good') cholesterol levels.

Daily intake about 8g from (g): margarines, fats, oils, 2.8, dairy products, 2.6; cereals, 1.3; meat, fish, eggs, 1.0. The OPCS Dietary and Nutritional Survey 1986-7 found a daily intake by men of 5.6g and by women of 4.0g.

---

fatty acids, volatile, acetic, propionic and butyric acids. Products of fermentation by bacteria in the colon. *See* fermentation, colonic.

---

fatty streaks, appear in artery walls of most adolescents and are the first signs of atherosclerosis.

---

favism, acute haemolytic anaemia produced on eating broad beans (*Vicia faba*) in people with an inherited deficiency of the enzyme glucose-6-phosphate dehydrogenase in red blood cells. The cells are susceptible to the toxins vicine and convicine in the beans. Seldom seen in N. Europeans but prevalent in Mediterranean and Middle Eastern countries.

FDA, Food and Drugs Administration. The USA equivalent of the UK DOH and MAFF combined.

---

feeding, intravenous, *see* nutrition, parenteral.

Feingold diet, excludes artificial colourings and flavourings and natural salicylates (aspirin-like compounds) from the diets of hyperactive children (sufferers from attention deficit disorder, *which see*), on the basis that there is a behavioural element in the adverse reaction of some people to these substances. A small percentage of the children certainly respond, but responses in others can be attributed equally well to placebo effect.

---

fermentation, metabolism that can be carried out by micro-organisms in the absence of oxygen (e.g., colonic fermentation in man). Made use of in food preparation, e.g., bread, cheese and beer in the UK. Many foods used in Asia and Africa are made by fermenting cooked soya-beans and cereal–legume mixtures with moulds or bacterial cultures, e.g., tofu, sufu, shoyu, koji, miso, soy sauce, natto, temper, kenkey. Nutritionally, fermentation can cheaply add flavours and destroy undesirable ones making monotonous food more appetizing, add vitamins B_{12} (important in vegan diets), B_6, niacin and riboflavin, inactivate anti-nutrients like trypsin inhibitors, etc.

---

fermentation, colonic, dietary fibre (about 20g), undigested starch and sugar (35–50g or 10–15 per cent of daily intake), some carbohydrate and protein from mucus, small amounts of other proteins and about 0.5g fat normally enter the large intestine of man on a Western diet every day. Bacteria ('friendly') secrete enzymes that ferment half to three-quarters of the fibre and most of the starch, sugar and protein. Dietary fibre comprises lignin, which is not a carbohydrate, is not fermented and may hinder fermentation of the other fibres, and cellulose and non-cellulosic components, which are unavailable carbohydrates. Up to 50 per cent of the cellulose and about 80 per cent of the non-cellulosic components are fermented. *See* carbohydrate classification, Figure 1, page 46.

Three important products of carbohydrate fermentation are volatile fatty acids (acetic, propionic and butyric), gases (carbon dioxide, hydrogen and, in some people, methane) and energy that the bacteria use for growth. The gases themselves are odourless but are often accompanied by traces of pungent by-products of protein breakdown in the colon (putrefaction). Man absorbs and utilizes the volatile fatty acids for energy production, some 70 per cent of the energy content of carbohydrate so fermented becoming available to him. On Western diets these acids are estimated to supply 5–10 per cent of human energy requirements, 2–3 per cent coming from those formed from the fibre. On high-fibre intakes of Third World populations and in the presence of intestinal malabsorption (e.g., of lactose), the proportion of the total energy obtained from these acids is increased.

Volatile fatty acids, or short chain fatty acids as they are sometimes called, are acetic, butyric and propionic acids (two, three and four carbons respectively). Acetic acid is absorbed and appears to act simply as a source of energy. Propionic acid has been suggested as responsible for the blood cholesterol lowering effect of soluble dietary fibre. *In vivo* studies indicate butyric acid is taken up by cells in the bowel wall and, while all the volatile fatty acids may have a growth stimulating effect on the large bowel and stimulate its blood flow, butyric acid has the greatest effect. Anti-bowel cancer effects have been attributed to butyric acid because it appears to favour growth of normal rather than cancer cells.

ferric,   the oxidized ion of iron.

ferritin,   readily available storage form of iron present mainly in the liver, spleen and bone marrow.

ferrous,   the reduced ion of iron.

fertility vitamin,   *see* vitamin E.

fever,   elevation of body temperature above normal. Basal metabolism rises and since it is usually accompanied by anorexia, there is muscle loss. Dietary management, particularly in prolonged fevers, includes liquid or semi-solid meals, rich in protein and carbohydrate and with a high energy value.

fibre, dietary,   roughage. Plant cell-wall supporting material that cannot be digested by man's own enzymes. Essential in the diet for the removal of waste matter as soft, bulky, easily eliminated stools. Acts as food for the fermenting bacteria in the colon that form 65–75 per cent of the wet weight of the stool.

Chemically comprises non-starch plant polysaccharides (cellulose and non-cellulosic substances). Though not a carbohydrate, lignin, a 'woody' material, was formerly regarded as a component of dietary fibre. The non-starch polysaccharides are complex carbohydrates described as 'unavailable' because they are indigestible by man's own enzymes. They differ widely in chemical and physical properties and comprise cellulose, hemicelluloses, gums, alginates, and mucilages, which are all fibrous in nature, and pectin, which is non-fibrous. (*See* carbohydrate classification: Figure 1, page 46). Lignin, cellulose and some hemicelluloses hold water but do not dissolve in it. The other dietary fibres are water-soluble and form viscous gels.

The average UK diet of 1986 (excluding out-of-home meals) was calculated to provide a daily average of 21.8g fibre using the Southgate method of estimation, which includes some starch resistant to digestion (*see* resistant starch), and lignins and 12.9g using the new Englyst method that measures non-starch polysaccharides only. This fibre was derived mainly from (Southgate/Englyst, per cent) cereals and products, 49/45; vegetables and products, 37/41. Official recommendations in 1983 (*see* NACNE) were to increase fibre consumption from the then estimated 20g daily (Southgate) to 30g. Third World populations consume about 50g daily and UK vegetarians 42g. The OPCS Dietary and Nutritional Survey 1986-7 found the average daily intake of fibre was 24.9g for men and 18.6g for women, while 25 per cent of men and 6 per cent of women achieved the NACNE recommendation of at least 30g daily.

The low intake of most Westerners is thought to contribute to their high incidence of constipation, bowel cancer, coronary heart disease, gallstones, diverticular disease, appendicitis, varicose veins, piles, diabetes, obesity and dental caries, compared with high-fibre eating communities.

Effects of dietary fibre The constituents of dietary fibre occur in foods in varying proportions, some foods such as wheat bran having a high proportion of lignin and other insoluble fibres, while others such as legumes have a high proportion of soluble fibres, e.g., gums. Wheat bran and insoluble fibres are particularly beneficial as regards colonic function (see 1. below), whereas the soluble viscous fibres are beneficial in modifying intestinal absorption (see 2. below). Both have side-effects (see 3. below). The behaviour of purified individual fibres in the gut may not be the same as when they are combined with other fibres and constituents of food.

1. *Beneficial effects of dietary fibre on colonic function*
Holds water so increasing bulk and softness of stools and thereby helping to prevent constipation and straining, the main cause of varicose veins. Increase in bulk dilutes concentration of toxic materials (e.g., carcinogens) in contact with bowel walls. Cereal fibres (e.g., wheat bran) and cellulose are specially effective.

Reduces high pressures in bowel, an important factor in relieving and preventing diverticular disease of the colon. Cellulose and hemicelluloses in wheat bran are particularly effective.

Normalizes transit time of food through the gut thereby reducing time of contact of toxic materials with bowel walls. Cereal fibres such as wheat bran and ispaghula are effective. Most viscous fibres slow transit time through the small intestine.

Resistant starch appears to behave like soluble dietary fibres in being fermentable in the lower bowel, modestly raising faecal bulk mainly by increasing bacterial cell content.

2. *Other beneficial effects of dietary fibre*

Lowers blood cholesterol and triglyceride ('fat') levels by binding bile acids and/or dietary cholesterol and fats and/or by other mechanisms. Particularly effective are pectins, some gums found in legumes and the soluble fibre in oat bran. Effectiveness of wheat bran is disputed. High blood-cholesterol and triglyceride levels correlate with incidence of coronary heart disease and cholesterol is the main constituent of gallstones.

Reduces and delays after-meal blood sugar rise. Legume fibres, forming viscous gels (e.g., guar gum), slow down absorption of sugars so reducing the after-meal blood sugar rise and consequent insulin secretion, a property of particular value to diabetics and potential diabetics.

Slows stomach emptying. Purified soluble fibres such as legume gums (e.g., galactomannan) swell in contact with water, forming a viscous gel that delays stomach emptying and gives a feeling of fullness.

Increases and/or reduces energy supply. Bacterial fermentation of fibres produces volatile fatty acids that are absorbed and contribute to the energy supply. There are also unproven suggestions that high fibre intakes increase potential energy loss in the stool, a property, if substantiated, of value to slimmers.

Fermentable fibres may decrease risk of bowel and breast cancer through their effects on steroid metabolism in the large bowel.

3. *Side-effects of dietary fibre*

Increased flatus production. Gases produced by bacterial fermentation of fibres in the colon may cause distension and discomfort on high-fibre intakes.

A high-fibre diet is unsuitable for young children and some elderly people because its bulk may make them feel full before they have consumed sufficient energy, protein, vitamins and minerals.

Decreased bioavailability of minerals. Have been reported to have an adverse effect on mineral balance, particularly of calcium, magnesium, iron, zinc and copper, partly due to presence in fibre-rich foods of phosphates and phytic acid that render some minerals insoluble and unavailable, but probably also by themselves binding minerals and preventing their absorption. However, high-fibre foods like wheat bran are themselves mineral rich, possibly thereby compensating for decreased mineral availability.

Affects pancreatic enzyme activity. In experimental animals, some dietary fibres and high-fibre foods (e.g., cellulose, hemicelluloses, wheat and oat brans) decrease the activity of some or all pancreatic enzymes, while others (e.g., pectin) increase the activity of some of them.

Affects intestinal mucosa variously. For example, in experimental animals, wheat bran increases mucus output, guar gum increases mucosal growth, pectin increases mucosal cell turnover. The long-term significance of such effects is unknown.

Measurement Results based on Englyst and Cummings' new analytical method indicate that traditional methods may have led to too high an estimate of total dietary fibre intake and that the actual current average intake in the UK is about 13g non-starch polysaccharides plus around 1g of substances analysing as lignin.

Traditional methods: *(a) Total dietary fibre* determined by Southgate's method involving complex analyses taking about five days. Values used in UK food tables, but now considered too high as they include resistant starch and lignins. However, as resistant starch appears to behave like true fibre (non-starch polysaccharide) in that it is indigestible by man and is fermented in the bowel like soluble fibre, Southgate values do appear to reflect roughage in the diet.

Van Soest's method is quicker but less informative, and gives values roughly comparable to Southgate's.

(b) Crude fibre Value often given in US food tables. Comprises the portion of a food that resists extraction with acid (sulphuric) and alkali (sodium hydroxide). Includes lignin, most cellulose and small amounts of hemicelluloses and so seriously underestimates the contribution of a food to the dietary fibre intake. Total dietary fibre values are five to seven times crude fibre values.

(c) Neutral detergent fibre (NDF) is the residue after boiling with neutral solutions of sodium lauryl sulphate and EDTA. Contains lignin, cellulose and hemicelluloses. A commonly used method that seriously underestimates total dietary fibre as it excludes constituents soluble in aqueous solvents.

(d) Acid detergent fibre is the residue after refluxing in sulphuric acid and cetrimide. Contains lignin and cellulose.

Distribution in foods Total dietary fibre (Southgate method) in g per 100g: wheat bran, 45.0; various bran cereals, 10–28; figs (dried, raw), 18.5; prunes (dried, raw), 16.1; almonds, 14.3; coconut, 13.6; peas (frozen, cooked), 12.0; soya flour (full fat), 11.5; wholemeal flour, 9.6; dates, 8.7; wholemeal bread, 8.5; various mueslis, 7.4; baked beans, 7.3; oatmeal (raw), 7.0; apricots (dried, raw), 6.7; spinach (boiled), 6.3; brown rice (cooked), 5.5; peas (fresh, cooked), 5.2; butter beans (cooked), 5.2; corn-on-the-cob (cooked), 4.7; broccoli tops (boiled), 4.1; leeks (boiled), 3.9; lentils (split, boiled), 3.7; cabbage (raw), 3.4; carrots (cooked), 3.0; cabbage (cooked), 2.8; jacket potato (cooked), 2.5.

There is more fibre on the outside of grains, fruit and some vegetables than on the inside, so milling and peeling remove a high proportion of the fibre content.

---

fibrin, insoluble fibrous protein formed in strands from the soluble plasma protein, fibrinogen, by the enzyme thrombin, trapping red blood cells and forming a blood clot.

---

fibrinogen, soluble protein precursor of fibrin.

---

fibrosis, formation of excessive fibrous tissue in a structure, as in the cirrhotic liver.

---

fish, for many, an important source of animal protein of high biological value. Lean or white fish store their fat as oils in the liver (e.g, cod and halibut liver oils), their flesh containing less than 3 per cent oils. Fatty or oily fish store oils in their muscles (e.g., mackerel, salmon) and their flesh contains up to 20 per cent oil (body oils). Fish oils are rich in vitamins A and D and in the omega 3 family of polyunsaturated fatty acids, particularly eicosapentaenoic and docosahexaenoic acids (EPA and DHA) (*see* omega 3) and in cholesterol (*which see*). The oils of fish from cold waters are richer in EPA and DHA than those from tropical waters. Fish synthesize EPA and DHA from the omega 3 polyunsaturated, alpha-linolenic acid, that they obtain from the minute marine algae in the plankton on which they live. Studies indicate that fish consumption (even one to two meals weekly — an average of 30g daily) protects against coronary heart disease, apparently, at least in part, due to their content of EPA and DHA (*see* cardiovascular disease). Marine fish are also the richest source of iodine.

Lean or white fish (e.g., cod, haddock, halibut, lemon sole, plaice, saithe) provide (per 100g): energy, 73–92 kcal; (g) water, 79.5–82.1; protein, 16.8–17.9, fat, 0.5–2.4.

Fatty fish (e.g., herring, mackerel, Atlantic salmon) in autumn provide (per 100g): energy, 182-234 (salmon, 182) kcal; (g) water, 63.9–68.0; protein, 16.8–19.0; fat, salmon, 12.0, herring, 18.5. The values for fat in herring and mackerel vary through the year from about 5g per 100g in spring to 20g in late summer. Herring, mackerel and Pacific, but not Atlantic, salmon also provide (in μg per 100g): vitamin A, 45–90; vitamin D, 12.5–22.5.

flatus, 'wind'. Gas in the stomach or intestine. Derived from three sources: swallowed air; produced in the gut by bacterial fermentation of contents; diffusion into gut lumen from blood. Oxygen and nitrogen diffuse from blood into the lumen, but carbon dioxide usually, and methane and hydrogen always, diffuse the other way. Nitrogen, oxygen, carbon dioxide, hydrogen and methane account for over 99 per cent of bowel gas. Hydrogen in the blood derived from bowel gas, is excreted in the breath, the amount being a measure of carbohydrate fermentation taking place and often used for that purpose, e.g., to indicate the severity of lactase deficiency.

flavin adenine dinucleotide, exists in oxidized (FAD) and reduced or hydrogen-rich ($FADH_2$) forms. A prosthetic group in the respiratory chain and other enzymes of oxidation. Derived from riboflavin.

flavin mononucleotide, a prosthetic group in the respiratory chain and other enzymes of oxidation. Derived from riboflavin.

flavour enhancers, additives that have no flavour themselves but enhance other flavours, e.g., monosodium glutamate, used in stews, meat pies, sauces, etc.

flavour perception, is largely a combination of taste (salt, bitter, sweet, acid), perceived by the tongue, and odour, perceived when any of 17,000 different volatile chemicals stimulate receptor cells in the nasal cavity. Pain, heat, cold, tactile and other sensations contribute to flavour.

flavourings, a list of permitted flavourings is being drawn up for adoption by members of the EC including the UK.

Foods themselves are often used to flavour other foods. 'Raspberry flavoured' is meant to indicate that all the flavouring is due to raspberries themselves, whereas 'raspberry flavour' or 'raspberry flavouring' is meant to indicate the reverse.

Synthetic chemicals mimic the flavour of many fruits and vegetables (e.g., benzaldehyde, n-propyl acetate and diethyl sulphite have the flavour of almond, pear and peppermint respectively) and are widely used in the food industry particularly in sweets. *See* additives.

flour improvers, are said to 'strengthen' the flour and produce bread that is well risen and stays fresh longer, e.g., cysteine. *See* additives.

---

flours, wheat, made by grinding the grain. Twelve per cent of the grain is made up of an outer layer of indigestible fibre surrounding a protein-rich layer (aleurone). Inside is the outer and inner endosperm, together comprising about 85 per cent of the weight of the grain, and the germ (or embryo), consisting of root and shoot, attached to the grain by the scutellum, together forming about 3 per cent by weight of the grain. The germ and scutellum are relatively rich in protein, fat and B vitamins, particularly thiamin. The outer layers of endosperm and the aleurone layer contain a higher concentration of protein, vitamins (especially nicotinic acid) and phytate than the inner endosperm, which contains most of the grain's starch and protein, though the latter is at a lower concentration than in the outer layers and germ.

If none of the grain is discarded on being ground, the flour formed is said to have a 100 per cent extraction rate and is described as wholemeal. When varying amounts of the outer layers and germ are discarded as bran, flours of lower extraction rate are formed. An 85 per cent extraction rate yields brown flour and a 72 per cent extraction rate, white flour. Because much of the thiamin, nicotinic acid and iron content are lost when bran is discarded and bread made from these flours is a staple food, brown and white flours are required by law to be fortified with these nutrients to specified minimum levels (mg per 100g: iron, 1.65; thiamin, 0.24; niacin, 1.60). Brown and white flours are also required to be fortified with calcium carbonate to provide a level of calcium nearly five times as great as that in wholemeal flour. Wholemeal flour must naturally contain the minimum quantities of iron, thiamin and riboflavin described above, but does not have to contain specified levels of calcium.

Though brown and white flours before fortification are less nutritious than wholemeal, since most of the fat and phytate are removed in the bran, they are less liable than wholemeal to go rancid (and so keep better) and to prevent absorption of minerals by forming insoluble phytate or fibre complexes. Wholemeal flour has about five times the amount of dietary fibre present in white flour. The limiting amino acid in wheat protein is lysine. *See* Table 3, page 107.

Table 3: Constituents of wheat flours per 100g

	Wholemeal	Brown	White Breadmaking	Plain household
extraction rate (%)	100	85	72	72
energy value (kcal)	318	327	337	350
protein (g)	13.2	12.8	11.3	9.8
fat (g)	2.0	2.0	1.2	1.2
total dietary fibre (g)	9.6	7.5	3.0	3.4
calcium (mg) before/ after fortification	35/—	20/150	15/140	15/150
iron (mg) before/ after fortification	4.0/—	2.5/3.6	1.5/2.2	1.5/2.4
zinc (mg)	3.0	2.4	0.9	0.7
total phosphorus (mg)	340	270	130	110
phytate phosphorus (mg)	240	100	30	30 about
thiamin (mg) before/ after fortification	0.46/—	0.30/0.42	0.10/0.31	0.10/0.33
riboflavin (mg)	0.08	0.06	0.03	0.02
niacin (mg) before/ after fortification	8.1/—	4.1/6.8	3.0/4.3	2.7/4.0
vitamin B_6 (mg)	0.50	0.30	0.15	0.15
total folate (µg)	57	51	31	22
vitamin E (mg)	1.0	trace	trace	trace

fluoride, an adult man contains about 2.6g of this non-metallic mineral. Whether it is essential in the diet is disputed but it plays an important role in preventing dental caries.

Daily supply in the UK, excluding that in water, averages 1.82mg (excluding cooking losses and out-of-home meals), derived mainly from beverages particularly tea (71 per cent) and cereals (8 per cent). Water in fluoridated areas provides an extra 1.1mg daily and, in unfluoridated areas, 0.11–0.21mg.

Functions Deposits in bone and in the enamel surface of the developing teeth of children, but does not affect adult dental enamel. Confers stability to bones and resistance to caries in teeth.

Absorption is rapid when in soluble form as in tea.

Excretion is rapid and via the urine.

Requirement No RDA. USA estimated safe and adequate daily adult intake is 1.5–4.0mg, with a maximum of 2.5mg for younger people to avoid mottling tooth enamel. Since fluoride levels in water of 1ppm (1mg per litre) reduce the incidence of dental caries in children, many countries and some authorities in the UK fluoridate water supplies in low-fluoride areas to this level.

Toxicity Excess is toxic to both teeth and bones. Fluorosis occurs with mottling of tooth enamel where water levels are greater than 3–5ppm. Severe poisoning occurs above 10ppm with loss of appetite and increased density (sclerosis) of the bones of the spine, pelvis and limbs and calcification of spinal ligaments producing 'poker back'.

Non-tea-drinking small children, even swallowing fluoride toothpaste, are unlikely to consume as much fluoride per kg body weight as an adult excessive tea drinker who, in a fluoridated area, may take in 9mg altogether daily. Prolonged consumption of 20–80mg daily is probably required before fluorosis occurs.

Fluoride treatment for osteoporosis has been tried with conflicting results. Supplementation can increase bone density but high intake can result in bone of inferior quality and hence poor mechanical strength.

FMN, *see* flavin mononucleotide.

---

folacin, generic name for folic acid itself and its conjugates with glutamic acid residues.

---

folic acid, water-soluble vitamin and member of the B complex. Includes folic acid (pteroylmonoglutamate) and the polyglutamates that are folic acid linked with additional glutamic acid units. Folinic acid is a stable form of reduced folic acid. Total folates equal free folic acid plus polyglutamates. Folacin is the generic name for all substances with folic acid activity.

Functions Biochemically, the reduced, active, coenzyme form, tetrahydrofolate, acts as carrier for one carbon units used in synthesis of purine and pyrimidine bases, components of DNA and RNA. It is therefore required for transmission of hereditary characteristics, formation of blood and for protein synthesis. *See also* vitamin B_{12}.

Required for growth, healthy digestive and nervous systems, and formation of red blood cells.

Deficiency leads to megaloblastic anaemia. Deficiency at time of conception and during the first six weeks of pregnancy in those with a genetic susceptibility, may lead to spina bifida (neural tube defect) in the foetus in which the foetal vertebrae fail to completely enclose the spinal cord.

Requirement UK RDA 300µg total folates. EC and US RDA 200µg. Seventy per cent of folic acid is absorbed and 55 per cent of polyglutamates. The better than previously thought absorption of polyglutamates was taken into consideration when the US RDA was lowered from 400µg in 1989.

Daily UK household supply in 1986 (not allowing for 10 per cent wastage and excluding out-of-home meals) averaged 230µg (261µg with contributions from alcoholic drinks and confectionery) derived mainly from (per cent): vegetables, 39 (potatoes, 15); cereals and products, 23 (bread, 15); milk and products, 10.

Toxicity None in itself, but doses above 500µg daily may mask vitamin B_{12} deficiency. Stored in liver.

Stability Canning, prolonged heating, leaching into cooking water and reheating can cause serious losses. Overall losses from vegetables, fruits and dairy products during processing and cooking may reach 45 per cent. Reducing agents in food, such as vitamin C, protect it. Unstable to light particularly in the presence of riboflavin.

Distribution in foods (free/total folate in µg per 100g): dried brewer's yeast —/2,400; liver, chicken, 290/590, pig, 59/110; broccoli, 89/130; winter cabbage, 60/90; eggs, free-range, 39/not known, deep litter, 32/not known, battery, 25/25; lentils, 25/35; wholemeal bread, 22/39; lettuce, 19/34; milk, 9/45; cod, 8/12; meat, trace–4/3–10; apples, 2/5; butter, trace/trace.

---

folinic acid,   *see* folic acid.

Food Advisory Committee (FAC),   an independant committee that advises government on matters referred to it by Ministers relating to the composition, labelling and advertising of food and on additives, contaminants, etc., in food or used in its preparation.

---

food allergy,   describes the adverse effects brought about by immunological reactions in sensitized people to certain food components (allergens), which are usually proteins. Also known as food sensitivity. Not to be confused with food intolerance where the mechanism is nonimmunological.

Everybody absorbs some large molecules, like proteins, whole. The body's immune system removes these foreign substances (antigens) by producing antibodies that form antigen/antibody complexes. These are metabolized by the liver and in most people cause no reactions. In some, however, they cause allergic reactions either immediate or delayed, through the allergen-antibody complex leading to the release of histamine from mast cells. (An allergen is an antigen that causes allergic reactions.) Symptoms may be gastrointestinal (vomiting and diarrhoea, e.g., reaction to gluten) and/or general (eczema, oedema, urticaria, asthma, e.g., reactions to eggs, strawberries, shellfish). Has been suggested as causing some cases of rheumatoid arthritis. Classical antigens include egg, fish, shellfish, wheat, nuts, cow's milk (in perhaps 1 per cent of infants), soya and peanuts.

---

food chains,   chains of food sources enabling animals and plants without chlorophyll (e.g., fungi) to obtain solar energy. Only green plants that contain chlorophyll can use the sun's energy to synthesize complex organic molecules (carbohydrates, proteins and fats) from simple molecules (carbon dioxide, water, ammonia, sulphates and phosphates). These complex molecules are energy stores that animals can release for their own use by oxidation. So animals eat green plants and are themselves eaten by other animals higher up the food chain. Man, at the top end of several food chains, eats both green plants and animals, which themselves have fed either directly on green plants (e.g., cattle, sheep) or on other animals that have eaten green plants (e.g., fish). *See also* photosynthesis.

---

food components,   comprise carbohydrates, proteins, fats, dietary fibres, water, vitamins and minerals, including trace elements.

---

food composition tables,   indicate the quantities of the food components present in foodstuffs. Because food composition varies with season, the soil on which it is grown, source and processing and results vary with sampling methods and analytical techniques used, values inevitably vary from table to table and alter with time as analytical techniques improve. They are, nevertheless, useful guidelines for those interested in and concerned with composing diets.

---

food efficiency,   is the ratio of energy accumulated as body mass to energy consumed. It is increased on resuming feeding after fasting, an effect of survival value in aiding recovery from illness, injury or starvation. This may help to explain the rapid regain in weight that often follows resumption of normal food intake following a low-calorie slimming diet.

food groups, food may be divided into five principal groups:
1. cereals (including bread, rice, porridge, biscuits, cakes, pasta);
2. meat and fish, etc. (including meat, poultry, fish, offal, eggs);
3. milk and dairy foods (including milk, cream, cheese, yogurt, butter);
4. fruit and vegetables (including leafy and other vegetables, potatoes, pulses, all fruits);
5. non-dairy fats and foods (including cooking fats and oils, margarine).
Dietary advice used to be based on balancing the diet by daily consumption of some food from each of these groups. Currently they are seldom referred to because there is more concern over reducing total consumption of fat present in foods in groups 2, 3 and 5 and increasing consumption of foods from groups 1 and 4. Foods in other groups (preserves, confectionery and alcohol) are not nutritionally essential.

---

food intolerance, describes the adverse reactions to food constituents that are toxic only to certain individuals. Also known as food idiosyncracy or pseudo-allergy. Not to be confused with food allergy since the mechanism of the reaction is non-immunological. Most are probably due to genetically determined enzyme deficiencies, e.g., favism, lactose malabsorption.

Sometimes symptoms resemble those of food allergy because they are mediated by release of histamine either from the food itself in susceptible individuals (e.g., fish, tomato, egg white, strawberries, chocolate) or the food releases histamine from mast cells (e.g., cheese, herring, salami, spinach, anchovy, tomato) or the food is rich in tyramine, which releases histamine from mast cells (e.g., chocolate, cheese, fish, beans). Tyramine also causes release of pressor amines and hence hypertension.

Some individuals are sensitive to caffeine and monosodium glutamate, apparently because the enzymes responsible for their metabolism are less efficient or deficient in these cases.

Some people are sensitive to salicylates (aspirin-like substance) occurring naturally in foods such as dried and berry fruits, oranges, grapes, almonds, peppermint, honey, many herbs, tea, wine, port, etc. *See also* Feingold diet.

---

food labelling, most prepacked foods are required by law to have labels that show: the name of the food; the net quantity; a datemark to indicate durability; a list of ingredients including additives arranged in descending order of weight; instructions for use when necessary; any special conditions of storage or use; the name and address of the manufacturer or packer or a seller in the EC; and place of origin where necessary. Claims, such as that the food contains certain vitamins or minerals or has been specially made for slimmers, infants or diabetics, etc., must be backed up with supporting information on the label.

---

food poisoning, has many causes including:

1. *Bacterial* from contamination of food that may not appear to be spoiled. This is the most common cause and the one generally understood by the term food poisoning. Produced by three different mechanisms:

(a) Toxic, caused by toxins or poisons produced outside the bacteria (exotoxins) as they grow and multiply in food before and after it is eaten. *See Staphylococci, Clostridium botulinum, Bacillus cereus.*

(b) Infective, caused by bacteria themselves that, as they grow and multiply in food, produce poisonous substances within the bacterial cell (endotoxins) which are only released when the bacteria die within the intestines. *See Salmonellae, Listeria, Campylobacter.*

(c) Intestinal, caused by bacteria that liberate exotoxins only when growing and multiplying in the intestines, not in the food before it is eaten. *See Clostridium welchii.*

2. *Mycotoxins* produced by fungi. Food appears mouldy or spoiled, e.g., aflatoxin B_1 from *Aspergillus flavus.*

3. *Inherent* caused by substances naturally present in food and affects everyone if they eat enough of them:

(a) Bananas and some fruits contain serotonin, adrenaline and noradrenaline, which have effects on the central and peripheral nervous system.

(b) Some cheeses contain tyramine, which raises blood-pressure, the effect being enhanced by monoamine oxidase inhibitor drugs.

(c) Almonds, cassava and other plants contain cyanide, which interferes with tissue respiration.

(d) Some fish, meat and cheeses contain nitrosamines, which can cause cancer.

(e) Legumes contain lectins or haemagglutinins, which cause red cell and intestinal damage. Rapidly destroyed by boiling, e.g., kidney bean.

(f) Some beans contain vicine and other agents, which cause haemolytic anaemia (favism), interfere with collagen formation and have toxic effects on the nervous system (lathyrism).

(g) Brassica seeds and some other *Cruciferae* (cabbage family) contain thiocyanate and other agents, which cause goitre.

(h) Green potatoes contain solanine, which causes gastrointestinal upset.

(i) Paralytic shellfish poisoning (PSP), which can be fatal, is caused by the concentration in shellfish (mainly mussels and other filter feeders) of toxins from a particular kind of naturally occurring alga.

4. *Allergy* causes adverse immunological reactions to food constituents, usually proteins, in sensitized individuals. *See* food allergy.

5. *Intolerance* causes adverse non-immunological reactions to food constituents that are toxic only to certain individuals. *See* food intolerance.

6. *Chemical*:

(a) Unintentional, e.g., fungicides on grains, insecticides on fruit, antibiotics or hormones given to animals, contaminant of tryptophan causing EMS.

(b) Pollution, e.g., organic mercury, cadmium, radioactive fall-out.

(c) Additives, some of which may cause adverse reactions in a minority of individuals, e.g., tartrazine and other azo dyes, monosodium glutamate, benzoate and sulphite preservatives.

---

food processing, includes the preparation, cooking and preservation of food.

Preparation comprises cleaning and removing inedible and toxic matter (e.g., rhubarb leaves, green parts of potatoes) and making ready for cooking.

Cooking Apart from fruits and salads, man seldom eats fresh, raw food. Cooking tenderizes meat, making it easier to chew into a form accessible to digestive enzymes. Cooking makes the starch in the cells of cereals, roots, legumes and green vegetables swell, bursting the indigestible cell walls of plant material, so allowing digestive enzymes access to the nutritious contents. Cooking improves the nutritive value of legumes such as soya beans and peanuts by destroying digestive enzyme inhibitors. Proper cooking also improves the palatability of the food.

Preservation stops food decomposing by autolysis due to its self-digesting enzyme content and by the action of putrefying bacteria and fungi present as spores in the air. Methods of preservation include heating, drying, refrigerating, freezing, canning, packaging in plastic and other synthetic packets, irradiation and use of chemical preservatives including salt, sugar, acetic acid (e.g., vinegar for pickling) and alcohol, as well as permitted preservative additives.

Though fresh foods are usually most nutritious, in an urbanized society the diet of most would be very restricted if they depended only on unpreserved food. Preservation also reduces the danger of food poisoning.

---

food processing, adverse effects, on individual food components:

Carbohydrates, such as the sugars and starches, suffer little loss and that by leaching or breakdown, the latter sometimes being a gain where it assists digestibility. Any loss is simply of 'energy'.

Dietary fibre is mainly lost in food preparation since there is more fibre on the outside of grains, fruit and some vegetables than inside, so milling (e.g., preparation of white flour) and peeling remove a higher proportion of the fibre content.

Proteins Other than high temperatures, most processes have little effect on protein quality and though even mild conditions can damage proteins, this apparently does not affect their nutritional value since amino acids remain relatively intact. The amino acid most readily damaged is lysine, but cystine and methionine can also be affected and those with reactive side chains (lysine, arginine, tryptophan and histidine) can form linkages with reducing substances (e.g., sugars) present in food (Maillard reaction) that render the protein resistant to digestive enzymes and so biologically unavailable.

Lipids Changes caused lead to unpalatability rather than loss of nutritional value except as regards essential fatty acids (EFA) and associated fat-soluble vitamins. EFA and other polyunsaturated fatty acids (PUFA), which readily undergo peroxidation, lose their nutritive properties and form substances (hydroperoxides and free radicals, etc.) that can initiate a chain reaction of damage to other PUFA. An antioxidant like vitamin E rapidly reacts with free radicals, preventing the spread of the chain reaction. At deep-freeze temperatures, some hydroperoxides are more stable than at room temperature and so lead to destruction of vitamin E in frozen foods.

Hydrogenation is the process by which oils are 'hardened' by converting some of the double bonds of their PUFA to single bonds by saturating them with hydrogen in the presence of a nickel catalyst. This is necessary for making oils into solid foods like margarines and cooking fats. The double bond of naturally occurring PUFA are in the *cis* form, but during hydrogenation may be converted to the *trans* form, and/or moved in position within the molecule forming *trans* and positional isomers. Isomers of the EFA no longer have special nutritional properties and isomers of PUFA are unable to lower blood lipid (e.g., cholesterol) levels. The isomers appear to be metabolized like saturated fatty acids. (*See also* fatty acids).

Vitamins Some loss of vitamins is inevitable during food processing, but in a properly cooked, well-varied diet this will not usually be of nutritional significance. Vitamin C, followed by thiamin, is the most vulnerable to destruction by food processing. The water-soluble vitamins (B complex and C) are vulnerable to loss into cooking and processing water and by drips from frozen foods, so these fluids should be utilized. The vitamin content of food is reduced by light (e.g., riboflavin, vitamins A and K), by oxygen (air) (e.g., vitamins A, C and E, folic acid and thiamin), by heat (e.g., vitamin C, thiamin and pantothenic acid, and vitamin A at high temperatures), by alkalis such as baking powder (e.g., thiamin and vitamin B_{12}), by deep freezing (vitamins E and K and pantothenic acid), by simple storage (e.g., vitamin C) and, in the case of thiamin, by the sulphur dioxide preservatives. Some vitamins such as niacin and vitamins D and B_6 are stable to most food processing techniques.

Minerals including trace elements cannot be destroyed by food processing techniques though they may be leached out into cooking or processing water and in drippings from cooked meats, poultry and fish and thawing foods and thereby lost unless these are utilized. Greatest losses are sustained in some industrial refining techniques used in the preparation of foods, as in the milling of white flour when the wheatgerm, which is the richest source of minerals in the wheat grain, is discarded leading to the loss, for example, of about half of the calcium and about three-quarters of the iron, zinc and copper content of the wheat grain; in the polishing of rice when the husk, a rich source of minerals as well as B vitamins, is removed; and in the refining of sugar, leaving nothing but potential calories.

---

food processing benefits, include destruction by cooking of toxins (e.g., phytohaemagglutinin in raw pinto beans that agglutinates red blood cells) and substances that inhibit digestive enzymes (e.g., trypsin inhibitors in soya beans and wheat flour); release of bound niacin in maize by soaking grain in alkali and by baking wheat flour with alkaline baking powder; addition of minerals such as calcium, in cooking water; reduction of phytate content of cereals and legumes; fermentation of cereals and pulses (traditional in Far East) that considerably increases content of riboflavin, niacin and vitamin B_6.

Food Safety Directorate, is based within MAFF and brings together under the Food Minister all the main aspects of food safety work for which MAFF is responsible.

---

food supplements, concentrates, usually, of important nutrients such as vitamins, minerals and polyunsaturated fatty acids, but also of herbs and other food substances, presented in tablet, capsule or elixir form. Used to remedy dietary deficiencies; to provide extra nutrients for those with special requirements because of physiological conditions or way of life; and as safeguards to ensure an adequate intake of essential micronutrients.

Energy requirement in the UK has fallen steadily over the last 20–30 years as motorized transport replaces walking and central heating maintains body warmth. As energy intake falls, so too does intake of essential micronutrients and, unless greater care is taken to balance the diet, it can become more difficult to obtain the full requirement from the diet alone. However, the OPCS Dietary and Nutritional Survey 1986–7 showed that, although energy intakes were below currently recommended levels, average intakes of vitamins were well above recommended levels, though average intakes of iron by women were below those recommended. Those who took supplements had higher intakes of vitamins and minerals from food than those who did not, confirming observations in other surveys, i.e., that supplements were being taken by those least at risk of dietary deficiencies. Women, especially older women, were more likely to take supplements than men. Those in Social Classes I and II were more likely to take supplements than others.

Groups of people at risk of dietary deficiencies, besides those whose diet is unbalanced or poorly cooked, include those who eat inadequately through apathy, disability or inability such as some elderly, students and people living on their own; slimmers on unbalanced diets; faddy children and adolescents; many in hospital; others who depend considerably on kept-hot and over-processed foods, which may lose much of their vitamin and mineral content. Those with extra requirements because of:

1.   special physiological conditions include: pregnant and lactating women; the physically very active, including athletes in training; menstruating women; convalescents with nutritional leeway to make up; children and adolescents in winter and the housebound who may get insufficient vitamin D from sunlight;

2.   way of life include: smokers; heavy drinkers of alcohol; women on the contraceptive pill.

---

foods, acidic or basic,   after metabolism, foods leaving a mineral residue that is predominantly acid- or anion-forming (phosphorus, sulphur and chlorine) are described as acidic; those leaving a mineral residue that is predominantly basic- or cation-forming (sodium, potassium, magnesium and calcium) are described as basic. Cereals, cheese, eggs, fish and meat are acid-forming, while milk, vegetables and some fruits are base-forming. Foods such as fats and sugar contain no minerals and so are neutral.

The only minerals present in the organic acids that give fruit juices their acid taste are potassium and sodium (as salts). Since the organic acids are completely metabolized, the potassium and sodium residue makes such foods basic.

---

foods, convenience,   are prepacked and either already cooked, partly cooked or very easy to cook. Increasingly used and can add beneficial variety as a component of a balanced diet. However, they usually contain many additives, sugar, salt and sometimes unsuspectedly high levels of fat. Because highly processed, may have lost much of their original vitamins and minerals.

---

foods, fast, describes substantial snacks, already prepared or cooked to order within minutes for consumption on the premises or to take away. Includes beef-, ham-, and cheeseburgers, fried chicken pieces, fried fish, milk shakes, chips, salads, pizzas, stuffed baked potatoes and sandwiches. Many are of good nutritional value and acceptable as part of a balanced diet, particularly if freshly cooked. As main constituents of the diet, however, they may result in a high intake of salt, energy and fat and a low intake of folic acid, biotin, pantothenic acid and iron, but provide adequate protein, thiamin, riboflavin, ascorbic acid and calcium.

---

foods, health, are primarily prepared with the specific intention of maintaining and/or improving health. They are as naturally based as possible and contain no additives not comparable to substances found in nature. Include wholefoods, food supplements to remedy or prevent dietary deficiencies and specially selected and dietetic foods desirable for particular nutritional requirements (e.g., high-fibre, gluten-free and low-sodium).

---

foods, intermediate moisture, partially dried to contain 15–40 per cent moisture. Shelf-life a few weeks. Lose lysine from proteins, and vitamin C.

---

foods, junk, describes foods that contain little or no nutrients apart from energy. Some, such as sugary drinks and confectionery, etc., if consumed in large amounts can cause marginal malnutrition, e.g., of thiamin.

---

foods, snack, describes small meals taken between or instead of main meals. Vary widely in nutritive quality and include junk foods and fast foods.

---

fortification, addition of vitamins, minerals or amino acids to a food. Term usually restricted to addition of nutrients to foods from which they were absent or present in unimportant amounts. Addition of certain nutrients to a legal specified level to replace those lost in food processing, e.g., thiamin, niacin and iron to white flour, is known as restoration (*which see*). Fortification is used to provide nutrients in a food replacing a staple food that normally contains them, e.g., vitamins A and D are added to margarine by law because it replaces butter, which naturally contains them, though vitamin D is added above the level found in butter. Voluntary fortification is practised for both genuine nutritional purposes (e.g., infant formulas, iodized salt) and as a marketing ploy.

The UK is unusual in allowing fortification of any food with any nutrient to any level without restriction, apart from white and brown flours and margarine. However, Section 7 of the Food Safety Act 1990 requires that nothing be added to a food that would make it injurious to health.

---

free radicals, molecules with an unpaired electron that makes them highly reactive. Usually electrically neutral (e.g., hydroxyl radical OH·, lipid peroxide radical RCOO·) but can be charged (e.g., superoxide anion radical O_2^-). Seek to stabilize themselves by attracting an electron from any other nearby molecule to make a pair. Particularly vulnerable are the polyunsaturated fatty acids of lipids in cell membranes in which oxygen free radicals cause lipid peroxidation, an ever-amplifying series of chain reactions (a cascade) leading to tissue destruction. A free radical starting a cascade is known as an initiator.

Initiators are produced by radiation (nuclear, X-rays), light, metal ions (e.g., iron and copper), tobacco smoke, urban smog, even uncooked broad beans, but most importantly from oxidative metabolism and the presence of oxygen in the tissues. A few enzymatic reactions work via free radicals, and white blood cells (neutrophils) kill bacteria using them. But, as initiators of cascades producing more free radicals they are very harmful.

Protective mechanisms Vitamin E is both a primary scavenger of initiator free radicals, and a secondary scavenger that interrupts the process of lipid peroxidation once started. Beta-carotene may also be a primary scavenger. Superoxide dismutase (SOD) enzymes capture superoxide anions forming hydrogen peroxide, itself harmful as it forms hydroxyl radicals unless destroyed by catalase and glutathione peroxidase enzymes. The latter also catalyses the destruction of fatty-acid peroxides, thereby being an important secondary scavenger.

Oxygen free radicals probably play major roles in any disease process involving hyperoxidation, inflammation and chronic degeneration such as heart disease. They are the primary means by which radiation injures malignant and normal tissue and by which drugs, carcinogens and other toxic agents exert their effects. They play a significant role in ageing.

freeze-drying, or, lyophilizing. Low-temperature dehydration of foods. Probably the best method of preserving the vitamin content of the preserved food, but process is little used.

---

freezing, best method of preserving food both from the organoleptic and nutritional viewpoints. Storage is usually at -18°C. Nutrient losses occur mainly during the preliminary blanching needed to destroy enzymes. The greatest losses in vitamins during frozen storage itself appear to be in C, E and pantothenic acid. The nutritive values of frozen compared with fresh foods are higher in some cases because foods are frozen immediately after harvesting and lower in other cases because of losses in blanching. Small nutrient losses and textural changes can occur at thawing stage. The drips from thawing foods may contain water-soluble nutrients such as B vitamins and should be used. Reheating leads to variable losses, mainly in vitamin C. Whether microwave or infra-red heating is superior to conventional ovens for nutrient retention in reheating is still disputed.

---

fructose, fruit sugar. Occurs free (g per 100g) in fruit (e.g., grapes, 7.3; apples, 5.9) and honey (38.8) and combined with glucose as sucrose or common sugar. Now synthesized commercially for use in sweetening food products and as a table-top sweetener. It is absorbed more slowly than glucose, 80–90 per cent being absorbed intact, with conversion of the rest to glucose or lactate. Many incompletely absorb larger doses. Unlike glucose it does not stimulate insulin secretion. It is taken up into the liver where it is metabolized either to glucose, which is usually stored as glycogen, or else oxidized or converted to fat. May raise blood lipids. It tastes sweeter than sugar so fewer calories are consumed for the same amount of sweetening. It is only slightly less cariogenic than sucrose.

---

fruitarian, vegan who consumes mainly fruit, but also other produce of plants that do not involve destroying the plant to obtain the food, e.g., peas, beans, nuts.

---

fruit, dried, e.g., apricots, sultanas, raisins, prunes, figs, dates. Provide (per 100g): energy, 161–250 kcal; (g) protein, 1.1–3.6; total dietary fibre, 6.8–24.0 (raisins, 6.8; apricots, 24.0); (mg) potassium, 270–1880 (figs 270; dates,1010; apricots, 1880); iron 1.6–4.1, (apricots, 4.1); calcium 52–280 (figs, 280).

fruits,   their most important nutritive contribution is vitamin C. Also provide dietary fibre. Most contain small amounts of beta-carotene and traces of B vitamins and little or no protein or fat. Ripe fruit contains no starch. Fructose and glucose are the chief sugars, often in equal proportions, though apples and pears contain more fructose, while apricots and peaches contain sucrose. Contain a great variety of acids responsible for the sourness of unripe fruit. As the fruit ripens the acid levels fall and sugars rise. The acids do not cause acidosis as they are readily metabolized.

Fruits provide (per 100g as purchased): energy, 20–80 kcal; (g) protein, 0.2–2.0; carbohydrate, 2–20; fat, 0–1; water, 75–90; (mg) calcium, 5–40; iron, 0.1–1.0; vitamin C, 0–300; (μg) beta-carotene, 0–2,000.

---

frying,   fast cooking at high temperatures in fat. In deep-frying the food is immersed in very hot fat and water on the food surface is evaporated, causing bubbling. Cooking is so fast that loss of minerals and proteins is minimal. In shallow-frying fat is used just to prevent food sticking to the heated pan, in which the food is cooked one side at a time.

Over-heating the fat to the point at which blue smoke appears causes decomposition of the fat, with formation of acrid-smelling acrolein.

Frying adds fat, and hence energy value, to food. Leaching of nutrients is minimal. Vitamin loss appears to be similar to roasting, heat sensitive thiamin and vitamin C being most affected.

---

fuels, tissue,   the main energy fuels for most body tissues are glucose and fatty acids, with ketone bodies being used mainly in starvation. Fatty acids are derived either from adipose tissue or lipoprotein triglycerides (chylomicrons and VLDL) in the blood. Muscles use fatty acids in preference to glucose. Red blood cells can only use glucose. The brain must have glucose but can adapt to using up to 50 per cent ketone bodies during starvation. It cannot use fatty acids as fuel since it cannot oxidize them to any significant extent. Within tissues, stores of glycogen and triglycerides may be used as fuel.

---

fungi,   simple plants that cannot utilize the sun's energy to synthesize their food since they contain no chlorophyll and so grow on dead or living organisms which they use as a food source. Some are responsible for spoiling food and cause food poisoning by producing mycotoxins, e.g., *Aspergillus flavus*. For edible fungi *see* mushrooms.

G

GABA, *see* gamma-amino butyric acid.

---

gadoleic acid, a monounsaturated fatty acid of the omega 11 family, with 20 carbons (C20:1 n-11). Found mainly in fish.

Distribution in foods (as percentage of total fatty acids): herring, 13.2; halibut, 6.1; cod, 1.8.

---

galactomannans, gums from the cell walls of the endosperm of all endospermic leguminous seeds. Polysaccharides of mannose and galactose sugars.

Water-soluble dietary fibres that swell in water forming viscous gels which delay stomach emptying and slow the diffusion of glucose, etc., through the intestinal contents to the absorbing surface. This slows and delays glucose absorption after a meal, producing a smaller blood sugar rise and consequently reduces the amount of insulin secretion required to deal with the glucose influx. Reduces blood and liver cholesterol levels by preventing cholesterol absorption and the reabsorption of bile acids. Examples: guar and locust bean gums.

Because of the danger of them swelling and blocking the oesophagus, their addition to foods at more than 15 per cent by weight is prohibited, effectively removing their use as slimming aids by reducing appetite through their bulking action in the stomach.

Guar gum, also known as jaguar gum and guar flour. Obtained from *Cyamopsis psoraloides* or *tetragonalbus* seeds. Forms unpalatable viscous gel with water.

Foods incorporating guar gum successfully used in dietary management of non-insulin dependent diabetics. Possible adverse effects of consuming large quantities are flatulence, nausea, vomiting and intestinal obstruction.

Used as stabilizer for ice-cream, salad dressings, processed cheese and as a 'cloud' stabilizer in fruit drinks.

Locust bean gum, also known as carob gum and carob flour. Obtained from *Ceratonia siliqua* seeds. Used as an emulsifier, stabilizer, thickener and binder in foods.

galactosaemia,   raised levels of galactose in the blood. Due to absence or reduced activity of enzymes converting galactose to glucose. If galactose (and hence lactose and all milk products) is not excluded from the diet, cataracts and blindness ensue and sometimes mental and physical retardation.

---

galactosan,   a polysaccharide of galactose, e.g., agar, carrageenan.

---

galactose,   a hexose monosaccharide. Occurs combined with glucose in milk sugar, lactose, and as a major constituent of some soluble dietary fibres (e.g., pectin and galactomannan) and in glycolipids found chiefly in the brain and in the myelin sheaths round nerve fibres. Can be changed to glucose in the liver.

---

galactosuria,   presence of galactose in the urine.

---

galacturonate,   acid form of galactose. Found in gum and mucilage dietary fibres.

---

gall-bladder,   stores and concentrates bile.

---

gallstones,   formed when excess cholesterol in the bile precipitates out as crystals.

---

gamma-amino butyric acid (GABA),   a neurotransmitter formed in the brain from glutamic acid, a reaction for which vitamin B_6 is the coenzyme. Brain levels of GABA are reduced in vitamin B_6 deficiency. Drugs that facilitate GABA activity (Valium, Librium, etc.) have marked anti-anxiety, sedative and muscle relaxant action.

---

gamma-linolenic acid (GLA),   a polyunsaturated fatty acid of the omega 6 family, with 18 carbons and three unsaturated bonds (C18:3 n-6). Important as an intermediate in the conversion of linoleic acid to its biologically active derivatives, dihomo-gamma-linolenic and arachidonic acids. Rarely found in foods. Occurs in human milk (colostrum and mature milk, 0.34 and 0.35 per cent respectively of the fatty acids) and in various seed oils, e.g., as per cent of total fatty acids in seed oils from: borage, 25–27, blackcurrant, 19, gooseberry, 12, hemp, 10–12, evening primrose, 8–10, redcurrant and hop, 4–6.

---

garlic, *Allium sativum*, a pungent herb with eight to 12 cloves (about 2–3g each) forming a bulbous corm. Used through the centuries in cooking and herbal medicine. High sulphur content (0.5–4g/kg, depending on how it has been grown), mainly as sulphur-containing amino acids, particularly alliin, a non-odorous, medicinally inactive compound. When garlic is crushed, chopped or sliced, the alliin comes into contact with the enzyme allinase and is converted to odorous, medicinally active but unstable allicin. Cooking, distilling or standing a few days unprotected, converts allicin to other compounds including oily, odorous mono-, di- and trisulphides such as methyl allyl trisulphide (MATS) and less odorous ajoene, many of which are medicinally active. Together these form essential oil of garlic whose exact composition depends on the method of extraction used, e.g., water or steam distillation or alcohol extraction.

Allicin is anti-infective with anti-microbial and anti-fungal actions and is used to treat infections of the mouth, throat and digestive tract, bronchitis, coughs and catarrh, cystitis, fungal infections of the skin and candidial infections of the mucous membranes.

Garlic is sometimes suggested as part of a healthy diet for the prevention of atherosclerosis and hence of coronary heart disease because allicin and/or its derivatives lower blood cholesterol (mainly LDL and VLDL) and triglyceride levels in the blood and reduce blood clotting rate and help to prevent blood clots forming (fibrinolytic), both anti-thrombotic properties. An association between garlic consumption and the low level of heart disease in Mediterranean countries has been suggested. The mechanisms may be through inhibition of cholesterol synthesizing enzymes and increasing cholesterol excretion in the bile, inhibition of fatty acid synthesizing enzymes so decreasing triglycerides and inhibition of the enzyme synthesizing thromboxane, a platelet aggregating, and hence thrombotic, prostanoid.

Requirements for beneficial effects will continue to be debated until based on alliin/allicin levels. Suggested intakes of fresh garlic for cardiovascular protection range from 3 or 4g (1 large clove) to 50g daily, while about 9g (3 large cloves) has been proposed for anti-infective activity. High intakes of fresh garlic can have adverse effects including nausea, burning sensation, loss of appetite and diarrhoea.

Garlic supplements (to minimize odour) include preparations of dehydrated whole garlic and garlic oil.

---

gas, *see* flatus.

---

gas storage, fruit and vegetables can be stored by replacing air with carbon monoxide, which destroys the enzymes, and then with ethylene, which destroys micro-organisms. Causes loss of vitamin C.

---

gastric juices, secreted into the lumen of the stomach by the chief and parietal cells, glands in the gastric mucosa. Juices are 97–99 per cent water, pale gold, of high acidity (pH about 1.0). Contain the enzymes rennin and pepsin that respectively coagulate milk protein and commence the digestion of protein. *See* digestion.

---

gastrin, a hormone secreted by the gastric mucosa on entry of food into the stomach that causes a further flow of gastric juices.

---

gastritis, inflammation of the stomach, especially its mucosa.

---

gastroenteritis, inflammation of mucous membranes of stomach and small intestine. Commonest cause of acute diarrhoea and usually the result of food poisoning. Usually mild and of short duration, but if prolonged and severe can cause dehydration and serious consequences in the young and old.

---

gastrointestinal, pertaining to the stomach and intestines.

---

gelatin, soluble protein derived from collagen. Obtained by boiling bones, skin, tendons, etc., in water. Unlike most animal proteins it is nutritionally of poor quality as it contains no tryptophan.

---

gelatin, vegetable, agar.

geophagia, practice of eating dirt or clay, usually for medicinal purposes.

---

germanium, a semi-conductor element used in the electronics industry. Widely distributed in nature in small amounts. In organic form, said to enhance the immune system, but its safety has not been fully established. Has no known biological function.

---

ghatti gum, Indian gum. Exudate from stems of *Anogeissus latifolia* (India and Ceylon). Complex, water-soluble polysaccharide and dietary fibre forming a viscous mucilage in water. Used as substitute for acacia and as an emulsifying agent in pharmaceuticals, oils and waxes.

---

ghee, Indian ghee is butter, clarified at 100–200°C for 10 minutes.

GI, *see* glycaemic index.

---

gingivitis, *see* periodontal disease.

---

ginseng, a herbal product derived from the roots of *Panax ginseng C.A. Meyer*, grown in Russia, Korea and China. Often called Korean ginseng to distinguish it from Siberian ginseng, which is obtained from a member of the same family but a different genus, *Eleutherococcus senticosus*. Both are adaptogens and are used therapeutically in many countries and as food supplements in the UK, their active constituents being ginsenosides. They appear to act via hormonal stimulation and are reputed to increase the capacity for work and to normalize numerous pathological states. They should not be taken by people with hypertension.

---

glands, organs or structures that form secretions. Some are ductless, their hormone secretions passing straight into the bloodstream, which carries them to their site of action, e.g., thyroid. Others have ducts that carry their secretions, e.g., digestive juices, straight to their site of action, e.g., salivary glands. The pancreas is both a ducted (pancreatic juices) and ductless gland (insulin and glucagon).

glands of Lieberkühn,   in the walls of the jejunum, produce intestinal digestive juices.

---

gliadin,   a component of the wheat protein, gluten. A prolamine.

---

globulins,   proteins insoluble in plain water but soluble in salt water. Found mainly in blood serum and milk (lactoglobulin).

---

glossitis, nutritional,   disorders of the tongue caused by nutritional deficiencies. Sudden severe deficiencies of niacin, riboflavin, vitamin B_{12}, folic acid or iron cause the acute form characterized by a clean, red, swollen, inflamed and painful tongue. A symptom therefore of pellagra, sprue, and nutritional anaemias. The chronic atrophic form, characterized by a clean, pale, smooth, small tongue, is seen if the deficiency is partial and extends over years.

---

glucagon,   a protein hormone secreted by the alpha-cells of the islets of Langerhans in the pancreas. Stimulates output of glucose by the liver. Secretion stimulated by a fall in blood glucose levels (e.g., on fasting) and by a rise in blood amino-acid levels (e.g., after a high-protein, low-carbohydrate meal).

---

glucans,   glucosans. Polysaccharides of glucose, e.g., starch, cellulose.

---

glucomannan,   polysaccharide gum of glucose and mannose. Water-soluble dietary fibre forming a viscous gel, e.g., konjac mannan derived from tuber of *Amorphallus konjac*, grown in Japan. Used to make popular Japanese foodstuff, konnayaku.

Viscosity of its gel is even greater than that of guar gum. Used in weight-control diets to give a feeling of fullness, so making it easier to reduce energy intake. Reduces blood and liver cholesterol levels. Not a permitted additive in the UK.

---

gluconates,   salts and chelate-like compounds of gluconic acid, which is formed by fermentive oxidation of glucose.

gluconeogenesis, formation of glucose from non-carbohydrate precursors, such as the glucogenic amino acids, lactate and glycerol from fats. Takes place in the liver, particularly in the absence of a dietary supply of carbohydrate when the liver glycogen has become exhausted (e.g., on fasting) in order to maintain the blood glucose level that is essential for providing fuel for the brain and red blood cells.

---

glucosans, or glucans. Polysaccharides of glucose, e.g., starch, cellulose.

---

glucose, also known as dextrose or grape sugar. A simple (mono-saccharide), six carbon sugar. Tastes less sweet than sucrose. It is only slightly less cariogenic than sucrose. Found naturally as such in honey (33.9 per cent) and fruit (e.g., grapes, 7.3 per cent) and as a constituent of many polysaccharides (e.g., as sole constituent of starches, glycogen and cellulose and with other monosaccharides as in glucomannan) and disaccharides (e.g., as sole constituent of maltose and with fructose in sucrose and with galactose in lactose).

Readily absorbed from the intestines, its absorption causes the pancreatic hormone, insulin, to be secreted, which aids uptake into the tissues. It is the principal sugar in the blood where its level is closely controlled by hormones (*see* blood sugar). It is found in the urine when glycosuria occurs as in uncontrolled diabetes mellitus.

Glucose is metabolized by the tissues to provide energy both for immediate use as high-energy phosphate compounds such as ATP (adenosine tri-phosphate) and for longer term storage as liver and muscle glycogen. During production of ATP, oxygen is used up and carbon dioxide and water are produced as waste products. It is the only energy food red blood cells can use. The brain also uses glucose for energy, though during starvation it can derive up to 50 per cent of its energy from ketone bodies. The muscles use glucose as an energy source but prefer fatty acids.

Dietary sources of glucose include, besides glucose itself, sucrose (common sugar) and lactose (milk sugar). Both the fructose and galactose from sucrose and lactose respectively are converted into glucose in the liver. Sugars are quickly digested and so provide a readily available dietary source of energy. However, starch-rich foods, which are also rich in dietary fibre, particularly soluble dietary fibre as in pulses (beans and peas), but also wholemeal bread, are better food sources of glucose carbohydrate energy than sugars or even than potatoes, which do not contain much soluble dietary fibre. This is because not only does glucose become available for absorption more slowly because starch takes longer than sugars to digest, but dietary fibres, particularly the soluble variety, then delay its absorption, providing a more prolonged and even supply for absorption into the bloodstream. This reduces the peaks and troughs in blood glucose and insulin levels that give temporary 'lifts' soon followed by tiredness. High intakes may contribute to body fat by sparing the use of dietary and body fat as fuel. Starch-rich foods are accompanied by other nutrients and so are not just 'empty calories' like the sugars.

Some amino acids (the glucogenic ones), lactate and glycerol from fat are converted into glucose in the liver, particularly during starvation, a process known as gluconeogenesis. Excess glucose not used for maintenance of blood sugar levels, production of ATP or storage as glycogen, is converted into fat and stored.

---

glucose syrup, a sweet colourless syrup made by hydrolysing (splitting) with acid, maize or other cereal starch, forming a mixture of dextrins, glucose and maltose. Used to make jams, preserves and boiled sweets.

glucose syrup, hydrogenated, a permitted bulk sweetener made by catalytic hydrogenation of glucose syrup forming a mixture of sorbitol, hydrogenated oligosaccharides and hydrogenated polysaccharides (*see* hydrogenation, catalytic).

---

glucose tolerance factor (GTF), organic form of chromium.

---

glucose tolerance test, measures the ability of the subject to secrete sufficient insulin to cope with a large intake of glucose. Used as a diagnostic test for diabetes mellitus. The fasting person drinks a solution containing 50g glucose and his blood glucose levels are estimated every half-hour. In the normal person the level rises to a maximum of about 150mg/dl and returns to 80–100mg within two hours. In the diabetic, the rise is greater and more prolonged and glucose may spill over into the urine (glycosuria). A glucose tolerance curve is the plotted results of the test.

---

glucoside, a glycoside where the monosaccharide is glucose, e.g., amygdalin (laetrile) of bitter almonds and salicin of willow bark.

---

glucuronate, acid form of glucose.

glutamic acid, a non-essential acidic amino acid. Metabolically a key substance in transamination. Precursor of the neurotransmitter, gamma-aminobutyric acid in the brain. Predominant amino acid in gliadin of wheat. Its sodium salt is the flavour enhancer, monosodium glutamate.

---

glutamine, amide of glutamic acid. Storage form of amino nitrogen for amino acid synthesis. In plants, acts as a store of ammonia for use in amino acid synthesis during growth.

---

glutathione, a tripeptide of glutamic acid, cysteine and glycine. Thought to help in maintaining the body's correct oxidation-reduction state. Required for the action of several enzymes (e.g., glutathione peroxidase) and insulin.

---

glutathione peroxidases, enzymes that catalyse the destruction of hydrogen peroxide and of harmful fatty acid peroxides liberated from membrane lipids attacked by free radicals, thereby protecting membrane lipids and possibly protein and nucleic acids from further oxidative damage by free radicals. One contains selenium.

---

glutelins, plant proteins insoluble in water but soluble in weak acids and alkalis. Present in cereals (e.g., glutenin in wheat, hordein in barley, oryzenin in rice).

---

gluten, a mixture of the proteins glutenin and gliadin, present in wheat. When mixed with water it becomes sticky, enabling the particles of wheat flour to be bound together by moderate heat with the production of dough for bread making. Rye has a small content of gluten-like protein and so can be made into bread with difficulty, but oats and barley, having little, and maize, millets and rice, having none, cannot be made into bread.

Sufferers from coeliac disease are allergic to gluten.

---

gluten enteropathy, coeliac disease (*which see*).

---

glutenin, a component of the wheat protein, gluten. A glutelin.

glycaemia, blood glucose level.

---

glycaemic index (GI), is a measure of a carbohydrate-rich food's effect on the blood glucose level of a fasting subject compared with that of a reference food (usually white bread or glucose) providing an equal amount of available carbohydrate. A food with a low GI produces a less acute and lower hyperglycaemia than one with a high GI.

Wholemeal bread, brown rice, muesli, have similar GIs to white bread. Maltose, glucose, honey, instant or baked potatoes have GIs 10–50 per cent greater than white bread. Pulses, fruit, fructose, white rice, spaghetti, oats, biscuits, new potatoes, milk, yogurt and sucrose have GIs 14–70 per cent lower than white bread. Compared with white bread, glucose has a GI of 130, fructose of 30 and sucrose of 86.

Factors contributing to a low GI include: a high proportion of non-glucose sugars in the carbohydrate (e.g., fructose or galactose); a high amylose/amylopectin ratio in the starch present; presence of soluble dietary fibre; presence of antinutrients; slow digestibility; and certain food forms, e.g., whole compared with ground rice; pasta wheat compared with bread wheat. These factors in reverse contribute to high GIs. Whatever the GI of a food, the glycaemic effect in a mixed diet is modified by the other dietary constituents.

Whether a low or moderate GI means that the food is automatically suitable as a part of a complex carbohydrate/high dietary fibre, low-fat diet for people with diabetes mellitus is still debated.

---

glycerin(e), glycerol.

---

glycerol, or glycerin, a compound with three alcohol groups that can therefore form esters with up to three acids. Esters with three fatty acids are triglycerides (fats and oils). Glycerol forms about 5-10 per cent by weight of most triglycerides. Other esters include the phosphatidylglycerides, e.g., lecithin.

---

glycerophospholipids, phospholipids containing glycerol.

---

glycine, the simplest amino acid. Nutritionally non-essential, though vitally important in the synthesis of many important body substances, e.g.,

porphyrins (haem), purines, conjugated bile acids, creatine.
Sweet tasting with 70 per cent of the sweetness of sucrose.

---

glycocalyx, *see* intestinal wall.

---

glycogen, the storage form of carbohydrate in animals. Sometimes called 'animal starch'. A polysaccharide of glucose in the form of highly branched chains. Occurs chiefly in the liver and muscle. It forms some 6 per cent by weight of the liver after a carbohydrate-rich meal, but is depleted almost to nothing after 12–18 hours of fasting. It rarely forms more than 1 per cent by weight of muscle and is only depleted significantly after prolonged vigorous exercise. Higher concentrations of muscle glycogen can be induced by feeding high-carbohydrate diets after depletion by exercise.

The function of liver glycogen is to provide glucose for maintaining the blood glucose level particularly between meals. During fasting or starvation, the liver maintains the blood sugar level, albeit at a lower level than normal, by converting certain (glucogenic) amino acids, lactate and glycerol (from fat) into glucose.

The function of muscle glycogen is to act as a readily available source of glucose phosphates for energy release within the muscle itself.

---

glycogenesis, the synthesis of glycogen from glucose. Takes place in the liver and muscles.

---

glycolipids, always contains galactose, a long-chain fatty acid and a complex alcohol called sphingosine. Found chiefly in the brain and in the myelin sheath round nerve fibres.

---

glycolysis, the oxidation of glucose or glycogen to pyruvate with the conversion of some of glucose's energy content into adenosine triphosphate (ATP), a readily available energy store. Glycolysis can take place in the absence of oxygen (anaerobic) when less energy is produced and lactate is formed. In the presence of oxygen (aerobic conditions), pyruvate is further oxidized via the citric acid cycle and respiratory chain to carbon dioxide and water with the formation of much more ATP.

Fermentation of sugars by yeasts is also glycolysis, with alcohol instead of lactate being the end product.

glycoproteins, proteins covalently attached to oligosaccharides. Differ from proteoglycans in the chemical nature of their oligosaccharides. Their many functions include: structural (cell walls, collagen, elastin, bone matrix); lubricant and protective (mucins and mucous secretions); transport (of vitamins, lipids, minerals including trace elements); immunological (immunoglobulins, antigens, interferon); hormones (e.g., thyrotrophin); many enzymes; attachment/recognition sites for viruses, bacteria, etc.; antifreeze in Antarctic fish; lectins.

glycosaminoglycans, oligosaccharides that have been removed from the original protein backbone of their proteoglycan precursor.

glycosides, compounds of a monosaccharide and a molecule such as methyl alcohol, glycerol, a sterol, a phenol or another monosaccharide. Found in many spices, animal tissues, drugs and antibiotics.

glycosuria, glucose in the urine. Found when the renal threshold is exceeded either because the blood glucose level is abnormally high (e.g., in diabetes mellitus) or because the threshold is unusually low.

goblet cells, secreting cells shaped like goblets, found in mucous membranes such as those lining the stomach and intestines where the mucus they secrete lines and protects the gastrointestinal tract.

goitre, enlargement of the thyroid gland due to dietary deficiency of iodine.

goitrogens, are naturally occurring inhibitors of the thyroid gland preventing the production of thyroid hormones. Found in the *Brassica* (cabbage) family, peanuts, cassava and soya-beans. There is no proof that they have caused goitre in man.

gooseberry-seed oil, forms 18 per cent by weight of the seeds and is rich in polyunsaturated fatty acids, linoleic acid forming 40 per cent of its total fatty acids and gamma-linolenic acid 10–12 per cent.

gout, a characteristic arthritis that affects single joints, often the big toe, in episodes lasting a few days. Tends to recur. Most common in middle-aged men and tends to be familial. Caused by a deposition in the joint of urate crystals and is associated with hyperuricaemia. Uric acid is the end-product of purine metabolism in man and only 50 per cent of blood urate is derived from food purines. Sufferers should avoid feasting particularly on high-purine/high-fat foods, obesity, fasting and a high fructose consumption; restrict alcohol consumption; and drink plenty of other fluids. High-purine foods include liver, kidneys, sweetbreads, sardines, anchovies, fish roes, meat extracts and yeast.

---

grams, black, green, red. Dahls. Green grams also known as mung beans.

---

grape sugar, *see* glucose.

---

grilling, *see* dry heat cooking.

GTF, *see* glucose tolerance factor.

---

guanine, a purine found in RNA and DNA. *See* nucleic acid.

---

guar gum, a galactomannan (*which see*).

---

guarana, fruit of a vine grown in Brazil. Traditional food of Amazonian Indians. Contains caffeine or a caffeine-like stimulant.

---

gum arabic, *See* acacia.

---

gums, water-soluble, gel-forming viscous polysaccharides mainly of glucose, galactose, mannose, arabinose, rhamnose and their uronic acids, which may be methoxylated and acetylated. Used in food processing as emulsion stabilizers (e.g., salad dressings), thickeners and in confectionery. Extracted from seeds (guar gum, locust bean gum, quince), tubers (*Konjac* *mannan*), sap or exudates (gum arabic, karaya gum, tragacanth, ghatti), and seaweeds (agar, carrageenan) or made from starch (dextrins) or cellulose or by bacterial fermentation of carbohydrates (xanthan), or synthetic (vinyl polymers). All except dextrins and synthetics are dietary fibres.

H

haem, red, iron-containing pigment linked to a protein in: (1) haemoglobin, which transports oxygen in the red cells of the blood from the lungs to the tissues and carbon dioxide back, and (2) myoglobin, which stores oxygen in red muscles.

haemagglutinins, lectins (*which see*).

haemochromatosis, disruption of cell and organ function by deposits of excess iron as haemosiderin in liver, pancreas, skin and joints.

haemoglobin, haem- (iron-) containing protein responsible for the red colour of blood in which it carries oxygen to the tissues from the lungs and carbon dioxide back.

haemosiderin, storage form of iron deposited when ferritin levels (normal storage form of iron) are large. Less readily available than ferritin.

haemosiderosis, *see* siderosis.

hair, in mal- or under-nourished people frequently becomes dull and lustreless and stands up straight or 'stares'. Colour may change. Grey or white hair and baldness in middle age are of no nutritional significance.

hair mineral analysis, data used to determine mineral deficiencies and the presence of toxic minerals in the body. Interpretation controversial. Results affected by hair colour and diameter, location on body, age, sex, season, pre-collection hair treatments, collection procedure, washing, analytical problems, etc. Can be useful in measuring exposure to environmental toxic elements, but hair trace mineral pattern is rarely well related to nutritional or disease status of an individual.

HDL, *see* high density lipoproteins.

health, is defined by WHO as 'a state of complete physical, mental and social well-being and not merely the absence of disease or infirmity'.

heart, offal. Lamb, ox and pig hearts provide (per 100g): energy, 93–119 kcal; (g) water, 75.6–79.2; protein, 17.1–18.9; fat, 2.7–5.6; (mg) iron, 3.6–4.9; zinc, 2.0; thiamin, 0.45–0.48; riboflavin, 0.8–0.9; niacin, 10.3–10.6; vitamin C, 5–7; (μg) vitamin B_{12}, 8–13.

heart disease, *see* coronary heart disease.

Hegsted score, summarizes the lipid composition of the diet — a high score indicating a relatively high intake of saturated fatty acids and cholesterol and a relatively low intake of polyunsaturated fatty acids. Similar to the Keys score (*which see*).

As modified for use in epidemiological surveys:

$$\text{Hegsted score} = 2.16S - 1.65P - 0.0677C$$

where S = percentage of calories from saturated fat; P = percentage of calories from polyunsaturated fat; C = dietary cholesterol in mg/day.

hemicelluloses, polysaccharides found in plant cell walls, indigestible by man's enzymes so forming dietary fibre. They are insoluble and include xylans, mannans, glucomannans, galactans and arabinogalactans. Composed of polyuronic acids combined with xylose, galactose, mannose and arabinose.

They hold water, increase stool bulk, reduce transit time of food in bowel, reduce abnormally high pressures in bowel and may bind bile acids. Some 80 per cent of hemicelluloses may be fermented in man's colon.

hemp seed oil, forms 25 per cent by weight of the seed and is rich in polyunsaturated fatty acids, linoleic acid forming 41.5 per cent of its total fatty acids and gamma-linolenic acid, 10–12 per cent.

hepatic, *see* liver.

hepatic-portal vein, carries blood direct from the intestines to the liver.

hepatitis, inflammation of the liver.

hesperidin, a bioflavonoid (*which see*).

hexosans, polysaccharides of hexoses, e.g., glucosans and fructosans.

hexose, a monosaccharide containing six carbon atoms, e.g., glucose, fructose.

hiatus hernia, protrusion through the diaphragm most commonly of the stomach at the oesophageal opening. Heartburn is felt, typically on changing posture, if condition allows reflux of gastric juices into oesophagus. A common cause of dyspepsia and dysphagia. Occurs most often in obese women.

high frequency irradiation, microwave cooking (*which see*).

high-temperature, short-time, food-processing technique that destroys micro-organisms more effectively with less loss of nutrients than conventional heating. Used in pasteurizing milk.

histamine, a neurotransmitter derived from histidine. Stimulates acid secretion in the stomach. Stored in granules in mast cells from which it is released in many allergic and other reactions. In skin it gives rise to nettlerash and in lungs to constriction of the bronchi, causing the symptoms of asthma.

---

histidine, a basic amino acid. Whether it is essential in the diet of adults is not fully established, but probably essential in children. Precursor of histamine.

---

history, some landmarks in the development of present-day knowledge of nutrition:

1752 Reaumur using a kite, a bird that regurgitates its food, demonstrated that chemical changes took place during digestion and that gastric juice had a solvent action on food. This destroyed the old theory that digestion was a process of fermentation.

1757 Lind, a naval surgeon, in the first controlled trial, showed that citrus fruit cured and prevented scurvy.

1789 Lavoisier and Seguin measured oxygen consumed and carbon dioxide exhaled when at rest, at work and following ingestion of food.

1803 Young proved that acid was a normal solvent in gastric juice.

1807 Rickets first successfully treated with cod-liver oil.

1810 Wollaston discovered cystine.

1819 Magendie showed that proteins were necessary in animal nutrition.

1828 Chevreuil showed that fats are a combination of fatty acids and glycerol.

1832 Appert (France) invented the canning of foods.

1834 Prout summarized the knowledge of nutrition at that time, classifying proteins, fats and carbohydrates as albuminous, oleaginous and saccharine. He showed that stomach acid was hydrochloric acid.

1835 Schwann identified pepsin in gastric juice.

1844 Schmidt identified glucose in blood.

1845 Boussingault, in a controlled experiment with geese and ducks, demonstrated the metabolic conversion of carbohydrate to fat.

1850s Lawes and Gilbert demonstrated that proteins were not of equal value. This work was confirmed and extended by Osborne and Mendel in Yale in the early 1900s.

c.1855 Bernard demonstrated that the liver synthesizes glycogen and that pancreatic juices dissolve proteins not digested in the stomach and convert starch to glucose, and fatty foods to fatty acids and glycerol.

1852–1919 Fisher's life span, during which he did much of the work on the chemical structure of glucose, showed that proteins were made up of chains of amino acids and proved the chemical structure of the purine ring.

1873 Forster established that minerals are essential as accessory food factors required for maintaining life in dogs and pigeons fed solely on carbohydrates, proteins and fats.

1880s–90s Rubner, Atwater, Bryant and others produced calorimeters and carried out calorimetry.

1909 Thomas introduced the term 'biological value of a protein' and methods of measuring it.

1912 Funk, a Pole, coined the name 'vitamine' (changed in 1920 to 'vitamin') for substances that must be present in food to maintain health and asserted that scurvy, beri-beri, pellagra and probably rickets were to be classed together as due to deficiencies of accessory food factors.

1913–15 Discovery of the first fat- and water-soluble vitamins that turned out to be vitamins A and B by two groups of Americans, Osborne and Mendel and McCollum and Davis.

1921 Banting and Best, in Toronto, isolated insulin.

1922 Warburg and Christian showed riboflavin was a coenzyme — the first of the B vitamins to be shown to have this function.

1922 Evans discovered vitamin E.

1923 Hevesy was the first to use a radioactive isotope (of lead) in metabolic experiments.

1924 Nutrient fortification of food began in the USA with iodization of table salt.

1925 Goldberger showed vitamin B to be a mixture of anti-beri-beri, anti-pellagra and other factors.

1928 Szent-Gyorgi isolated ascorbic acid but did not discover it was anti-scorbutic until 1932.

1929 Burr and Burr showed that the polyunsaturate, linoleic acid, is an essential nutrient.

1935 Rose and co-workers discovered the last of the essential amino acids, threonine and, in 1938, identified eight essential amino acids for adult humans.

1943 The USA National Academy of Sciences first published a list of recommended dietary allowances.

1949 Block and Mitchell developed the chemical score method of determining protein quality.

1950 The British Medical Associations Committee on Nutrition first produced their recommended dietary allowances.

1964 Discovery that opaque-2 maize had twice the lysine content of ordinary maize pointed the way to present work seeking to improve the nutritive quality of specific foods by genetic manipulation.

1969 Burkitt pointed out that cancer and other diseases of the large intestine prevalent in Western society were rare in countries in which there was a high intake of dietary fibre. This stimulated research in the 1970s into the chemical, physical and physiological properties of fibres and into their medical aspects.

1983 NACNE report presenting short- and long-term guidelines on improving the British diet with regard to general good health.

1984 DHSS COMA report on diet and cardiovascular disease.

holoenzyme, the complete or active enzyme, consisting of apoenzyme (a protein) plus coenzyme or prosthetic group (usually formed from a B vitamin).

homeostasis, regulation of the constancy of equilibria and character of body fluids (e.g., blood) and of energy, protein, vitamin and mineral status of the body.

hominy, a preparation of the starch endosperm of maize. Low nutritive value.

honey, a food derived from the nectar of flowering plants, collected by the honey bee that provides an enzyme, invertase, which converts most of the sucrose in the nectar to glucose and fructose. Provides energy but little else of nutritive value. Cariogenic. Provides (per 100g): energy, 288 kcal; (g) water, 20; sugars, 75; protein, 0.6; traces of a few minerals but no vitamins.

hop seed oil, forms 7 per cent by weight of the seed and is rich in polyunsaturated fatty acids, linoleic acid forming 52.8 per cent of its total fatty acids and gamma-linolenic acid 4–6 per cent.

hordein, barley protein, a glutelin. Harmful to coeliac patients.

hordenin, an alkaloid present in germinated barley, millet, and sorghum. May cause hypertension and respiratory inhibition.

hormones, many are secretions of ductless glands carried in the blood to excite activity in another tissue, e.g., insulin, glucagon and the thyroid and steroid hormones. Others are also important neurotransmitters synthesized and released from neurons and active in the same organ, e.g., the catecholamines and cholecystokinin, gastrin and secretin. Chemically they include proteins, small polypeptides, single amino-acid derivatives, and steroids.

hospitalization, as many as 50 per cent of hospitalized patients may suffer from some degree of malnutrition and often are severely malnourished. A high percentage even of those well nourished on admission show nutritional deterioration when hospitalized for two weeks or more. Causes include loss of appetite, unappetizing, poorly cooked, kept-warm food, drug therapy and the nature of the illness.

Poor nutritional status compromises recovery and may result in secondary complications, poor wound-healing, impaired immunity, anaemia, muscle and organ degeneration, prolonged hospitalization and even death.

humectants, additives used in foods to prevent them drying out, e.g., sorbitol, glycerine.

hyaluronic acid, a polysaccharide present in the synovial fluid of joints acting as shock-absorber; between cells in loose connective tissue holding them together; and in vitreous fluid of the eye.

hyaluronidases, enzymes that depolymerize polysaccharides like hyaluronic acid. Because of this, when subcutaneously injected, they promote the absorption of drugs or of considerable volumes of glucose solution, etc., injected subcutaneously.

hydrogen peroxide, formed by many dehydrogenase enzymes containing FAD and FMN and during destruction of the superoxide radical anion by superoxide dismutase. Can form harmful hydroxyl radical unless destroyed by catalase or glutathione peroxidase.

hydrogenation, catalytic, addition of hydrogen to a molecule in the presence of a catalyst. Used to solidify plant oils in the making of margarine, and in the preparation of the bulk sweetener, hydrogenated glucose syrup.

hydrolysis, splitting into simpler substances with the addition of water, e.g., as in the digestion of polysaccharides and proteins.

---

hydroxyl radical, a highly reactive form of oxygen (OH'). *See* free radical.

---

hydroxyproline, a non-essential amino acid. Prevalent in collagen in which it is formed by hydroxylation of some of the proline present, a reaction requiring vitamin C.

5-hydroxytryptamine, *see* serotonin.

---

hyperactivity, *see* attention deficit disorder *and* Feingold diet.

---

hypercalciuria, above average urinary excretion of calcium. Present in about 8 per cent of the healthy population when it is accompanied by low faecal outputs of calcium. Also present in some disease states and when enforced confinement to bed leads to bone decalcification. Predisposes to formation of urinary stones.

---

hyperchlorhydria, production of too great a volume of hydrochloric acid by the stomach.

---

hyperglycaemia, above normal blood glucose levels. *See* blood sugar.

---

hyperkalaemia, high blood levels of potassium.

---

hyperlipidaemias, metabolic disorders characterized by raised blood levels of lipoproteins and therefore of the lipids cholesterol and/or triglycerides and often, also, of phospholipids.

---

hyperllpoproteinaemias, the more precise term for hyperlipidaemias.

hypernatraemia,   high blood levels of sodium.

---

hyperphagia,   above normal food consumption.

---

hypertension,   high blood-pressure. Diastolic blood-pressures over 90, 105 and 120mm mercury are usually taken to indicate mild, moderate or severe hypertension respectively. Essential hypertension has no known cause. Risk of hypertension is increased by obesity, by high alcohol intake and may be influenced by intake of common salt (sodium). It is a risk factor for cardiovascular disease (*which see*), particularly strokes.

---

hyperuricaemia,   raised blood levels of uric acid. Present in sufferers from gout. Significantly associated with hypertension and atherosclerotic diseases.

---

hypoglycaemia,   below normal blood glucose levels. *See* blood sugar.

I

iatrogenic,   describes a condition or illness arising as a result of treatment for another condition, e.g., side-effects from a drug or mineral deficiency arising as a result of excessive intake of bran to relieve constipation.

---

icosanoids; icosapentaenoic acid,   *see* eicosanoids; eicosapentaenoic acid.

IDL,   intermediate density lipoprotein. *See* fats.

---

ileum,   lower three-fifths of small intestine. Site of absorption of bile salts, vitamin B_{12}, some electrolytes and some water.

immune system, mechanisms by which the body resists invasion by antigens — foreign molecules (usually proteins) or cells, e.g., bacteria, tissues, or by free radicals. Comprises:

1. Humoral responses — involving the production of specific antibodies (immunoglobulin proteins) by certain white blood cells (B lymphocytes) that combine with their antigen, forming harmless antibody-antigen complexes. However, if these complexes cause release of histamine, an allergic reaction ensues.

2. Cellular responses — involving the mobilization of other white blood cells (T lymphocytes) etc., that engulf and destroy the invading organism or reject foreign tissue.

3. Antioxidants — include repair enzymes; antioxidant enzymes such as superoxide dismutases; dietary antioxidants including vitamins C, D, and E and beta-carotene

A deficiency of vitamins A, B_{12}, folic acid, iron or zinc has been shown to produce failure in immune system functioning. Deficiencies in riboflavin and vitamins C and B_6 or excesses of iron, vitamin E, cholesterol and polyunsaturated fatty acids also may impair immune functions in man.

---

in vitro, in the test-tube. Used to describe biological experiments not carried out on living material.

---

in vivo, in the living state. Opposite of *in vitro*.

Indian gum, *see* ghatti gum.

---

indigestion, *see* dyspepsia.

---

indole, and skatole are putrefaction products of tryptophan particularly responsible for the odour of faeces.

---

infarction, death of an area of tissue because its blood supply has been cut off. In the brain it leads to one type of stroke; in the heart to myocardial infarction.

inorganic compounds, do not contain carbon in their molecules. Carbon dioxide, carbon monoxide and carbonates are therefore organic compounds, but are usually described in textbooks of inorganic chemistry.

---

inositol, a member of the B-complex but not a vitamin for man since it can be synthesized in the body. Also known as myo-inositol. As the phospholipid, phosphatidylinositol, it is a structural component of cell membranes and found in high concentrations in the brain, heart and liver. Functions as a lipotropic agent, preventing accumulation of fat in the liver. Its hexaphosphate is phytic acid. Good food sources include heart and liver.

---

instantized legumes, partially pre-cooked to loosen seed-coats and so shorten cooking time. Losses of B vitamins relative to other processes are variable.

---

insulin, a protein hormone secreted by the beta-cells of the islets of Langerhans in the pancreas. Stimulates uptake of glucose, amino acids and triglyceride fatty acids by tissues, synthesis of glycogen and the deposition of fat in adipose tissue. Secretion stimulated by a rise in blood glucose or amino acid levels, e.g., after a meal. Its deficiency or diminished effectiveness causes diabetes mellitus.

---

intelligence, inborn mental ability. A person is born with a potential level of intelligence that is only likely to be fully realized if he is healthy, properly nourished and mentally stimulated. Supplementation of a diet deficient in vitamins, minerals, etc., may optimize health so that scores in intelligence tests improve up to the maximum of which the individual is capable, but cannot increase the individual's actual intelligence or IQ (Intelligence Quotient — the ratio of mental age to actual age).

---

international units (IU), quantification of substances such as vitamins, enzymes and hormones in terms of their biological activity. As chemically pure preparations of such substances become available, IU are replaced by weights. Vitamins A and D are still often quantified as IU in addition to μg or the percentage of the RDA present. Vitamin E is usually quantified as IU in food supplements.

intestinal digestive juices, produced by the glands of Brunner and Lieberkühn in the walls of the duodenum and jejunum respectively. Contain enzymes that split polypeptides into smaller peptides and amino acids (aminopeptidases, dipeptidases); sucrose into fructose and glucose (sucrase); maltose into glucose (maltase); lactose into glucose and galactose (lactase); release free phosphate from organic phosphates (phosphatases); complete breakdown of RNA and DNA to nucleotides (polynucleotidase) from which phosphate is removed forming nucleosides (phosphatases) that are absorbed as such or further degraded to purine and pyrimidine bases, ribose and deoxyribose sugars (nucleosidases).

Most digestion is carried out in the lumen, but enzymes carrying out the final stages project from or are within the mucosal epithelium of the intestinal wall.

---

intestinal wall, the wall of the small intestine is five-layered, including two layers of muscle. The innermost folded layer, the mucosa, is composed of minute projections called villi separated by hollows called crypts. Each villus is 0.5–1.5mm long and there are 10-40 per sq mm. The villi are supplied with blood and lymph vessels for transporting away absorbed nutrients and are covered by a single layer of cells, the epithelium (mucosal epithelium) composed of goblet cells that are mucus secreting and absorptive cells that also secrete the intestinal digestive juices. Epithelial cells in the crypts divide actively, the cells formed passing over the course of two days up the shafts of the villi to replace those worn away at the tips by the movement of the semi-digested food and enzymes in the lumen. The surface of the epithelial cells facing the lumen is made up of minute projections called microvilli (1/1,000mm long; 200,000 per sq mm) and is known as the brush border. The resulting total surface area of the intestine is about 300 sq m. The surface membrane of the microvilli facing the lumen is covered by a carbohydrate coat, the glycocalyx. Enzymes and transport systems are incorporated into this membrane, which is the actual site of absorption of nutrients.

---

intestine, large, portion of the intestine between small intestine and anus. About 1.83m long, so shorter than small intestine, but larger in diameter. Comprises the colon, which is the main portion, and the rectum.

---

intestine, small, portion of intestine between stomach and large intestine. About 6m long. Divided into the duodenum, jejunum and ileum. Glands of Lieberkühn and Brunner in its walls secrete digestive juices containing enzymes that, with those from the pancreatic juices, continue and complete digestion of food in the slightly alkaline medium created by the bile and pancreatic juices.

---

intracellular, within the cell.

---

intrinsic factor, a glycoprotein secreted by the stomach and required for the absorption of vitamin B_{12}.

---

inulin, the storage form of carbohydrate found in tubers and roots of artichokes, dahlias and dandelions. A polysaccharide of fructose. Cannot be digested by man or other mammals, so a dietary fibre.

---

iodide/iodine, the adult body contains 20–50mg of this essential non-metallic mineral, of which about 8mg is intensely concentrated in the thyroid gland in the hormones it stores and secretes.

Daily intake in UK (excluding cooking losses and out-of-home meals) averages 225µg, derived mainly from milk, 36 per cent; meat and meat products, 14 per cent; cereals, 12 per cent; fish, 5 per cent.

Functions as a component of the hormones triiodothyronine (T3) and thyroxine (T4). Their output is controlled by the hormone thyrotropin from the pituitary gland.

Thyroid hormones determine the rate of metabolism in many cells. If secretion is deficient, basal metabolism falls, the circulation is reduced and the whole tempo of the person's life slows down. Mucinous material accumulates under the skin, etc., coarsening the features and giving a characteristic appearance (myxoedema).

Absorption usually as inorganic iodide from food and water, takes place readily. The proportion taken up by the thyroid gland depends on its activity but is usually about half.

Excretion of any not taken up by the thyroid takes place in the urine. The kidneys cannot reduce clearance when plasma iodide levels are low.

Deficiency leading to goitre, an enlargement of the thyroid gland, is largely endemic and occurs where the level of iodide in the soil is low so that a population depending on locally grown food has an insufficient dietary supply. Goitres result from an increased secretion of thyrotropin, which stimulates the thyroid gland to enlarge. In places where endemic goitre is severe, cretinism is also endemic. Cretinism is due to congenital thyroid deficiency and results in a dull-looking child, underdeveloped both mentally and physically. In the UK, increased access in low-iodide areas such as Derbyshire to iodide-richer foods has very greatly reduced endemic goitre. Sporadic instances of goitre still appear in non-endemic areas.

Goitrogenic substances are naturally occurring inhibitors of the thyroid gland. Seeds, and to a lesser extent the leaves and roots of the *Brassica* (cabbage) family contain substances known to be goitrogenic in cattle, but there is no proof that they have produced goitres in man. Other foods with goitrogenic properties include peanuts, cassava and soya beans.

Requirement UK RDA 140μg. Figure based on scant evidence and may be unrealistic as physiological need is influenced by many dietary and environmental factors. EC and US RDA is 150μg.

Toxicity Though average intake in the UK is nearly twice the RDA, there is no evidence that it is causing thyrotoxicosis. The FAO/WHO in 1988 set a provisional maximum tolerable daily intake of 1,000μg.

The permitted red food colour erythrosine (E127) contains 577mg iodine per gram. However, foods containing the colour (e.g., glacé cherries, some pink or red confectionery items, biscuits, cherry cake, tinned strawberries, luncheon meat, salmon spread) are unlikely to contribute more than 10μg iodine daily to most UK diets. However, its use is soon likely to be restricted just to cocktail and glacé cherries.

Thyrotoxicosis is usually due to overproduction of thyroid hormone caused by excessive secretion of thyrotropin. Symptoms include anxiety, tachycardia, sweating, increased appetite with weight loss, prominence of the eyes. Like goitre, it is much more common in women than in men.

Distribution in foods (in μg per 100g): iodized salt, 3,100; haddock, 120; cod, 54–120; yogurt, 63; eggs, 53; Cheddar cheese, 20–58; salt, 40; butter, 23–49; winter milk, 29–50; soft margarine, 27; almonds, 10; summer milk, 5–11; meat, 3-9; white bread, 6, wholemeal bread and fruit juices, 5; cabbage, 2.

---

iodine number, a measure of the degree of unsaturation of fatty acids.

---

ion, charged particle formed when an atom or group of atoms loses or gains one or more electrons, forming a positively charged cation or negatively charged anion respectively. Anions and cations are attracted towards each other, forming compounds held together by electrovalent bonds. In solution, electrovalent compounds separate into their constituent ions. Examples include salts such as sodium chloride or common salt (formed between the sodium cation and chloride anion).

ionizing radiation, gamma rays usually, but also high-energy electrons and X-rays, are used: (1) in very low doses of less than 1 kilogray (kGy) to inhibit sprouting (potatoes, onions) and insect infestation (grains, citrus fruits) and delay ripening of fruits (tropical fruits, e.g., mangoes); (2) in slightly higher doses (1–3 kGy) to reduce the number of micro-organisms in food: (a) reduction of normal spoilage microflora extends shelf-life of soft fruit, meat and fish; (b) though slightly more resistant, a useful reduction in *Salmonella* and *Campylobacter* and, possibly, *Listeria* is achieved; *Clostridium botulinum* spores are much more resistant, viruses are highly resistant and doses high enough to reduce them cause unacceptable changes to food's sensory quality. (3) in higher doses (8 kGy) to decontaminate herbs and spices of their pathogenic micro-organisms, which is now considered to be the only acceptable means of doing this.

Increasing irradiation doses increases the changes to food's sensory and nutritional properties, mainly: (1) autoxidation of fats giving rise to rancid flavours; (2) slight breakdown of sulphur amino acids causing 'off' flavours, especially in dairy products; (3) breakdown of polysaccharides into smaller units, e.g., of pectin in cell walls leading to softening of fruit and vegetables; (4) loss of vitamins, e.g., thiamin and vitamin C, comparable to that arising from storage or cooking — this loss being additional to the subsequent loss on cooking.

Potential toxicity problems with irradiated foods include: (1) irradiation not removing toxins already present in food or restoring spoiled food so, if irradiation stops the food appearing 'bad', it may be eaten; (2) irradiated potatoes exposed to light synthesizing poisonous solanine but not developing the warning green colour; (3) irradiated cereals, potatoes and onions producing more aflatoxin when inoculated with *Aspergillus parasiticus* than if not irradiated; (4) irradiated crab-meat staying apparently fresh for 40 days, allowing time for considerable accumulation of toxin if contaminated with *Clostridium botulinum*.

Irradiation of food up to an overall average dose of 10 kGy will be permitted and does not increase the natural radioactivity of the food. The label of an irradiated food will have to state 'irradiated' or 'treated with ionizing radiation'.

IQ, Intelligence quotient, the ratio of mental to actual age. *See* intelligence.

Irish moss, *see* carrageenan.

iron, the healthy adult body contains about 4g of this essential mineral, 2.5g as haemoglobin in red blood cells, 0.3g as tissue iron (myoglobin and cytochromes) and 1.0g in iron stores. Haemoglobin, myoglobin and cytochromes contain oxidized (ferric) iron in the form of a complex organic molecule called haem, which is linked to proteins. The iron in non-haem compounds is found as the oxidized (ferric) ion in a protein complex.

The daily intake in the UK is around 11.6mg, but only about 10 per cent of this is absorbed by normal men, 14 per cent by menstruating women and 20 per cent by iron-deficient subjects.

Functions Haem-iron, as haemoglobin in red blood cells and as myoglobin in muscles, transports oxygen and, as cytochrome enzymes in the respiratory chain, takes part in the oxidation of foodstuffs for the release of energy.

Absorption is finely controlled and takes place in the duodenum and jejunum. An adult needs to absorb only 1mg daily to replace excretory losses. However, a woman must absorb an extra 1mg daily to replace the 28mg lost monthly in menstruation and 5–6mg extra daily during the last three months of pregnancy for foetal stores, etc.

Haem-iron is well absorbed and little affected by the composition of the diet, though depressed by vitamin C. For non-haem iron to be absorbed it has first to be released from its complexes with proteins, etc. (a process assisted by stomach acid) and reduced from ferric to ferrous ions both of which readily form insoluble salts with phytates, phosphates, tannins and polyphenols. However, the low availability of iron in cereals and vegetables may be mainly due to their dietary-fibre content.

Iron in phosphate-rich egg is poorly available and tannin-rich tea and coffee depress non-haem iron absorption. Vitamin C (ascorbic acid, reducing agent) and other organic acids like citric acid, form soluble complexes with ferrous iron and so iron absorption from vegetables rich in such acids is enhanced.

In the intestinal mucosal cells, iron is released from haem and ferrous ions are oxidized to the ferric form, which is either bound to a plasma protein forming transferrin that transports iron to the tissues or, if the person is not iron deficient, it is combined with another protein, forming ferritin, which remains in the mucosal cells that are eventually sloughed off and lost in the faeces. Mucosal cell ferritin levels help regulate iron absorption.

In tissues such as the liver, spleen and bone marrow, iron is stored as ferritin. If large amounts of ferritin are formed, the molecules join, forming haemosiderin, a less readily available iron store. Haemoglobin for new red blood cells is synthesized from ferritin in the bone marrow. The life of a red blood cell is about 120 days. It is then destroyed (haemolyzed) and the iron in its haemoglobin recycled via ferritin into fresh haemoglobin.

Excretion is low, only about 1mg daily being lost mainly by sloughing of cells into the alimentary tract, shed skin and into the urine.

Deficiency occurs when dietary iron and/or its absorption is insufficient to meet losses due to menstruation, haemorrhage, etc. When iron stores (ferritin levels) and the amount of iron being transported in transferrin are low, the person is said to be iron deficient, a symptomless condition widespread among women, infants and children, particularly in under-priviledged countries, who are consequently at risk of becoming anaemic. Only when haemoglobin levels fall does the person become anaemic, a condition seldom found in men unless they are haemorrhaging. Among Western children and menstruating women, 30 per cent are iron deficient and 2 per cent anaemic. Symptoms of anaemia include general fatigue and lassitude, breathlessness on exertion, giddiness, headache, pallor, insomnia and loss of appetite. In some countries, iron fortification of foods (e.g., of wheat in the US, salt in India, flour in Sweden) is carried out to reduce prevalence of iron deficiency.

The OPCS Dietary and Nutritional Survey in 1986–7 found for women, particularly young women, average intakes of iron were 10.5mg, i.e., below the RDA. Four per cent of all the women were anaemic and one third of all the women and 42 per cent of those under 50, had low iron stores.

Requirement UK RDA 12mg. Sufficient for all except 10 per cent of menstruating women whose monthly iron loss is too great to be met by the normal diet and who therefore require supplementation. Ferrous iron preparations protected against oxidation are the most effective.

Toxicity Siderosis or excess iron in the body in the form of haemosiderin deposits in the liver, pancreas, skin and joints, may be caused by excessive dietary intake (e.g., of cheap wine, which can contain 3.0mg per 100ml), excessive haemolysis or failure to regulate absorption. When deposits disrupt cell and organ function the disorder is called haemochromatosis. Iron overload syndrome is an inherited haemochromatosis affecting one to three individuals per 1,000, caused by over-absorption of dietary iron and treatment is by bleeding.

Accidental poisoning in children eating iron supplements as sweets quickly leads to nausea, vomiting, diarrhoea and even death. Supplemental iron causes epigastric pain, colic and diarrhoea or constipation in some people and may interfere with zinc absorption.

Distribution in foods (in mg per 100g): black (blood) sausage, 20; liver, 7.0–21.0; cocoa powder, 10.5; treacle, 9.2; parsley, 8.0; lentils, 7.6; haricot beans, 6.7; wholemeal bread, 2.5; meat, 0.9–2.1; eggs, 2.0; peas, 1.9; watercress, 1.6; winter cabbage, 0.6; potatoes, 0.5; cod, 0.3; yogurt, 0.09; milk, 0.05.

irradiation, three main types used in food processing: *see* microwave, ionizing radiation and ultraviolet.

irritable bowel syndrome, symptoms: diarrhoea (usually abdominal pain/distension) and/or constipation. Causes may include: nervous state; food allergy/intolerance.

ischaemia, deficient blood supply.

ischaemic heart disease, coronary heart disease (*which see*).

isinglass, dried swimming bladder of sturgeon containing about 80 per cent collagen protein. Used for clarifying beers and wines.

isinglass, Japanese, *see* agar.

isoascorbic acid, D-ascorbic acid or crythorascorbic acid. Isomer of ascorbic acid with one-twentieth of its vitamin C activity.

isoleucine, a branched chain essential amino acid. Seldom if ever limiting in foods.

isomalt, a permitted bulk sweetener. A mixture of synthetic glucose-mannitol and glucose-sorbitol compounds which are partly metabolised in the small intestine to free glucose, mannitol and sorbitol. The remaining isomalt is fermented by bacteria in the large intestine. Consumption of large quantities may cause flatulence and have a laxative effect.

isomers, substances that have the same molecular formula but which differ in the way their constituent atoms are arranged. Isomers particularly important nutritionally include:
1. *Amino acids* Only the L form occurs naturally. Synthetic ones are a mixture of the D and L forms. The body absorbs the D form more slowly than the L and converts it to the L.

2. *Sugars* Some occur naturally in the D form, others in the L form. Most involved in mammalian metabolism are D isomers.

3. *Vitamin E* Only the D form occurs naturally. The L form has some but not all of the biological activity of the D isomer.

4. *Ascorbic acid* Only the naturally occurring L form has full vitamin C activity.

5. *Alpha- and gamma-linolenic acids* Both 18 carbon fatty acids with three unsaturated bonds. Differ only in the position of the unsaturated bonds, the position of those in the alpha acid making it a member of the omega 3 family of polyunsaturated fatty acids and those in the gamma acid of the omega 6 family. There are many such isomers among the unsaturated fatty acids.

6. *Linoleic and linoelaidic acids, cis* and *trans* Isomers of the same fatty acid. The unsaturated bonds in fatty acids may be either *cis*, in which the hydrogen atoms are on the same side of the double bond, or *trans*, when they are on opposite sides. Naturally occurring isomers are always in the *cis* form. Chemical hydrogenation or 'hardening' of fats converts some or all *cis* bonds to *trans*. Linoelaidic has none of the essential fatty acid properties of linoleic acid. *Trans* fatty acids appear to behave metabolically like saturated fatty acids.

---

isotopes, of an element differ only in the number of neutrons (uncharged particles) they contain. Because they contain the same number of protons and electrons (charged particles), isotopes do not differ in chemical properties. Radioactive and stable isotopes can be measured in very small amounts and they are used to 'label' dietary nutrients so their metabolic fate in man and animals may be studied.

---

ispaghula, mucilage derived from husk of seed of *Plantago ovata*. Like psyllium, it is a mixed polysaccharide with xylose the main constituent sugar. A dietary fibre. Used as thickener or stabilizer in certain American dairy desserts. Used in Europe as a bulk laxative, as an emollient and demulcent, and in slimming diets as an appetite depressant because of the feeling of fullness it gives as it swells in contact with water. Unlike most soluble dietary fibres it contains an unfermentable soluble residue that enables it to act as a bulk laxative to treat chronic constipation. Some, sensitized by inhaling it, experience allergic reactions on consuming it.

IU, international units.

J

JACNE, *see* Joint Advisory Committee on Nutrition Education.

jaguar gum, guar gum, a galactomannan (*which see*).

jaundice, raised blood levels of the bile pigment, bilirubin, formed from breakdown of haemoglobin. High levels lead to yellowing of whites of eyes, skin and urine. May be caused by excessive breakdown of red blood cells (haemolytic) or obstruction of entry of bilirubin with bile into the duodenum (obstructive) or through liver cell damage as in viral hepatitis (hepato-cellular). In the latter two, stools are pale and urine dark yellow or brown.

jejunum, middle section of small intestine between the duodenum and the ileum. About 2.4m long. Walls contain glands of Lieberkühn that produce intestinal digestive juices. Site of absorption of most substances except vitamin B_{12}, some electrolytes, bile salts and water.

Joint Advisory Committee on Nutrition Education, an independent panel of experts commissioned by the DHSS following their COMA Report, to prepare a layman's guide to healthy eating that is entitled, 'Eating for a Healthier Heart'.

joule (J), is a unit of energy. It is the energy expended when 1kg is moved 1m by a force of 1 newton (N). The units used in nutrition are the kilojoule (kJ) and megajoule (MJ), equal to 1,000 and 1,000,000 J respectively. 4.2 kJ = 1 kcal for practical purposes.

juices, fruit, nutritional composition as in the fruit from which they were derived except for loss of pectin. Most important nutrient is vitamin C, citrus juices providing 30–50mg/dl, pineapple and tomato about half this amount, but apple little. Low in sodium (about 0.057g/l) and rich in potassium (about 1.17 g/l), with a potassium:sodium ratio at least 20:1, and so useful for those on low-sodium diets or diuretics.

K

karaya gum, also known as sterculia gum. Dried exudate of East Indian tree, *Sterculia*. A polysaccharide of galacturonic acid, galactose and rhamnose. A dietary fibre that forms a viscous mucilage in water. Used as a stabilizer (meringues, water-ices) and as denture adhesive. Cathartic. Lowers blood cholesterol levels in normocholesterolaemic men.

Kashin-Beck disease, caused by a deficiency of selenium (*which see*).

kelp, a seaweed (principally *Ascophyllum nodosum*, bladderwrack or knotted wrack) often dried and used as a food supplement. Contains minerals, being a good source of iodine, and small amounts of vitamins D and K, most water-soluble vitamins and carotene. Its protein is of poor quality.

Dried provides (in g per 100g): protein, 5.7; fat, 2.6; fibre, 7.0; water, 10.7; minerals, 15.4; iodine, 0.067 to 0.11, depending on season.

Kempner diet, based on rice and fruit and very low in sodium (100–150mg daily). An original very low-salt diet, but difficult to follow as it is so unpalatable.

kenkey, African fermented and cooked maize, whole grain or husked. Products using whole grain show little nutrient loss compared with the raw grain, whereas losses are considerable in products produced from husked grain.

keratin, chief protein of hair, nails, horns, hooves, feathers, scales. Insoluble, fibrous and elastic. Contains 11 per cent of sulphur amino acids. Indigestible by man or other animals.

keratomalacia, ulceration of the cornea of the eye due to vitamin A deficiency.

Keshan's disease, caused by selenium deficiency.

---

ketoacidosis, a possible complication of diabetes mellitus arising as a result of severe and chronic ketosis caused by the incomplete oxidation of fatty acids, resulting in the formation of ketone bodies. Two of the ketone bodies are strong acids that upset the body's acid-base balance by depleting base that is lost in the urine during neutralization of the acids for excretion.

---

ketone bodies, collective term for acetoacetic acid and its derivatives beta-hydroxybutyric acid and acetone. Produced by the liver in ketosis.

---

ketosis, arises as a result of glucose or insulin deficiency, which causes free fatty acids to be mobilized from fat stores. These saturate the oxidative mechanisms in the liver, leading to the release of ketone bodies (acetoacetic acid, beta-hydroxybutyric acid and acetone), products of incomplete fatty-acid oxidation. The ketone bodies (apart from acetone) are oxidized readily by other tissues.

Occurs in starvation or when carbohydrate supply is short, when it is controlled and beneficial, providing an alternative energy source for the brain; and more severely in uncontrolled diabetes mellitus when it can lead to ketoacidosis. Characteristic odour of ketotic subjects is due to excretion of acetone in the breath.

Keys score, summarizes the lipid composition of the diet, a high score or 'phi' value indicating a relatively high intake of saturated fatty acids and cholesterol and a relatively low intake of polyunsaturated fatty acids. Similar to the Hegsted score (*which see*).

The Keys equation is:

$$\Phi \text{ ('phi')} = 1.35 (2S - P) + 1.5\sqrt{Z}$$

where S = % calories from saturated fat; P = % calories from poly-unsaturated fat; and Z = amount of cholesterol in mg per 1,000 kcal.

---

kGy, *see* kilogray.

---

kidneys, organs responsible for: formation of urine (on average 1,500ml daily) in which are excreted nitrogenous waste products (urea, uric acid, creatinine) and other metabolites (sulphate, hydrogen ions) and surplus nutrients (sodium, potassium, calcium, chloride, phosphate, water-soluble vitamins, etc.) and water; regulation of total body-water content and maintenance of sodium, potassium, hydrogen ion and magnesium balance; the final activation of vitamin D; the synthesis of a stimulant to red blood cell production by the bone marrow; renin synthesis; hormone degradation. Effects of kidney failure include uraemia, acidosis, hypertension, oedema, hyperkalaemia, bone disease, and anaemia.

Dietetic measures in kidney disease include decreasing their work-load by reducing intake of water, sodium, potassium, magnesium and protein to the minimum.

As offal food lamb, ox and pig kidneys provide (per 100g): energy, 86–90 kcal; (g) protein, 15.7–16.5; fat, 2.6–2.7; (mg) vitamin A, 0.10–0.15; vitamin E, 0.18–0.45; thiamin, 0.32–0.49; riboflavin, 1.8–2.1; niacin, 9.4–11.8; vitamin B_6, 0.25–0.32; vitamin B_{12}, 0.014–0.055; vitamin C, 7–14; sodium, 180–220; iron, 5.0–7.4; copper, 0.42–0.81; zinc, 1.9–2.6.

---

kilogray (kGy), unit of irradiation. *See* ionizing radiation.

---

kinky hair syndrome, Menke's disease. *See* copper.

---

koji, oriental fungal proteolytic enzyme preparation from the mould *Aspergillus oryzae* grown on steamed rice. Used in preparation of miso.

---

konjac mannan, *see* glucomannan.

---

kosher, foods, are those allowed and prepared in accordance with Jewish laws. *See* Table 16, page 295.

Krebs cycle, *see* citric-acid cycle.

---

kwashiorkor, a form of protein-energy malnutrition seen in children, especially the newly weaned, in whom energy intake is adequate but with quantitative and qualitative deficiency of dietary protein. Oedema, failure to grow, general unhappiness or apathy, characteristic skin disease and sparse hair are obvious symptoms. (*See also* proteins: deficiency.)

L

LACOTS, Local Authority Coordinating Body on Trading Standards. Local authorities, not MAFF, enforce food law. This is in contrast to medicine's law, which is enforced by the Ministry itself, the DoH. In the event of any dispute an authority may refer specific issues to its local liaison group, which may choose to seek the advice of the appropriate LACOTS panel.

lactase, enzyme that splits lactose into glucose and galactose. Present in intestinal digestive juices.

lactase deficiency, the activity of lactase is always limited and appears to decline from childhood onwards in about 60 per cent of all humans, who exhibit various degrees of lactase deficiency and consequent lactose malabsorption. Deficiency is particularly prevalent among non-white populations. About 20 per cent of North Europeans and 90 per cent of some African tribes are lactase deficient. In Europe, prevalence of deficiency increases as one passes from north to south.

Symptoms of lactose malabsorption, which include abdominal cramps, diarrhoea and flatulence, are attributed to the undigested lactose holding water and to its fermentation by colonic bacteria producing gases and intestinal irritants. Lactase deficiency from birth is a rare inherited disease.

lactation, similar dietary principles apply to those followed during pregnancy (*which see*).

lactic acid, formed in muscles from glucose breakdown for energy release during vigorous exercise when the oxygen supply is inadequate. Converted by the liver back to glucose (*see* Cori cycle *and* gluconeogenesis). Formed by fermentation of milk sugar giving sour milk its taste and causing precipitation of casein curd for cottage cheese production.

lactic acid cycle, *see* Cori cycle.

lactitol, a permitted bulk sweetener. Synthetic compound between galactose and sorbitol. In large quantities has a laxative effect.

---

lacto-ovo-vegetarians, vegans who also consume dairy products and eggs. *See* vegetarians.

---

lacto-vegetarians, vegans who also consume dairy products. *See* vegetarians.

---

lactose, commonly called 'milk sugar', being the main sugar in milk (5–8g/dl in human milk and 4–6 in cow's) and sometimes 'sand sugar' as it crystallizes in gritty prisms. A disaccharide of glucose and galactose. Less soluble and one-sixth the sweetness of sucrose and digested more slowly than sucrose and other disaccharides. Enzyme lactase hydrolyzes it to its constituent monosaccharides for absorption (*but see* lactase deficiency). Synthesized and found almost exclusively in the mammary gland of lactating mammals. Cariogenic when used with sucrose.

---

lactose intolerance or malabsorption, mainly attributable to lactase deficiency.

---

lactulose, a synthetic compound between galactose and fructose. Sweeter than lactose but less sweet than sucrose. On consumption passes essentially unchanged into the colon where it is fermented by bacteria. Large amounts may cause flatulence and diarrhoea. Used medicinally e.g. in the treatment of constipation. Not permitted for use as a bulk sweetener.

---

laetrile, a B complex factor but not a vitamin. Also known as amygdalin, B_{17}, and incorrectly as vitamin B_{17}. Bitter tasting, extracted from apricot kernels. Used controversially in some 'alternative' treatments for cancer, chiefly in the USA. Forms cyanide on digestion, often causing toxic symptoms and sometimes even death.

---

lager, *see* beer.

lamb, meat of young sheep. Lean lamb provides (per 100g): energy, 162 kcal; (g) water, 70.1; protein, 20.8; fat, 8.8; (mg) iron, 1.6; zinc, 4.0; thiamin, 0.14; riboflavin, 0.28; niacin, 7.1; vitamin B_6, 0.25; (μg) vitamin B_{12}, 2.0.

lathyrism, a disease of the spinal cord producing permanent paralysis that is caused by high consumption of the seeds of *Lathyrus sativus* (Khesari dahl), sown with wheat in dry districts of Asia and N. Africa and eaten if drought causes the wheat crop to fail.

lauric acid, a 12 carbon, saturated fatty acid. Forms 48 per cent of the total fatty acids of coconut oil.

law, important provisions of the Food Safety Act 1990 are:
1. to make it an offence to sell to the prejudice of the purchaser food that is not of the nature, substance or quality demanded;
2. to prohibit the use of a label or advertisement that falsely describes the food or misleads as to its nature, substance or quality;
3. to prohibit the addition to or abstraction of any substance from food so as to render the food injurious to health;
4. to make it an offence to sell unsound food.
These general provisions are backed up by many regulations that lay down requirements as to the labelling of all foods, the composition of the major foods in the diet and the type and level of additives and contaminants permitted in food.

layer, unstirred, *see* unstirred layer.

LCAT, (pronounced L cat), lecithin: cholesterol acyltransferase. Plasma enzyme that catalyses the transfer of a fatty acid, usually polyunsaturated, from lecithin (phosphatidylcholine) to cholesterol forming a cholesteryl ester and lysolecithin.

LDL, *see* lipoproteins, low density.

lead, a 70kg man contains about 120mg of this non-essential mineral. It can accumulate in the body until toxic levels are reached. Daily food supplies 200–400µg. Intake is considerably increased by inhaling traffic exhaust fumes and proximity to an industrial plant, by drinking water supplied by old-fashioned lead pipes and from lead paints — now banned. Children are more susceptible than adults to comparable doses. Lead poisoning may lead to anaemia and nerve and brain damage. Lead is more easily absorbed from drinks than food, but on average uptake from the gut is about 10 per cent of dietary intake. Some reports (but not others) indicate that iron deficient humans absorb about 24 per cent of ingested lead — important if true, considering that 30 per cent of Western children and menstruating women are iron deficient. About 20 per cent of absorbed lead is excreted in the faeces and urine in a 12 day period.

---

lecithin,   term applies chemically only to the phospholipid, phosphatidyl-choline, but in the food industry it describes a complex mixture of at least 50 per cent mixed phospholipids with vegetable oils, fatty acids and sugars, such a mixture being liquid. When purified, a granular solid can be obtained containing 98 per cent phospholipids that is used as a food-supplement source of choline and inositol. Lecithin from plant sources, e.g., soya beans, contains a higher proportion of polyunsaturated fatty acids than that from animal sources.

Used in the food industry as an emulsifying agent, being partly soluble in water as well as in fat.

---

lectins,   toxic proteins or glycoproteins, also known as haemagglutinins or phytoagglutinins. Present in many legumes but destroyed on boiling for ten minutes. Cause vomiting and diarrhoea. *In vitro*, cause red blood cells to agglutinate, or, clump together. *See* food poisoning.

---

legume gums,   galactomannans (*which see*), e.g., guar and locust-bean gums.

---

legumes,   *see* pulses.

---

lente carbohydrate,   a food from which the carbohydrate is released slowly because it is only slowly digested. Tends to have a low glycaemic index.

leucine, a branched chain essential amino acid. Seldom if ever limiting in foods.

---

leukocytes, *see* blood cells, white.

---

leukotrienes (LT), formed by the action of lipoxygenase enzyme on 20 carbon polyunsaturated fatty acids. Series 3 are derived from gamma-linolenic acid, Series 4 from arachidonic acid and Series 5 from eicosapentaenoic acid (EPA). Little is known about Series 3 and 5, but many of Series 4 are very potent constrictors of smooth muscle and constrict small airways in the lungs, cause oedema and constrict blood vessels. Some of Series 4 are linked with amino acids and are known as the slow-reacting substances (SRSs) because of the slow onset of the smooth muscle contraction they cause. When SRSs are generated as the result of allergic reactions, they are known as the slow-reacting substances of anaphylaxis (SRS-A). *See* eicosanoids *and* Figure 2, page 79.

---

licorice, black substance used in medicine, to flavour chewing tobacco and as a sweetmeat made from the root of *Glycyrrhiza glabra*. In some people, its long-term consumption produces symptoms similar to those of an excess of the mineralocorticoid steroid hormone, namely hypertension, sodium retention, and excretion and low blood levels of potassium. The mechanism may be inhibition by glycyrrhetinic acid compounds in licorice of the enzyme that inactivates the mineralocorticoid hormone normally produced by the body, resulting in its accumulation.

---

lignans, substances structurally resembling synthetic oestrogens but with anti-oestrogenic activity. Present in grain dietary fibres other than bran. Converted by intestinal bacteria into animal lignans (e.g., enterodiol and enterolactone). Suggested as the colon and breast cancer protecting factors of high-fibre, low-meat-eating communities.

---

lignin, contributes to structural rigidity of plant cell wall. Only non-carbohydrate component of dietary fibre. Holds water. Possibly an anti-oxidant. May bind trace minerals. Affects faecal steroids. Polymer of aromatic alcohols. Probably not itself broken down by colonic fermentation and reduces fermentation of other components of dietary fibre, both by preventing bacterial access and inhibiting bacterial growth. The average UK diet provides about 1.7g daily, which is about 7 per cent of the total dietary fibre intake.

---

linoelaidic acid,   *trans* isomer of linoleic acid. *See* fatty acids, *trans*.

---

linoleic acid,   a polyunsaturated fatty acid of the omega 6 family with 18 carbons and two unsaturated bonds (C18:2 n-6). An essential fatty acid. Oils from cereals, pulses and other vegetables are rich dietary sources.

Distribution in foods (as percentage of total fatty acids): safflower-seed oil, 75; evening primrose oil, 72; sunflower-seed oil, 58; soya bean and corn oils, 53; polyunsaturated margarines, 52; cotton-seed oil, 50; sesame oil, 43; chicken, 18; hard vegetable source margarine, 10; pork and fish oil, 7; beef, butter, cream and milk, 2.

---

linolenic acids,   alpha- and gamma-. Both are polyunsaturated fatty acids (PUFA) with 18 carbons and three unsaturated bonds, but while alpha- belongs to the omega 3 family of PUFA, gamma- belongs to the omega 6 family, resulting in completely different physiological roles for the two acids. *See also* alpha-linolenic acid; gamma-linolenic acid; isomers.

---

linseed oil,   rich in polyunsaturated fatty acids, alpha-linolenic acid forming at least 50 per cent of its total fatty acids and linoleic acid 14 per cent.

---

lipases,   enzymes that split off one or more fatty acids from triglycerides. Lingual lipase is secreted by glands at the back of the tongue and commences fat digestion in the buccal cavity and continues it in the stomach. Pancreatic lipase is secreted with the pancreatic juices into the duodenum where it continues fat digestion, assisted by the emulsifying action of bile. *See also* lipoprotein lipase.

---

lipid peroxidation,   a complex, ever-amplifying series (cascade) of free radical reactions causing harmful oxidation of polyunsaturated fatty acids. Peroxidized food fats and oils are described as rancid. They have an unpleasant odour and taste. Process delayed by excluding oxygen and by the presence of an antioxidant like vitamin E.

Peroxidation in cell membranes disrupts their structure and may lead to cell rupture or inhibition of enzyme and transport systems in the membrane, while toxic end-products may inhibit certain enzymes. Vitamin E in cell membrane lipids prevents their peroxidation by scavenging free radical initiators. *See* free radicals.

lipids, biochemical term for fats and fatty substances.

lipofuscin, pigments that accumulate with age in tissues. Probably products of reactions between malonaldehyde (formed by peroxidation of all lipids) and amino groups of proteins, amino acids or nucleic acids. Vitamin E has been reported to inhibit lipofuscin accumulation.

lipolysis, splitting of triglycerides (fats and oils) into fatty acids and glycerol.

lipoprotein lipase, enzyme that catalyses the breakdown of plasma lipoprotein triglycerides to fatty acids and glycerol. Responsible for the uptake into the tissues of triglyceride fatty acids in chylomicrons and VLDL.

lipoproteins, combinations of lipids with particular proteins called apoproteins. They mix with water and so enable large quantities of water-insoluble lipids to be transported in an aqueous medium — blood plasma. They differ from each other in density, particle size and composition and comprise chylomicrons and very low-density, intermediate-density, low-density and high-density lipoproteins (VLD, IDL, LDL and HDL respectively). *See* fats.

lipoproteins, high-density, (HDL, alpha-lipoproteins), originate in the liver and small intestines. Newly formed their lipid content is almost entirely phospholipid, but they pick up cholesterol from the tissues and possibly from other lipoproteins, eventually containing almost as much cholesteryl ester/cholesterol as phospholipid. Sometimes known as 'good' cholesterol as they represent cholesterol being transported from peripheral tissues to the liver for excretion. *See* fats.

lipoproteins, intermediate-density, (IDL), an intermediate in the formation of low-density lipoproteins from very low density lipoproteins. *See* fats.

---

lipoproteins, low-density, (LDL, beta-lipoproteins) are formed in the blood from VLDL. Up to 58 per cent of their lipids are cholesteryl esters and cholesterol that they deposit in peripheral tissues like blood-vessel walls (so sometimes being known as 'bad' cholesterol) and the liver. *See* fats.

---

lipoproteins, pre-beta, very low density lipoproteins.

---

lipoproteins, very low density, (VLDL, pre-beta lipoproteins), are formed in the liver. About 56 per cent of their lipid content is triglycerides and 23 per cent cholesteryl esters and cholesterol. As a result of the action of lipoprotein lipase, they deposit much of their triglycerides in peripheral tissues as they pass through them in the capillaries and eventually form LDL. *See* fats.

---

lipotropic factors, methyl donors, e.g., choline, betaine, methionine, which help to prevent certain types of fatty livers.

---

lipoxygenase, enzyme that catalyses the conversion of 20 carbon polyunsaturated fatty acids to leukotrienes.

---

liqueurs, alcoholic drinks produced by distillation from fermented sugars, sweetened and variously flavoured. Drunk in very small amounts.
   Advocaat/cherry brandy/curaçao provide (per 100ml): energy, 272/255/311 kcal; (g) alcohol, 12.8/19.0/29.3; carbohydrate, 28.4/32.6/28.3.

---

liquorice, *see* licorice.

Listeria monocytogenes, causes the food poisoning, listeriosis in humans. A common bacterial contaminant of foods, especially chicken, raw milk, soft ripened cheeses, vegetables, chilled meals and pâté. Unusual among bacteria in that it can grow at temperatures as low as 2°C (lower than refrigerator temperatures) and as high as 42°C. In low numbers it is not a significant threat, but if allowed to grow in food that is then eaten without thorough cooking, it can cause the infection listeriosis, which has become more common in recent years. Most at risk are pregnant women in whom it may only cause mild diarrhoea, but, because it can cross the placenta, may give rise to meningitis in the foetus or newborn baby, which can cause disabilities or be fatal. Also at risk are the elderly and those with weakened immune systems, e.g., transplant patients. At-risk groups should avoid soft ripened cheeses such as Brie, Camembert and blue vein-type, cooked-chilled meals, any type of pâté and ready-to-eat poultry should be re-heated until piping hot rather than eaten cold.

---

listeriosis,   food poisoning caused by *Listeria monocytogenes*.

---

liver,   largest gland in the body, weighing 1.3–1.8kg in the adult. Via the hepatic portal vein, it receives the water-soluble products of digestion that have been absorbed straight into the blood, e.g., sugars and amino acids and short chain fatty acids.

Functions are numerous. Responsible for 25 per cent of basal metabolism. Fundamentally concerned with metabolism of carbohydrates, proteins, fats and vitamins, it metabolizes over 90 per cent of ingested alcohol. It inactivates many hormones and toxic substances. It synthesizes proteins (e.g., albumin, lipoproteins), amino acids, urea, triglycerides, fatty acids, ketone bodies, cholesterol, bile acids, glucose and glycogen. It excretes cholesterol, activates vitamins and stores glycogen, vitamins A, E and K, B_{12} and folic acid.

Diseases   Obstruction of the bile duct or other restriction on entry of bile into the duodenum leads to failure in fat and fat-soluble vitamin digestion and absorption and consequently, to fatty stools. It may also lead to high blood levels of bilirubin, causing jaundice.

Fatty infiltration of the liver is the first and reversible change following liver damage seen in kwashiorkor or caused by alcohol. Prolonged heavy drinking may then lead to cirrhosis.

As a food, highly nutritious offal. Calf, chicken, lamb, ox and pig livers provide (per 100g): energy, 135–179 kcal; (g) protein, 19.1–21.3; fat, 6.3–10.3; (mg) vitamin A, 9.2–18.1; vitamin E, 0.17–0.46; thiamin, 0.21–0.36; riboflavin, 2.7–3.3; niacin, 14.3–19.2; vitamin B_6, 0.40–0.83; vitamin B_{12}, 0.025–0.11; total folate, 0.17–0.59; pantothenic acid, 6.1–8.4; biotin, 0.027–0.21; vitamin C, 10–23; copper, 0.52–11.0; zinc, 3.4–7.8; iron, 7.0–21.0.

locust-bean gum,   a galactomannan (*which see*).

---

loupe,   a stone fruit, e.g., coconut.

---

lumen,   space inside a tubular structure such as the intestines.

---

lyophilized,   freeze-dried. Frozen and dried by evaporation of ice under a high vacuum.

---

lysine,   an essential basic amino acid. The limiting amino acid in many cereals, e.g., wheat. Sometimes added to fortify cereal foods. Likely to be deficient in poor vegetarian diets.

---

lysolecithin,   phosphatidylcholine minus the fatty acid on position 2. Formed during digestion and during formation of cholesteryl ester from cholesterol catalysed by the enzyme LCAT in the blood.

M

---

macrobiotics,   the art of choosing food according to a set of principles, with the objective that man, in order to live naturally, actively and healthily must eat natural foods. Foods are accordingly classed as predominantly Yin or Yang, representing negative and positive life forces respectively, and a balanced diet is achieved by a balance of Yin and Yang foods. Weak conditions and characteristics are said to be caused by an excess of Yin foods (e.g., sugar, liquids, alcohol, fruit, dairy products, chemicals and drugs) and over-strong conditions and characteristics by an excess of Yang foods (e.g., meat, animal produce, salt). Either condition can be corrected by avoiding extremes in food. Grains and vegetables are at the centre and so form the bulk of a macrobiotic diet. In cold climates more Yang foods should be consumed and in hot climates more Yin ones. Manual labourers need more Yang foods than creative workers. In practice it may be difficult to achieve a nutritional balance for infants and young children with this diet.

macrophages, *see* blood cells, white.

mad cow disease, *see* bovine spongiform encephalopathy.

MAFF, Ministry of Agriculture, Fisheries and Food.

magnesium, an adult man contains about 25g, mostly in the bones as the phosphate and bicarbonate that appear to act as a reserve of this essential mineral. About one-fifth is present in soft tissues. Magnesium ions are present in all living cells being next to potassium, the main intracellular cation (positively charged).

Daily UK household supply in 1986 (not allowing for 10 per cent wastage and excluding out-of-home meals) averaged 247mg (294 with contributions from alcoholic drinks and confectionery), derived mainly from (per cent): cereals, 33 (bread, 19); vegetables, 19 (potatoes, 7); milk and products, 18.

Functions Essential for all reactions involving ATP and therefore required for the synthesis of all proteins, nucleic acids, nucleotides, lipids, and carbohydrates and the activation of muscle contraction.

Absorbed throughout the small intestine in amounts mainly depending on the load presented, though vitamin D may help. On a low-magnesium diet three-quarters can be absorbed, reducing to a quarter on a high dietary intake. High levels of calcium, protein and phosphate in the diet reduce absorption.

Excreted by the kidneys, which can conserve it in times of shortage.

Deficiency not uncommon though unlikely to arise from low dietary intake as, being an essential component of chlorophyll, it is present in most foods of vegetable origin. However, alcoholism and illnesses leading to excessive losses in the urine and faeces (diarrhoea) may lead to deficiency. Symptoms include apathy and muscular weakness and sometimes tetany and convulsions. Magnesium salts given by mouth are poorly absorbed and tend to cause diarrhoea.

Requirement No UK RDA. US RDA is 350mg. EC RDA is 300mg.

Toxicity rare if kidney function is normal.

Distribution in foods (in mg per 100g): Brazil nuts, 410; soya bean flour, 290; wholemeal flour, 140; plain chocolate, 100; wholemeal bread, 93;

lentils, 77; parsley, 52; peas, 30; mustard and cress, 27; white bread, 26; cod, 23; winter cabbage and watercress, 17; cauliflower, 14.

Maillard reaction,   complex reaction between amino acids with reactive side chains such as lysine, arginine, tryptophan and histidine and sugars or other reducing substances causing brown discoloration, e.g., on prolonged storage of foods such as dehydrated vegetables or concentrated or dried milk and in dry heat cooking (*which see*). *See also* food processing, adverse effects.

---

maize,   a grain second only to wheat in world food production. Mostly used as food for livestock, but a staple food for man in central America, parts of Africa and South America made into a porridge or flat bread. Other forms include 'corn on the cob' or sweet corn, and hominy. Used in the food industry in manufacture of cornflour, glucose and some whiskys.

Unlike other grains, one form, yellow maize, contains carotenoids with vitamin A activity. Zein, which is 50 per cent of its protein, is lacking in tryptophan and lysine. Since in addition its nicotinic acid content is bound and unavailable (unless treated with alkali (lime-water) as in Mexico), maize eating is associated with pellagra. Geneticists are working on a strain, opaque-2, which is relatively rich in lysine and tryptophan.

Wholemeal maize provides (per 100g): energy, 356 kcal; (g) protein, 9.5; fat, 4.3; (mg) calcium, 12; iron, 5.0; thiamin, 0.33; riboflavin, 0.13; (μg) beta-carotene up to 800 in yellow maize.

---

malabsorption syndrome,   a defect of absorption of essential nutrients as a result of reduced absorptive surface, defective digestion, competition with bacteria for nutrients or defects of the gut mucosa. Some or all of the following symptoms are present: diarrhoea, steatorrhoea, abdominal distension, loss of weight, anaemia, hypoproteinaemia, deficiencies of vitamins and minerals producing stomatitis, glossitis, dermatitis, paraesthesia or tetany.

---

malonaldehyde,   substance produced during lipid peroxidation (*which see*). *See also* lipofuscin.

---

maltase,   enzyme that splits maltose into glucose molecules. Present in intestinal digestive juices.

maltodextrins, partially digested starch. Include varying proportions of starch oligosaccharides and maltose. A thickening agent in foods. Used in foods such as drinks for athletes where both quickly digested and more slowly digested carbohydrate energy sources are required.

---

maltose, a disaccharide of glucose. Produced during digestion of starch and glycogen by the enzyme amylase and found in germinating cereals and malt. Enzyme maltase in the small intestine hydrolyses it to glucose for absorption. About one-third as sweet as sucrose. Cariogenic.

---

maltotriose, trisaccharide of three glucose molecules formed during digestion of starch and glycogen by amylase.

---

manganese, the adult body contains 12–20mg of this essential mineral mainly in bones, liver and kidneys.

Daily UK household supply in 1986 (not allowing for 10 per cent wastage and excluding out-of-home meals) averaged 3.43mg (4.02mg with contributions from alcoholic drinks and confectionery) derived mainly from (per cent): cereals, 50 (bread, 31); tea, 21; fruit and vegetables, 20. Total intake has dropped due to declining consumption of tea, a rich source, in the UK.

Functions as a cofactor in enzymes concerned in synthesis of cartilage components and as a constituent of several metalloenzymes.

Absorption About 5 per cent of the dietary intake is absorbed by a mechanism similar to that of iron, which can inhibit its absorption, and like iron it is transported in the blood as protein complexes including transferrin.

Excretion is via the bile.

Deficiency is unknown in man.

Requirement No RDA but the USA estimated safe and adequate daily intake is 2.0–5.0mg.

Toxicity Poisoning due to food contamination is unknown, but mineworkers inhaling it may develop 'manganese madness'.

Good food sources include tea, whole cereals, legumes and leafy vegetables. Meat, milk and refined cereals are poor sources.

---

manioc, *see* cassava.

mannitol,   a permitted bulk sweetener. A six-carbon sugar alcohol. Less cariogenic than sucrose. Consumption of large amounts may cause diarrhoea and flatulence.

mannose,   a hexose monosaccharide. A constituent of plant gums (e.g., glucomannan and galactomannan) and associated with many important animal proteins.

maple syrup,   derived from maple tree sap. Mainly sucrose and water. Cariogenic.

marasmus,   a form of protein-energy malnutrition seen mostly in children deficient in both dietary energy and protein, as well as other nutrients. Characterized by generalized loss of body tissues, resulting in a wizened, shrunken child, often with diarrhoea, who may be generally unhappy or apathetic.

margarine,   flavoured and coloured emulsion of vegetable, fish or animal oils containing not more than 16 per cent water. To obtain the right consistency, the oils in some have been hardened by hydrogenating their unsaturated bonds (*see* fatty acids).

The polyunsaturated to saturated fatty acid ratio (P/S) of margarines depends on the sources of oils and fats used to make them. P/S: hard (animal and vegetable), 0.46; hard (vegetable), 0.32; soft (animal and vegetable), 0.64; soft (vegetable), 0.70; polyunsaturated, 3.15.

By law, margarine must be fortified with between 760 and 940 IU vitamin A, and 80–100 IU vitamin D per 28g.

mast cells,   wandering cells found in large numbers in connective tissue. Release histamine into blood in response to an allergen/antibody complex, certain foods (e.g., fish, tomatoes, egg white, strawberries, chocolate) and foods rich in tyramine (chocolate, cheese, fish, beans). *See* food allergies *and* food intolerance.

matoke,   a banana eaten green, staple diet of many Africans. High content of serotonin.

MCT, medium chain triglycerides. *See* triglycerides, medium-chain.

---

mead, fermented honey and water, used as alcoholic drink.

---

mead acid, a polyunsaturated fatty acid of the omega 9 family with 20 carbons and three double bonds. Its concentration in the blood rises during deficiency of essential fatty acids (*see* fatty acids, essential).

---

meat, commonly refers to the muscle tissue or flesh of animals, e.g., beef, lamb, veal, mutton, pork, or poultry. By law, it is flesh including fat and the skin, rind, gristle and sinew in amounts naturally associated with the flesh and includes diaphragm, head meat (not brain), heart, kidney, liver, pancreas, tail meat, thymus and tongue and the gizzard, heart, liver and neck of poultry. Legally, lean meat content means the total weight of lean meat, free, when raw, of visible fat.

Animal protein is not essential for man's health. Communities eating large amounts of meat and other animal products usually have high rates of coronary heart disease. Much more land and energy are required for the production of meat than grain.

Muscle protein is more easily digested than connective tissue proteins (mostly collagen) and fat. The proportion of connective tissue varies with the cut and increases with age, so meat from an old animal is tougher than from a young one. Fat delays the emptying of the stomach, so fat cuts are more indigestible than lean. Tenderness depends on treatment after slaughter, a low proportion of coarse muscle fibres and connective tissue, its marbling with fat and the age and species of animal. Flavour decreases on storage, even when frozen, due to the evaporation of volatile substances.

The energy value of meat varies greatly with its fat content, but even lean meat, which contains about 20 per cent protein, also contains 5 per cent fat, and is a good energy source — half the energy being provided by the fat. The protein is of high biological value, though this is reduced if there is a high proportion of connective tissue. The fat is largely saturated, that from pork and chicken having a higher polyunsaturated/saturated ratio than that from beef and mutton.

Meat provides as per cent of UK daily intake: energy, 16–17; protein, 31; fat, 27; zinc, 36; copper, 28; selenium, 28; iron, 24; sodium, 21; phosphorus, 20; potassium, 14; magnesium, 9; calcium, 3; vitamins: B_{12}, 59; A, 36; niacin, 35; B_6, 23; riboflavin, 18; thiamin, 14; folic acid, 7; C, 2; D, 1.

meat substitutes, vegetable proteins (e.g., from soya beans) are increasingly used as alternatives or to replace meat in the diet, being cheaper. Meat is an important source of high-quality protein, thiamin, riboflavin, vitamin B_{12}, iron and zinc in the average diet. A DHSS report therefore recommended that vegetable protein foods that simulate meat, whether textured or not, shall contain, on a dry weight basis, at least 45 per cent and preferably 50 per cent protein with either a PER of not less than 1.6 (compared with casein, 2.5) or an NPU of not less than 60; and, per 100g protein, not less than 2.0mg thiamin, 1.6mg riboflavin, 10μg vitamin B_{12}, 20mg iron and 20mg zinc.

---

medicinal claims, a claim that a food is capable of preventing, treating or curing human disease, is prohibited by law unless it is a licensed medicine.

---

medicine, orthomolecular, aims to prevent or cure disease by giving megadoses of essential nutrients such as vitamins, to achieve optimum concentrations in the body of substances normally present and essential for health. Examples include the treatment of cancer with vitamin C, of skin tuberculosis with vitamin D and of schizophrenia with niacin. Efficacy is often, as yet, unproven and megadoses of many vitamins are toxic.

---

medium chain triglycerides (MCT), *see* triglycerides, medium chain.

---

megadose, of a vitamin or mineral is ten or more times the recommended daily amount (RDA) for normal nutritional requirements. Used: to correct a deficiency; by those who have an extra requirement for a nutrient; to obtain the pharmacological (non-nutritional) effects of a nutrient; and in orthomolecular medicine. Megadoses of many vitamins and minerals are toxic.

---

melanin, brown pigment present in skin. Increases on exposure to sun. Absent in albinos. Derived from tyrosine.

---

membranes, cell, are viscous solutions surrounding all living cells, separating them from each other and from the outside environment. Also

surround structures within the cell such as the nucleus. Act as barriers
allowing some, but not other, substances and information through. Composed predominantly of lipids (phospholipids, glycolipids and sterols —
cholesterol in mammalian membranes) and proteins, but also some
carbohydrates, different membranes having different ratios of proteins to
lipids.

---

menadione, menaphthone, menaquinones, *see* vitamin K$_3$.

Menke's disease, kinky or steely hair syndrome, caused by rare,
inherited inability to absorb copper (*which see*).

---

mercaptans, intestinal putrefaction products of the sulphur amino acids.
Themselves undergo bacterial decomposition, forming methane and
hydrogen sulphide gases.

---

mercury, does not appear to be an essential element for man. Poisoning
can result from eating foods contaminated with mercury, such as fish living
in polluted waters and seed grains treated with a mercury fungicide.

---

metabolism, series of chemical changes in the living body that maintain
life. Made up of anabolic changes that build tissues up and catabolic ones that
break them down.

---

metal-activated enzymes, require a metal ion for their activity but can
exist separately.

---

metalloenzymes, enzymes in which a metal ion is a functional and
inseparable component.

---

methionine, an essential sulphur amino acid. Frequently the limiting
amino acid in food proteins, e.g., vegetables, soya beans, beef. The other
sulphur amino acids, cystine and cysteine, in part spare methionine, and so
all are considered in assessing protein quality. Contains a labile methyl group
and is one of the chief dietary methyl donors.

methyl alcohol, is present in methylated spirits to which it is added to denature the ethanol, making it undrinkable and so free from duty and cheaper than alcoholic beverages. It is highly toxic, being oxidized in the liver to formaldehyde that damages the retina, causing blindness and leading to mental disturbances and, with chronic intake, to death. Obtained commercially from wood.

methyl donors, substances with a labile (readily transferable) methyl group ($-CH_3$). Chief dietary sources are methionine, betaine and choline. Methyl donors are lipotropic factors in that they prevent the development of certain types of fatty liver.

methyl group, $=CH_3$. A metabolically important group of atoms found in choline, methionine, methylcobalamin, etc.

methylcobalamin, coenzyme form of vitamin B_{12} (*which see*).

methylene interrupted, describes the carbon chain of polyunsaturated fatty acids in which the unsaturated bonds are separated or interrupted by a methylene group ($-CH_2-$). *See* fatty acids.

methylxanthines, are methyl derivatives of xanthine, a purine. Those commonly occurring in foodstuffs are caffeine, theophylline and theobromine. Found in tea, coffee, cocoa, chocolate and many cola-type soft drinks. Caffeine has a thermogenic effect, is a nervous system and muscle stimulant, a mild diuretic and, in excessive amounts, may cause sleeplessness. Theobromine and theophylline have greater influences on the cardiovascular system, on smooth muscles and as diuretics. Amounts producing physiological effects in adults are 100–150mg caffeine; 200–250mg theophylline; and 500–1,200mg theobromine. Caffeine is the predominant one in coffee and tea and theobromine in cocoa.

micelles, minute emulsified lipid particles consisting of a core of water-insoluble (non-polar) components surrounded by more water-soluble (polar) components. Formed for the solubilization of digested lipids in the duodenum.

micro-flora, intestinal, usually describes bacteria in the colon that carry out fermentation of undigested foodstuffs.

---

micronization, an extremely rapid method of heating food with infra-red radiation. Proposed as an alternative to steam heating or toasting where the shorter heating time might be less damaging to the foodstuff.

---

micronutrients, substances required in the diet only in milli- or micro-gram amounts, but essential for life and health. Comprise the vitamins and minerals including trace elements.

---

microvilli, *see* intestinal wall.

---

microwave cooking, or high-frequency irradiation. Uses high-energy electromagnetic radiation to heat throughout the bulk of the food by making its constituent molecules vibrate. In spite of the shorter cooking time and lower surface temperatures employed than in traditional cooking, nutrient losses vary with the food tested, sometimes showing improved retention and, sometimes, no change.

---

migraine, periodic, unilateral, throbbing headache, often preceded by visual disturbances and accompanied by nausea and vomiting. In some, attacks precipitated by a particular food, e.g., chocolate, cheese, wines — especially sherry and red wines.

---

milk, the natural food of the young mammal, that of each species being adapted to the needs of its own young. Cow's milk is nutritious food for children and adults, though for those over five years old (except the non-obese elderly) in Western societies with high dietary intakes of saturated fat, it is best taken semi-skimmed or skimmed, when the normal fat content (in g per 100g) of 3.8 (4.8 for Channel Island) is reduced to about 1.55 and 0.1 respectively. It is a good source of calcium, a useful but not rich source of vitamin A (unless skimmed) and B, but contains little vitamins C or D or iron. Pasteurization has little effect on nutrient composition except to reduce vitamin C, which is still further reduced by storage. Riboflavin is lost at the rate of 10 per cent per hour on exposure to sunlight.

Breast milk is the natural food of the human infant. By law, no substitute can be claimed as being equivalent or superior to the milk of a healthy mother. Breast milk, particularly during the first two weeks when it is known as colostrum and early milk, contains immunoglobulin A (IgA), lactoferrin and lysozyme, which have antimicrobial action and help protect against infection. Postponing for as long as practical the provision of cow's milk or foods other than breast milk helps to prevent development of food allergies in the infant, particularly important in families with a history of eczema, asthma, hay fever, etc. Human milk provides sufficient food energy, protein, fat, vitamins (except D) and minerals for the needs of the infant.

In preparing formulas for use when breast milk is unavailable, cow's or goat's milk has first to be diluted to reduce the concentration of protein, which is two and a half times that of human milk and too much for the infant kidney to cope with, and then fortified with lactose, which is in higher concentration in human milk and required for energy. Goat's milk is deficient in folic acid, required for blood formation, and, unless supplemented, infants on goat's milk may develop 'goat's milk anaemia'. Infants allergic to cow's milk protein may also be allergic to that in goat's milk.

Whole cow's milk/skimmed cow's milk/goat's milk/mature human milk provide (per 100g): energy, 65/33/71/69 kcal; (g) water, 87.6/90.9/87.0/87.1; protein, 3.3/3.4/3.3/1.3; fat 3.8/0.1/4.5/4.1; lactose, 4.7/5.0/4.6/7.2; (mg) calcium, 120/130/130/34; iron, 0.05/0.05/0.04/0.07; thiamin, 0.04/0.04/0.04/0.02; riboflavin, 0.19/0.20/0.15/0.03; niacin, 0.86/0.88/0.97/0.69; vitamin C, 1.5/1.6/1.5/3.7; (µg) vitamin A, 35/trace/40/60; carotene, 22/trace/0/0; total folic acid, 5/5/1/5.

millet, a grain of good nutritive value but less tasty than wheat or rice. Husked and made into porridge or ground into meal by poor peasants mainly in Africa. A variety, sorghum, provides (per 100g): energy, 343 kcal; (g) protein, 10.1; fat, 3.3; (mg) calcium, 30; iron, 6.2; thiamin, 0.40; riboflavin, 0.12; nicotinic acid, 3.5.

millimole, one thousandth of a mole. Abbreviated as mmol.

minerals, essential, elements that have defined physiological functions and are therefore nutrients essential in the diet for health. Some are required in amounts of more than 100mg daily: calcium, chloride, magnesium, phosphorus, potassium and sodium. Others required in less than 100mg amounts daily are often called trace minerals or trace elements: chromium, cobalt (only as vitamin B_{12}), copper, iodine, iron, manganese, molybdenum, selenium and zinc and probably fluoride. The elements arsenic, nickel, silicon, tin and vanadium may be essential trace elements but their requirement by man is not yet fully established. Some such as iron and zinc are metals, but others such as phosphorus and iodine are non-metallic.

Absorption Apart from the electrolytes sodium, potassium and chloride, most form insoluble compounds that are not readily absorbed, so their absorption often requires specific carrier proteins the synthesis of which serves as an important mechanism for controlling mineral levels in the body.

Absorption can be affected by chelating agents such as phytates and oxalates that form insoluble complexes with some such as zinc, reducing their absorption, and by others such as amino acids that assist their absorption; by protein, fat and other minerals and fibre in the diet. No guidelines on dietary practices for all-round optimum mineral nutrition have yet emerged. Iron, for example, is better absorbed from meat than from vegetables, but high-protein diets increase zinc and calcium requirements. Vitamin C increases the absorption of iron from vegetables but reduces it from meat and decreases copper absorption. Diets high in fibre inhibit the absorption of calcium and magnesium but not of phosphorus.

Transport and storage also require specific binding to carrier proteins such as transferrin in the case of chromium, iron, manganese and zinc.

Excretion is mostly via the kidneys into the urine (e.g., cobalt, chromium, molybdenum and zinc), but also via the bile (chromium, copper, manganese and zinc), pancreatic juices (e.g., zinc) and the sloughing off of cells lining the intestine (e.g., iron and zinc) eventually into the faeces and in the sweat (e.g., zinc).

Deficiency always leads to illnesses, e.g., of iron, copper or cobalt (as vitamin B_{12}) to anaemia; of iodine to cretinism in children and goitre in adults. Iron deficiency is the most widespread nutritional deficiency.

Toxicity is seen with excessive intake of most minerals and generally results from malfunction in the regulation of absorption.

Requirements RDAs, where available, are given for men (except for iron): UK RDAs are available only for: calcium, 500mg; iron, 12mg; and iodine, 140µg. US RDAs for these three are 15mg, 800mg and 150µg, respectively, and for zinc, 15mg; magnesium, 350mg; phosphorus, 800mg; and selenium, 70µg. EC RDAs are: calcium, 800mg; phosphorus, 800mg; iron, 14mg; magnesium, 300mg; zinc, 15mg; and iodine, 150µg.

For the other minerals, the US has a published list of estimated safe and adequate dietary intakes (mg): copper, 1.5–3.0; manganese, 2.0–5.0; fluoride, 1.5–4.0; chromium, 0.05–0.20; molybdenum, 0.075–0.25. *See* Tables 5–10, pages 224–232.

US estimated minimum daily requirements for sodium, chloride and potassium are (mg) 500, 750 and 2,000, respectively.

Food sources Widely distributed but usually in small amounts in wholegrain cereals, fruits and vegetables, dairy products, meats and seafoods, so a sufficient quantity and variety of food must be consumed to meet daily requirements.

Law From 1986, a food may legally be described as a 'source'/'rich or excellent source' of mineral(s) only if a reasonable daily intake of the food provides at least one-sixth/one-half of the RDA of calcium, iodine and iron. Unless the claim is made for a named mineral, the food must provide two or more of these three minerals, which are thought by MAFF to be most likely to be at risk of being deficient in the diet.

---

minerals, trace, minerals essential in the diet in amounts of less than 100mg daily.

---

mmol, abbreviation for millimole.

---

mol, abbreviation for mole.

---

molasses, thick brownish syrup. A by-product from the manufacture of cane or beet sugar, it is left after part of the sugar has been removed by crystallization. Contains significant amounts of some minerals. Blackstrap molasses is left after the third and final sugar extraction. A strong laxative for some people. May be mixed cautiously with other foods.

Blackstrap molasses provides (mg per 100g): potassium, 2,927; calcium, 684; magnesium, 209; sodium, 96; iron, 16.

---

mole, (abbreviated as mol). One mole of a compound is equivalent to the molecular weight (mass) of the compound in grams (g).

A millimole (mmol) is one-thousandth of a mole, so one millimole of a compound is equivalent to the molecular weight (mass) of the compound in milligrams (mg). Scientific papers frequently quantify intake of food constituents like common salt, as mmol per day; and concentrations of blood constituents such as glucose or cholesterol as mmol/litre; and amounts of substances in the urine such as urea as mol/24 hours. However, many find it easier to envisage such quantities as g per day; mg/100ml (dl) blood; and g excreted per 24 hr, respectively.

To convert mol into g or mmol into mg:
multiply the molecular weight of the compound by the number of mol or mmol respectively. Since the molecular weight of a compound is the sum of the atomic weights of its constituent atoms (*see* Table 14, page 294 for atomic weights), the molecular weight of common salt, sodium chloride, is 23 plus 35.5 = 58.5.

So a diet providing 200 mmol sodium chloride per day contains:
$$58.5 \times 200 = 11,700\text{mg or } 11.7\text{g salt.}$$
The quantity of sodium contained in 11.7g salt may be calculated:
$$\frac{23}{58.5} \times 11.7 = 4.6\text{g}$$
If the diet is said to provide 200 mmol sodium it contains:
$$23 \times 200 = 4,600\text{mg or } 4.6\text{g sodium}$$
and this may be provided by:

$$\frac{58.5}{23} \times 4.6 = 11.7\text{g salt.}$$

Similar calculations can be carried out for potassium which has an atomic weight of 40. A blood level of 5 mmol glucose/litre (Mol. Wt. glucose 180), or of 5.2 mmol cholesterol/litre (Mol. Wt. cholesterol 387) corresponds to 90mg/dl and 200mg/dl respectively.

---

molecular weight, of a compound relates its weight (mass) to that of the reference element, carbon, which is 12. It can be calculated by adding together the atomic weights of the compound's constituent atoms. (*See* Table 14, page 294, for atomic weights.)

---

molecule, the smallest particle (usually a group of atoms) into which matter can be divided and still retain its identity.

---

molybdenum, a 70kg man contains about 9mg of this essential mineral. Mean daily intake in UK is 99.3µg. Very variable as the food content is highly dependent on the soil type in which it is grown.
Functions as a component of several metalloenzymes.
Absorbed readily in the soluble hexavalent form.
Excreted mainly via the urine and may be half the total daily intake.
Deficiency unknown.
Requirement No RDA. USA estimated safe and adequate daily intake is 0.15–0.5mg

Toxicity High intakes of 10–15mg daily have been suggested as the cause of the high incidence of gout in Armenia (USSR), a molybdenum-rich area. High intakes may interfere with copper metabolism. Children reared in molybdenum-rich areas have a low incidence of dental caries.

Good food sources in descending order of importance: cereals, non-root vegetables, meat, fruit preserves.

---

monkey nut, *see* peanut.

---

monoamine oxidase, an enzyme that oxidizes tyramine and catecholamines.

---

monoglycerides, lipids that are esters of the alcohol, glycerol, with one fatty acid.

---

monosaccharides, simple sugars. Carbohydrates that cannot be hydrolysed into a simpler form. Include hexoses (e.g., glucose) and pentoses (e.g., ribose). All are sweet, soluble and crystalline.

---

monosodium glutamate (MSG), sodium salt of glutamic acid. Used as flavour enhancer in savoury foods because of its strong, meaty flavour. 'Chinese-restaurant syndrome' symptoms have been ascribed to high content in Chinese food of MSG to which some people are sensitive.

---

monounsaturates, food fats/oils rich in monounsaturated fatty acids, e.g., olive oil. *See* fatty acids.

---

mucilages, water-soluble polysaccharides from seeds and seaweeds used in small amounts in the food industry as thickeners and stabilizers because of their water-holding and viscous properties. Dietary fibres. Include ispaghula and psyllium, extracted from seed husks in which xylose is the main constituent sugar of their mixed polysaccharides and that are both used as bulk laxatives, and alginates from seaweeds.

mucin, mucoproteins. Highly viscous complex of protein and carbohydrate. One lines and protects the stomach wall that secretes it against stomach acid.

mucosa, mucous membrane.

mucous membrane, mucosa. Inner surface lining of hollow organs of the body, e.g., intestine, stomach. Rich in mucus-secreting cells. The whole mucosa of the gastrointestinal tract is replaced every three or four days.

mucus, sticky secretion of mucous glands, e.g., goblet cells, usually forming protective covering for mucous membranes.

multiple sclerosis, *see* disseminated sclerosis.

mushrooms, fungi. Contain the sugar trehalose. Nutritive value good but nutritive contribution low because of high water content. Their protein contains all essential amino acids and is especially rich in lysine and leucine.
    Provide (per 100g): energy, 13 kcal; (g) water, 91.5; protein, 1.8; fat, 0.6; (mg) potassium, 470.

mutagen, that which causes a mutation or change in a gene's DNA, the bearer of inherited characteristics, as a result of which the character of the cell changes. The diet contains natural mutagens, many of which may act through generation of oxygen free radicals. Mutations frequently precede, but are not always followed by, tumour formation.

mycotoxins, toxins produced in foods by fungal contamination, which cause toxic effects mainly in nervous system and liver. Examples: the fungal rust, ergot, that infects rye produces toxic alkaloids causing ergotism; aflatoxins produced by moulds (e.g., *Aspergillus flavus*) contaminating peanuts, nuts and grains usually grown and stored in warm moist climates — some like aflatoxin B_1 are liver carcinogens.
    Mycotoxins are potentially dangerous, often carcinogenic, and appear to be more widespread than hitherto realized. Foods grown and processed

without fungicides, preservatives and chemical additives are more likely to be contaminated by moulds.

---

myocardial infarction,   death of an area of heart muscle caused by failure of its blood supply, usually due to a blood clot blocking the lumen of a coronary artery narrowed by atherosclerosis, or even by atherosclerosis alone. May lead to sudden death or may heal, leaving a scar.

---

myocardial ischaemia,   deficient blood supply to heart muscles.

---

myocardium,   heart muscle.

---

myoglobin,   haem (iron) containing protein present in red muscles in which it stores oxygen.

---

myosin,   contributes 55 per cent by weight of muscle protein. A fibrous, insoluble, intracellular protein. Digestible.

   In resting muscle it is linked to another protein, actin. Muscle contraction results when energy derived from ATP releases myosin from actin so the two can slide past each other. Calcium ions are required for muscle contraction.

---

myristic acid,   a saturated, 14 carbon fatty acid, widely distributed in nature.

N

NACNE,   National Advisory Committee on Nutrition Education. A working party that included representatives from the DHSS, the British Nutrition Foundation and the Health Education Council, reported to this committee in September, 1983, on the urgent need for the provision of simple and accurate information on nutrition. The report sought to identify what is wrong with the diet of the British population as a whole, including the average typical diet, and how this can be remedied by changes that can be achieved in the short term (the 1980s) and the long term (over 15 years). Proposals include a reduction in total fat intake, particularly of saturated fat, a reduction in sugar, salt and alcohol consumption, an increase in dietary fibre and no change in total energy intake to be achieved by increasing consumption of complex carbohydrate/high-fibre foods. The proposed changes in energy sources as percentages of the total energy intake, are summarized in Table 4.

Table 4: Energy sources in the UK diet: present and proposed

| | As % of total energy (including alcohol) | | |
| | | Proposed | |
Energy source	1980	Short-term	Long-term
fat	38	34	30
(including saturated fatty acids)	(18)	(15)	(10)
protein	11	11	11
carbohydrate	45	50	55
alcohol	6	5	4

NAD and NADH, oxidized and reduced forms of nicotinamide adenine dinucleotide (*which see*).

NADP, nicotinamide adenine dinucleotide phosphate.

nails, in chronic iron deficiency anaemia, may be spoon-shaped. Brittle, thickened nails, surface-lined either longitudinally or horizontally may or may not be signs of nutritional deficiencies. Severe protein deficiency may result in transverse white bands on the nails of both hands.

NDF, neutral detergent fibre. *See* fibre, dietary.

necrosis, death of cells.

neohesperidin, permitted intense sweetener (*which see*).

---

neoplasm, tumour.

---

nervous system, structures controlling the actions and functions of the body. Includes the brain, spinal cord and nerves. Responsible for one-fifth of basal metabolism. Glucose is the main energy source and therefore B vitamins are particularly important for its health. Amino acids and lipids are required for its growth, regeneration and metabolism.

---

net dietary protein energy ratio, protein content of food or diet expressed by multiplying the protein energy ratio by the net protein utilization.

---

net dietary protein value, is the product of the protein intake and net protein utilization. It is a combined measure of both the quantity and quality of protein in the diet.

---

net protein utilization (NPU), is the percentage of the protein eaten that is retained in the body. Usually measured by providing the protein at 10 per cent of the dietary energy as the sole source of protein in the diet (NPU10). Unlike the biological value (BV), it takes into account the digestibility of the protein. The NPU of a good mixed diet is about 75. When 70 per cent or more of the dietary proteins come from a single staple food, e.g., maize, cassava or wheat, the NPU value of the food may determine whether or not protein requirements are met.

Examples of NPUs (determined in rats): eggs, 94; human milk, 87; cow's milk, 82; soya bean, 65; rice, 59; maize, 52; wheat, 48.

---

neural tube defect, or, spina bifida, failure of foetal vertebrae to completely enclose the spinal cord. May occur in those with a genetic susceptibility if folic acid is deficient at conception and during the first six weeks of pregnancy.

---

neurine, a toxic amine produced by bacterial decomposition of choline in the intestines. Also found in egg yolk, brain and bile.

neuritis, inflammation of a nerve. Seen in vitamin B_6 deficiency.

---

neuron(e), a nerve cell and the fibres conveying impulses to and from it.

---

neuropathy, disease of the nervous system, known as polyneuropathy when more than one nerve is affected.

---

neurotransmitters, substances that carry nerve impulses, for example from one neuron to another across the synapse (junction), or from a nerve ending to a muscle fibre. Examples: acetylcholine, catecholamines, GABA, serotonin, substance P, histamine.

---

niacin, water-soluble vitamin and member of the B complex. Includes nicotinic acid (formerly itself called niacin) and nicotinamide (formerly called niacinamide), which is the biologically active form into which the body readily converts nicotinic acid. Also formerly known as P-P or pellagra-preventative factor and as vitamin B_3 and even as vitamin B_5.

Functions As a component of the respiratory chain, nicotinamide adenine dinucleotide (NAD), it is concerned with the tissue oxidation of foodstuffs for the release of energy. As the coenzyme nicotinamide adenine dinucleotide phosphate (NADP), it is concerned in the synthesis of fatty acids and steroids.

Required for healthy nervous and digestive systems, skin and tongue.

Deficiency leads to pellagra. Early symptoms include anorexia, muscular weakness and fatigue, minor skin and nervous troubles.

Toxic in high doses, e.g., above 1.0g nicotinamide or 100mg nicotinic acid. Nicotinic acid at megadose level produces harmless flushing, a tingling sensation due to dilation of blood vessels and lowers blood cholesterol levels.

Niacin equivalents Niacin is obtained preformed in food and derived from tryptophan in the body at the rate of 1mg from 60mg tryptophan. Consequently the niacin content of food is often expressed as niacin (sometimes nicotinic acid) equivalents. Dietary tryptophan normally provides about two-thirds of the daily niacin requirement.

1 niacin equivalent (1 NE) = 1mg available nicotinic acid or 60mg tryptophan. The conversion from tryptophan requires vitamin B_6 as coenzyme.

Requirement In niacin equivalents, EC and UK RDA 18mg and US RDA 19mg. In the UK about 36 per cent of the daily intake is provided by meat and offal, 20 per cent by cereals and bread, 14 per cent by vegetables and 14 per cent by milk and milk products.

Stable to all cooking processes. Lost by leaching into cooking water and in drips from thawing frozen food unless those liquids are used.

Distribution in foods (as niacin equivalents mg/100g): brewer's yeast, 100; meats, 9–10; liver and kidney, 9–18; mackerel, 11.6; brown/white rice, 6.4/2.5; cod, 4.9; pulses, 3.0–5.9; maize meal, potato, vegetables, fresh fruits, eggs, milk and cheese, low.

In the UK and in many other countries, white flour and bread are required to be fortified with niacin.

Niacin in many cereals, e.g., maize, is often in bound form, niacytin, and so largely unavailable unless first released by alkali treatment.

niacytin, bound unavailable form of niacin found in many cereals.

nickel, may be an essential trace element for man. A 70kg man contains about 10mg. Its biological role is unknown.

nicotinamide, active form of niacin.

nicotinamide adenine dinucleotide, exists in oxidized (NAD) and reduced or hydrogen-rich (NADH) forms. A coenzyme component of the respiratory chain and of other enzymes concerned with oxidation. Derived from niacin.

nicotinamide adenine dinucleotide phosphate, exists in oxidized (NADP) and reduced or hydrogen-rich (NADPH) forms. A coenzyme that takes part in the synthesis of fatty acids and steroids and in carbohydrate metabolism. Derived from niacin.

nicotinic acid, *see* niacin.

night blindness, early symptom of vitamin A deficiency.

nitrates, naturally occurring constituent of many plant foods. Readily reduced to nitrites. Used as preservatives for meat and meat products.

---

nitrites, additives used as preservatives for meat and meat products. Also present in many plant foods formed by reduction of naturally occurring nitrates. With amines can form nitrosamines, which may be carcinogenic.

---

nitrogen balance, a subject is in nitrogen balance when the intake of nitrogen in the diet equals the output of nitrogen in the urine, faeces and skin. A person in nitrogen balance is taken to be in protein balance. When the balance is negative, output is greater than intake and it is interpreted as loss of tissue protein as seen in fasting, starvation, fevers and wasting diseases. When the balance is positive, intake is greater than output and the subject is assumed to be laying down tissue protein as in growth, repair and convalescence.

---

nitrogen conversion factor, the factor by which the nitrogen content of a food must be multiplied to determine its protein content. Varies with the amino acid content of the protein, e.g., milk, 6.4; rice, 6.0; most cereals including wheat, 5.8; soya bean, 5.7; most legumes and nuts, 5.3. Presence of nitrogenous compounds other than protein reduces accuracy.

In foods with mixed protein content, the factor 6.25 is used, e.g., in compiling food tables.

---

nitrosamines, potentially carcinogenic substances formed by combination of nitrites and secondary amines. Can be present preformed in pickled foods, or may be formed in the stomach if nitrite/nitrate additives are present in food.

---

nocebo, opposite of placebo. A person's expectation that a treatment will give pain causes him to feel pain though the treatment is actually a sham and painless.

---

non-cellulosic substances, term used for components of dietary fibre that are neither cellulose nor lignin, e.g., hemicelluloses, gums, mucilages, pectins.

noradrenaline, a catecholamine (*which see*). May be involved in the control of food intake.

---

norepinephrine, noradrenaline.

NPU, *see* net protein utilization.

---

nucleic acids, include deoxyribonucleic acid (DNA) and ribonucleic acid (RNA). Polynucleotides. Of fundamental importance in controlling reproduction, protein synthesis, growth and metabolism. Occur in close association with proteins, forming nucleoproteins. Dietary nucleic acids are broken down in the intestines to mononucleotides and thence to nucleosides that are absorbed as such or further digested to free purine and pyrimidine bases and sugars which are absorbed. It is thought that practically none of the bases in the diet serves as a direct precursor for tissue nucleic acids. Thus humans apparently synthesize all components of their RNA and DNA for themselves and do not obtain them direct from the diet.

Potential sufferers from gout should avoid foods rich in nucleic acids, like yeast, because of their high content of purine bases that are converted to uric acid by enzymes in the gut wall. Crystals of uric acid derivatives in the joints are responsible for the pain of gout.

DNA — deoxyribonucleic acid or desoxyribonucleic acid — is the essential component of chromosomes in cell nuclei. Carrier of genetic information with two functions: to be exactly reproduced in order to transmit its genetic information to future generations; and to contain information in chemical code to direct the development of the cell according to its inheritance.

Made up of a double-stranded molecule twisted into a helical spiral, the two strands being polynucleotides held together by hydrogen bonds between the purine and pyrimidine bases of the respective strands.

RNA — ribonucleic acid — is directly involved in protein synthesis. Found in both the nucleus and cytoplasm of cells. Consists of three types:
1. ribosomal RNA (rRNA), 80 per cent of total cell RNA. Important component of ribosomes, which play a central role in protein synthesis.
2. messenger RNA (mRNA), short-lived. Acts as template for protein synthesis carrying the 'message' from the DNA to ribosomes.
3. transfer RNA (tRNA), relatively small RNAs. Each binds with a particular amino acid and places it in the correct position on the mRNA template associated with the ribosomes for forming new protein.

See ribosomes.

nucleosidases, enzymes that split nucleosides into purine and pyrimidine bases, ribose and deoxyribose sugars. Present in intestinal digestive juices.

---

nucleoside, purine or pyrimidine base linked with a sugar (ribose or deoxyribose). A nucleoside linked with phosphoric acid forms a nucleotide.

---

nucleotide, a nucleoside linked with phosphoric acid. Many nucleotides linked into a chain form a polynucleotide.

---

nucleus, a body within the cell containing the genetic apparatus (DNA). *See* nucleic acids.

---

nutrient density, expresses the nutrient value of a food in terms of its nutrient and energy contents, each related to RDA:

$$\text{Nutrient density} = \frac{\text{Nutrient per 100g/energy per 100g}}{\text{RDA for nutrient/RDA of energy}}$$

Where the value is less than 1.0, the food is a poor source of the nutrient, where above 1.0, it is satisfactory. For example, bread made from unfortified, white flour would have a nutrient density for thiamin well below 1.0 and be a poor source of that vitamin, whereas made from wholemeal or fortified white flour, it would be well above 1.0, indicating that the food was a satisfactory source of this vitamin.

A useful value for new types of manufactured foods and foods enriched with synthetic ingredients (e.g., vitamins).

The term is also used to express the amount of a nutrient per 1,000 kcal of the diet or food.

---

nutrients, components of the diet essential to life and health. Usually include those required in considerable quantities to provide energy (carbohydrates, fats and proteins), dietary fibre, the essential fatty acids, the essential amino acids and the micronutrients comprising vitamins and essential minerals including the trace elements. However, the term as used by some authorities excludes the energy-producing components and dietary fibre.

---

nutrification, addition of nutrients to a food to a nutritionally significant level (e.g., of calcium to white flour).

nutrition,   processes by which the living organism receives and utilizes food materials for maintaining life, growth and tissue repair.

---

nutrition, parenteral,   feeding of patients other than via the alimentary canal, e.g., intravenously, intramuscularly, subcutaneously, because of disease or injury to the canal. Usually for a few days but may be for months or years.

---

nuts,   hard-shelled fruits of a variety of trees. Many have a high content of fat and protein, but are generally eaten in amounts that contribute to flavour rather than nutrition. Rich in potassium, low in sodium. High in dietary fibre. Include almonds, Brazils, cob or hazel nuts, chestnuts, walnuts (*which see*).

---

nuts, Brazil,   provide (per 100g): energy, 619 kcal; (g) protein, 12.0, fat, 61.5; total dietary fibre, 9.0; (mg) potassium, 760; thiamin, 1.0.

---

nuts, cob or hazel,   provide (per 100g): energy, 380 kcal; (g) protein, 7.6; fat, 36.0; total dietary fibre, 6.1; (mg) potassium, 350; vitamin E, 21.0.

O

---

oats,   a grain used for porridge, as a basis for muesli and for cattle fodder. Oatmeal contains 12g protein and 8.5g oil per 100g with about 45 per cent of the fatty acids as the polyunsaturate, linoleic acid. Oat starch is 23–24 per cent amylose and high amylose cereals give rise to smaller increases in blood glucose and insulin after meals than cereals with a lower amylose content. Oats contain oat gum, a soluble dietary fibre that is the reason for the high viscosity of porridge. Studies have shown that rolled oats (100–150g (three bowls of porridge) daily) reduce blood cholesterol levels in those with elevated and normal levels. More recently, total and LDL ('bad') cholesterol levels were shown to be reduced in those with high levels by 60g rolled oats daily (one large bowl porridge) and the reduction was in addition to that already achieved by a low-fat diet. Oat bran has been shown to reduce total serum cholesterol significantly.

Rolled oats, formed by crushing grain between heated rollers and thus partially cooking them, provide (per 100g): energy, 385 kcal; (g) protein, 13.0; fat, 7.5; fibre, 7.7; (mg) iron, 3.8; calcium, 60; thiamin, 0.50; riboflavin, 0.14; nicotinic acid, 1.3. Oat bran provides 14g fibre per 100g.

Oat gel is an almost tasteless fat substitute made from oats or oat bran that can be used in low-temperature foods such as ice-cream, powdered drink products, salad dressings and sauces. It contains only 10 per cent of the calories of fat and 2–10 per cent of beta-glucans, which are the soluble fibres responsible for oat bran's cholesterol-lowering effect. It is made by converting the oat starch into amylodextrins with the enzyme, alpha-amylase. The dextrins and soluble beta-glucans are separated from the insoluble material and made into gels with different textures or dried to a powder.

---

obesity, a state characterized by excess accumulation of body fat. Defined as a body mass index (BMI, i.e., weight in kg divided by height squared in m) of over 30. Overweight (BMI 25–30) is the most common nutritional disorder in the UK. The OPCS Dietary and Nutritional Survey 1986–7 revealed that the average BMI had risen in all age groups compared with a similar survey carried out in 1980. The prevalence of obesity had also risen to 12 per cent in women and 8 per cent in men from 8 and 6 per cent respectively in 1980.

Overweight and obesity arises only as a result of excess intake of food. Reducing energy intake below expenditure, a process assisted by increasing energy output by vigorous exercise (including brisk walking) will eventually achieve an acceptable weight. Unfortunately, energy expenditure decreases with decreased energy intake, which makes weight loss more difficult. Overweight people also have reduced energy requirements after slimming and return to pre-slimming energy intakes will lead to weight regain.

Obesity correlates with increased risk of hypertension and stroke, impaired cardiac function, diabetes mellitus, kidney disease, osteoarthritis and gout, cancer of the womb, gall-bladder disease, varicose veins, menstrual abnormalities and raised serum total cholesterol levels.

Evidence is increasing that the *distribution* of excess fat in the body is more important than BMI or per cent body fat, as an indicator for risk of coronary heart disease. Upper-body obesity (inferred from a high waist-to-hip circumference ratio) appears to be a better predictor of hypertension, LDL ('bad') and HDL$_2$ ('good') cholesterol levels, impaired glucose tolerance and premature coronary heart disease.

See Table 12, page 287 for Acceptable Weights.

---

oedema, dropsy. Abnormal infiltration of tissues with fluid. Subcutaneous oedema demonstrable by the 'pitting' produced by finger pressure. Seen in starvation (hunger or famine oedema) and as a result of heart and liver failure, and kidney disease. Quite often seen during pregnancy, usually in mild form though a doctor should be consulted. An inconvenient, but not serious, symptom ('bloating') of premenstrual syndrome (*which see*).

---

oesophagus, gullet. Muscular, membranous canal linking the oral cavity with the stomach.

---

offal, organ meat, refers to non-muscle tissue such as liver, kidneys, heart, tongue, sweetbreads (pancreas and thymus), tripe, feet (pig's and calf's), brains, chitterlings, lamb's fries and udders. Most provide good nutritional value. Liver, kidneys and pancreas are rich in purines and are, therefore, often avoided by sufferers from gout (*which see*).

Office of Population and Censuses Surveys, carried out for MAFF and the DoH. The Dietary and Nutritional Survey of British Adults in 1986–7, published in 1990 surveyed the diet and health of over 2,000 adults (aged 16–64 years) living in private households. Participants provided seven-day dietary records, blood and urine samples and their heights, weights and blood pressures were measured.

Among its findings were that, although average energy intakes were below current recommendations, a high proportion of people were overweight and 12 per cent of women and 8 per cent of men were obese. Only about one third of the respondents had cholesterol levels in the desirable range. Over 85 per cent were eating more fat than the recommended level of 35 per cent or less of food energy from fat. Women on average consumed 18.6g fibre per day and men 24.9g. Intakes of vitamins were well above current recommendations in all age groups. Men's iron intakes were above recommended levels but the average intake of women, particularly young women (10.5mg) was below recommended levels. One third of all women had low iron stores and 4 per cent were anaemic. Women were more likely than men to take vitamin and mineral supplements. People who took supplements tended to be those with the highest intake from food itself. Three quarters of the men and two-thirds of the women drank alcohol during the survey week. Of these, men on average obtained 9 per cent and women 4 per cent of their energy from alcohol. High blood-pressure was found in some who were not on treatment for hypertension.

---

oils, term applied to liquid digestible triglycerides (e.g., olive oil), and to indigestible mineral hydrocarbons (e.g., liquid paraffin) and to essential oils (*see* oils, essential).

---

oils, essential, sometimes called ethereal oils. Volatile, odorous substances soluble in alcohol, but only to a very limited extent in water. Distilled or extracted with alcohol from various parts of plants and used medicinally and for flavouring foods, e.g., garlic oil, oil of bitter almonds. Chemically they are a mixture of esters, aldehydes, ketones and terpenes and, in the case of garlic oil, of sulphur compounds. They are not lipids.

---

oleic acid, a monounsaturated, 18 carbon fatty acid of the omega 9 family (C18:1 n-9). Most widely distributed fatty acid in nature, forming up to 30 per cent or more of the total fatty acids of most fats.

As per cent of total fatty acids: olive oil, 72; canola oil, 55; sunflower oil, 33; butter, 28.

---

oligosaccharides, carbohydrates yielding 3–15 monosaccharide molecules on hydrolysis, e.g., digestible dextrins, indigestible raffinose and stachyose. Occur naturally in glycoproteins, proteoglycans and glycosaminoglyans. Formed during digestion of polysaccharides.

---

olive oil, rich in the monounsaturated fatty acid, oleic acid, that forms 72 per cent of its total fatty acids, linoleic acid forming 11 per cent and alpha-linolenic acid 0.7 per cent.

---

omega 3 polyunsaturated fatty acids (PUFA), or n-3 PUFA as they are often called, are a series or family of acids that all have a double (unsaturated) bond on the third carbon atom from the end of the chain distal to the acid end of the molecule. Several members of the series have vital functions in the body, but only the first — alpha-linolenic acid — is essential in the diet of man because the body can synthesize the others from it. The 18 carbon alpha-linolenic acid, which has three double bonds, is present in small amounts in a wide variety of foods and in large amounts in plant oils such as linseed, canola and soya oils. Besides having a structural function in cell membranes, the body adds carbon atoms to it (chain elongates) and removes hydrogen atomas (desaturates) to form the other members of the series, including the 20 carbon eicosapentaenoic acid (EPA) with five double bonds and the 22 carbon docosahexaenoic acid (DHA) with six double bonds (*see* Figure 2, page 79). Fish oils are the only rich food sources of EPA and DHA. EPA is the immediate precursor of particular series of prostanoids and leukotrienes, hormone-like substances that control many body processes. DHA is present in brain, nervous tissue, testes and the retina of the eye and can be converted back to EPA.

Omega 3 PUFA consumption from marine food sources, is associated with a reduced incidence of coronary heart disease via the following mechanisms:
1. through lowering plasma triglyceride (fat) levels (a risk factor for coronary heart disease) by inhibiting triglyceride synthesis in the liver;
2. by replacing in phospholipids, arachidonic acid (an omega 6 PUFA) with EPA and DHA. This depresses the output of prostanoids and leukotrienes derived from arachidonic acid that constrict blood vessels and encourage blood clotting, replacing those with ones derived from EPA, which do the reverse, so decreasing the risk of thrombosis;
3. omega 3 PUFA also reduce blood-pressure and blood viscosity and make cell membranes more fluid.

The synthesis of EPA and DHA in the body is not very efficient and may depend on the ratio of linoleic to alpha-linolenic acid in the diet since both compete for the same enzymes. This may account for the reduction in coronary heart disease in populations not depending on body synthesis because they consume dietary sources in the form of fish oils from marine animals (Greenland Eskimos) or oily or other fish (*see* cardiovascular disease).

---

omega 6 polyunsaturated fatty acids (PUFA), or n-6 PUFA as they are often called, are a series or family of acids that all have a double (unsaturated) bond on the sixth carbon atom from the end of the chain distal to the acid end of the molecule. Several members of the series have vital functions in the body, but only the first, linoleic acid, is essential in the diet of man because the body can synthesize the others from it. The 18 carbon linoleic acid that has two double bonds, is present in many foods in small amounts and in large amounts in many plant oils such as sunflower, safflower and corn oils. Besides having a structural function in cell membranes, the body adds on to it carbon atoms (chain elongates) and removes hydrogen atoms (desaturates) to form the other members of the series including the 18 carbon gamma-linolenic acid (GLA) and the 20 carbon dihomogamma-linolenic acid (DGLA) both with three double bonds and the 20 carbon arachidonic acid (AA) with four double bonds (*see* Figure 2, page 79). GLA is found in small amounts in a wide variety of common foods such as liver, beef and oats and in large amounts in borage, blackcurrant, evening primrose and fungal oils. Egg yolk, liver, beef, brain, fish and fish oils are food sources of AA in which it occurs in small amounts.

DGLA and AA are each immediate precursors of a separate series of prostanoids and leukotrienes, hormone-like substances that control many body processes. Those derived from AA are inflammatory and also vaso-constrictive and platelet aggregatory and hence increase the risk of thrombosis and coronary heart disease. Their production is decreased by those derived from eicosapentaenoic acid (EPA) (an omega 3 PUFA) and DGLA, which are anti-inflammatory. Prostaglandin E_1 derived from DGLA also vasodilates, i.e., reduces blood-pressure and inhibits platelet aggregation and thrombosis. The replacement of saturated fatty acids in the diet by omega 6 PUFA (linoleic acid), reduces serum cholesterol levels, a risk factor for coronary heart disease (*see* cardiovascular disease).

The synthesis of GLA from linoleic acid, and possibly of AA from DGLA, in the body is not very efficient, but DGLA is readily formed from GLA, which is therefore sometimes taken as a supplement to the diet, most frequently as evening primrose oil. Such dietary sources of GLA have been found to be helpful for some people suffering from atopic eczema, premenstrual syndrome and cyclical breast pain.

---

oncogenic, tumour producing.

OPCS, *see* Office of Population Censuses and Surveys.

---

oral cavity, or buccal cavity, cavity behind the mouth. Lined with mucous membrane. Opens into the oesophagus. Pierced by openings to nose, ears and larynx. Three pairs of glands secrete saliva and glands at the back of the tongue secrete lingual lipase into the cavity.

---

organic compounds, contain carbon in their molecules. Include those occurring naturally in living things, e.g., carbohydrates, proteins and fats, as well as many synthetic ones, e.g., azo-dyes, some used as food colours.

---

organoleptic, term used in food industry for taste and smell of a food. Bitter, sweet, acid and salt tastes are detected by the tongue and all other tastes by smell.

---

ornithine, an amino-acid component of the urea cycle (*which see*).

---

orotic acid, a member of the B complex but not a vitamin for man. Also known, incorrectly, as B_{13}. An intermediate in the synthesis of pyrimidine nucleotides. Present in all living cells. The only foods containing significant quantities are cow's milk (8mg/dl) and dairy products.

---

oryzenin, principal protein of rice. A glutelin.

---

osteoarthritis, disease characterized by degeneration of the cartilage in the joints and formation of bony outgrowths at edges of the joints. An exaggeration of normal joint ageing. General health unaffected. The prevention and correction of obesity, which hastens onset in load-bearing joints (hips and knees), is a valuable aid in managing the disease.

---

osteomalacia, adult form of rickets, brought about by vitamin D deficiency.

---

osteoporosis, loss of bone density with increased porosity and subsequent brittleness. Bone density peaks in early adulthood but naturally begins to decline in men around 50 years and in women by the age of 40 and more rapidly after the menopause. If depletion is severe, as in many postmenopausal women, osteoporosis results. Osteoporosis itself causes no disability except that bones are more liable to break and take a long time to heal. Loss in trabecular (inner) bone occurs first in the distal radius (leading to fracture of the wrist) and vertebra (leading to crush fracture and Dowager's Hump). Loss in cortical (outer) bone occurs later leading to hip fracture.

There are two overlapping forms, primary, Type 1, or, postmenopausal, usually associated with vertebral crush fractures, and secondary, Type 2, or, senile, usually associated with hip fractures. Type 1 can also occur in women whose ovaries have been removed and in men and is characterized by bone loss due to lack of oestrogen. Type 2 is protracted and slow in onset and is due to the natural ageing process. It occurs in men, women and children and is also caused by some diseases (e.g., hypogonadism), by drugs such as corticosteroids, which reduce bone mass, and by immolization.

Principal risk factors are: early menopause; childlessness in women; femaleness; white or Asian race; family history of the disease; leanness; immobility/lack of exercise; low-calcium, high-protein, low-fluoride, high-alcohol intakes; smoking; steroid therapy.

At the menopause, and with age, calcium absorption falls. Overnight urinary calcium loss in postmenopausal women also increases. Both factors would appear to increase the dietary calcium requirement in postmenopausal women. Whether low calcium intakes and/or low vitamin D states contribute to the development of osteoporosis is still disputed. Some, but not all, studies indicate that 1 to 1.5g daily intakes of calcium reduce, but do not prevent, postmenopausal bone loss. Several studies show a lower incidence of hip fractures among those with higher, compared with lower, intakes.

Hormone replacement therapy (HRT) prevents postmenopausal bone loss, but may not be tolerated. A single unconfirmed study in each case suggests that loss of bone mass may be prevented by calcium supplementation combined with low-dose HRT, while boron supplementation may reduce urinary calcium loss. Fluoride supplementation can increase bone density but high intakes may result in poor quality new bone of impaired mechanical strength.

See also calcium.

---

overweight,　*see* obesity.

---

oxalates,　salts of oxalic acid. Typical UK diet provides 70–150mg daily, about half from tea, 80–90 per cent of which is excreted in the faeces. About 25 per cent of urinary stones are pure calcium oxalate and, though most oxalate is formed endogenously, some susceptible people restrict intake of oxalate-rich foods and avoid megadoses of vitamin C, which is metabolized to oxalic acid.

Besides tea and cocoa, which are rich in oxalates, the distribution in foods is (in mg per 100g): rhubarb and spinach 250–800; beetroot and parsley 100–200; beans about 25; bread and cereal products 5–20; fruits, meat and fish less than 5.

oxidation, the removal of electrons, e.g., ferrous iron → ferric iron + 1 electron. Embraces loss of hydrogen or gain of oxygen. Foodstuffs are oxidized in the body for the release of their energy.

P

PABA, *see* para-aminobenzoic acid.

palmitic acid, a saturated, 16 carbon fatty acid. Widely distributed in nature. May contribute 10–50 per cent of the total fatty acids in any fat.

palmitoleic acid, a monounsaturated, 16 carbon fatty acid of the omega 9 family (C16:1 n-9). Common in seed oils.

palm oil, unusual among plant oils in its high content of saturated fatty acids. As per cent of total fatty acids: saturates, 47 (palmitic, 42); oleic, 43; linoleic, 8.

pancreas, gland that secretes pancreatic digestive juices into the duodenum (exocrine function) and the hormones insulin and glucagon into the bloodstream (endocrine function). Eaten as offal, when it is known as sweetbread.

pancreatic digestive juices, contain enzymes (in brackets) that: split proteins, proteoses and peptones into polypeptides, dipeptides and amino acids (trypsin, chymotrypsin and carboxypeptidase); starch and glycogen into dextrins, maltotriose and maltose (amylase); split off one or more fatty acids from triglycerides (lipase), phospholipids (phospholipase) and cholesterol esters (cholesteryl lipase); and split ribonucleic acids and deoxyribonucleic acids into nucleotides (ribonuclease and deoxyribonuclease).

pancreatitis, inflammation of the pancreas. Often associated with blockage of bile duct preventing flow of pancreatic juices into the duodenum. In the UK about a quarter of sufferers are heavy drinkers of alcohol.

---

pancreozymin, *see* cholecystokinin.

---

pangamic acid, a B complex factor but not a vitamin. Also known, incorrectly, as vitamin B_{15}. A naturally occurring compound including dimethylglycine and gluconic acid. Said to improve oxygen availability to the tissues.

---

pantothenic acid, water-soluble vitamin and member of the B complex. Sometimes known as vitamin B_5 and even as vitamin B_3.

Functions Biochemically, a main constituent of coenzyme A that acts as donor and receptor of acyl groups (e.g., acetyl) in many reactions concerned with carbohydrate and fat metabolism.

Deficiency leads to no specific disease except possibly burning feet syndrome (*which see*). Dietary deficiency unlikely as vitamin widespread in food, but on a diet made deliberately deficient other symptoms include anorexia, indigestion and mental disturbances.

Toxicity None reported.

Requirement EC RDA is 6mg. US estimated safe and adequate daily intake is 4–7mg.

Daily UK household supply in 1986 (not allowing for 10 per cent wastage and excluding out-of-home meals) averaged 6.07mg (6.41mg with contributions from alcoholic drinks and confectionery) derived mainly from (per cent): vegetables and products, 26; milk and products, 22; meat and products 17; eggs, 13.

Stable to oxygen and light. Normal cooking and baking causes little loss, but 40 per cent may be destroyed at temperatures above boiling. Destroyed by deep freezing. Leaches into cooking water.

Distribution in foods (in mg per 100g): dried brewer's yeast, 9.5; liver, 6.1–8.2; kidney, 3.0–4.3; wheat bran, 2.4; wheatgerm, 2.2; egg, 1.8 (yolk, 4.6); lentils, 1.4; meat and chicken, 0.7–1.2; peas, 0.8; wholemeal bread, 0.6; parsnips, 0.5; Cheddar cheese and milk, 0.3; winter cabbage, 0.2; fish, 0.1–0.2; butter and margarine, 0.

---

para-aminobenzoic acid (PABA), a B complex factor but not a vitamin for man. A constituent of folic acid but man is unable to utilize it to synthesize folic acid. Also known as anti-grey-hair factor as it prevents hair greying in rats. Used in lotions and creams as a sunscreen agent.

paralytic shellfish poisoning (PSP), which can be fatal, is caused by the concentration in shellfish of a toxin from a particular kind of naturally occurring alga. Mussels and other filter feeders are usually associated with PSP rather than crabs and lobsters, in which the toxin tends to be in low concentrations and in the non-edible parts. Occurs only occasionally during late spring and summer when particular climatic conditions cause a proliferation of the algae.

paraesthesia, any abnormality of sensation, e.g., numbness, pins and needles. Can be a symptom of malabsorption syndrome.

parenteral nutrition, *see* nutrition, parenteral.

parietal cells, found in stomach walls. Secrete gastric juices.

parotitis, nutritional, inflammation of the parotid salivary glands found under the ear. Common in Asia and Africa where associated with protein deficiency.

parsley, green leafy vegetable providing (per 100g): energy, 21 kcal; (g) protein, 5.2; fat, trace; total dietary fibre, 9.1; water, 78.7; (mg) potassium, 1,080; calcium, 330; beta-carotene, 7.0; vitamin C, 150; thiamin, 0.15; riboflavin, 0.30; niacin, 1.8.

pasteurization, destruction by mild heat treatment of the vegetative forms of many bacteria but not their spores. Prolongs storage life of the food for a limited period. Pasteurization of milk destroys pathogenic bacteria so that, though it sours in a few days, it is not a source of disease.

Vitamins most affected are C and thiamin.

pathogens, disease producing agents.

peas, pulses. Include:
chick pea (garbanzo beans) from *Cicer arietinum L.* Green or dried. Widely used in Middle East, served whole in sauce or with rice, as a rich cream/spread, called hummus, or fried in rissoles.
cow pea, seed of *Vigna unguiculata*.
garden pea, seed of *Pisum sativum*.
pidgeon pea, a dahl.

---

peanuts, also called ground-nuts and monkey nuts. Seeds of *Arachis hypogea*, a legume, and therefore properly a pulse and not a nut. Similar to other pulses in nutritive value, except contains about 40 per cent fat, twice as much as soya bean and ten times as much as other pulses. Dug up from underground where plant deposits them to ripen. Chiefly used for production of oil for cooking or making margarine or soap, the protein-rich but unpleasant tasting cake left being fed to cattle.

Provide (per 100g): energy, 570 kcal; (g) fat, 49.0; protein, 24.3.

---

pectin, water-soluble dietary fibre, though not fibrous in nature. A mixture of polysaccharides, composition depending on source but all contain methyl pectate (a polymer of galacturonic acid), araban and galactan. Only methyl pectate has gel-forming properties. Formed in fruit as it ripens and softens due to breakdown of protopectin that cements cell walls together.

Concentrated pectin extracts from citrus fruit or apples are used as setting agent for jam, in confectionery, chocolate, as emulsifying agent and stabilizer in ice-cream, jelly making, and anti-staling agent in cakes.

Slows down stomach emptying, may bind bile acids, and may affect trace mineral excretion.

---

pellagra, niacin deficiency disease. Occurs chiefly among poor peasants subsisting largely on maize (low in niacin and tryptophan). Symptoms include weight loss, debility, characteristic dermatitis, gastrointestinal disturbances especially diarrhoea and glossitis, mental changes, e.g., depression.

PEM, *see* protein-energy malnutrition.

---

pentosans, polysaccharides of pentoses, indigestible by man, so forming dietary fibres. Found in fruit, wood and oat hulls.

pentose, a monosaccharide containing five carbon atoms, e.g., ribose, deoxyribose, xylose.

pepper, black and white, obtained from peppercorns, fruit of the tropical vine, *Piper nigrum*. Black pepper is made from whole, sun-dried, unripe peppercorns and white from ripe ones that have been soaked and the outer skin rubbed off. Used as a condiment.

pepper, chil(l)i or red, fruit of *Capsicum frutescens* that is usually sun-dried. Hot and very pungent. Used in curry powder, pickles, tabasco sauce, and powdered as cayenne pepper. Active principle is capsaicin.

pepper, sweet, also known as paprika, bell pepper and pimiento (Spanish). Red and yellow fruit of *Capsicum annum*, often eaten when unripe and green. Used as vegetable both cooked and raw.
    Provides per 100g: (mg) vitamin C, 100; (μg) carotene, 200.

pepsin, enzyme in gastric juices that splits proteins into proteoses and peptones.

peptide bond, -CO-NH-, the bond formed between two amino acids when water is lost between the acid group (-COOH) of one and the amino group (-NH$_2$) of the other, resulting in the formation of a peptide.

peptides, are compounds formed when two or more amino acids are linked by peptide bond(s). Di- and tri-peptides are formed from two and three amino acids respectively. Ten or more amino acids so linked are polypeptides and very large polypeptides are proteins.
    Metabolically active peptides and small polypeptides include glutathione, the gastrointestinal hormones and glucagon.

peptones, polypeptides formed by breakdown of proteins and proteoses by pepsin in the stomach and trypsin in the duodenum.

PER, *see* protein efficiency ratio.

---

periodontal disease, causes the gum margin to fall away from the teeth. In the pocket formed, bacteria accumulate, which inflame the margin (gingivitis) and damage underlying tissues (periodontitis). In advanced cases, the teeth become loose and fall out (pyrrhoea alveolaris). A soft diet, rich in simple carbohydrates encourages bacterial growth and periodontal disease, while the massaging, cleansing effect of rough, tough foodstuffs prevents it. It is the major cause of tooth loss after the age of 45. Occurs independently from dental caries but may help to cause it. A form of the disease is present in scurvy.

---

peristalsis, wave of contraction followed by wave of relaxation of intestinal walls that moves food along the intestinal lumen.

---

peroxidation, *see* lipid peroxidation.

---

pfaffia, sometimes known as Brazilian ginseng, although not related to the ginsengs of Asian origin, because of its similar properties.

---

pH, abbreviation of 'potential hydrogen'. The pH of a solution is a measure of its hydrogen ion concentration and hence of its acidity. Values range from 0 to 14. The lower the pH, the greater is the hydrogen ion concentration and, hence, the acidity of the solution, and vice versa. Pure water is neutral with a pH of 7. The pH of the gastric juices is about 1, of pancreatic juices about 8, of normal blood, 7.4, and normal urine, 4.6–8.0, depending on diet.

---

pharynx, the rear part of the oral cavity (*which see*).

---

phenolases, e.g., tyrosinase, polyphenol oxidase, catechol oxidase, are copper-containing enzymes that catalyse the oxidation of phenols (e.g., tyrosine) to quinones. Phenolases present in potatoes and apples cause them to turn brown when exposed to air. *See* browning.

phenylalanine, an essential amino acid, seldom if ever limiting in foods. Precursor of tyrosine. An inherited inability to carry out the conversion causes phenylketonuria.

Constituent of the intense sweetener, aspartame.

---

phenylketonuria, a disease caused by an inherited inability to convert phenylalanine to tyrosine. The intermediate metabolite, phenylpyruvic acid (a phenylketone) that is excreted in the urine, affects the brain causing mental retardation. Very early detection followed by a diet containing minimal levels of the essential amino acid, phenylalanine, prevents or ameliorates the condition.

---

phosphatases, enzymes that release free phosphate from organic phosphates. Present in intestinal digestive juices.

---

phosphate, physiologically important form of phosphorus. An anion (PO_4^{3-}). Present in bones, teeth, ATP, nucleic acids, phospholipids, some proteins, etc.

---

phosphatides, e.g., phosphatidylglycerides such as lecithin.

---

phosphatidylcholine, *see* phospholipid. Also known as lecithin.

---

phosphatidylethanolamine, *see* phospholipid. Also known as cephalin.

---

phosphatidylglycerides, phospholipids (*which see*).

---

phosphatidylinositol, *see* phospholipid.

---

phosphatidylserine, *see* phospholipid.

phospholipase, enzyme concerned with digestion of phospholipids. Present in pancreatic digestive juices.

---

phospholipids, lipids that contain a phosphate group. Physiologically important ones include phosphatidylglycerides (or glycerophospholipids), which are esters of the alcohol glycerol with two fatty acids and a phosphate group linked to either choline (lecithin or phosphatidylcholine), inositol (phosphatidylinositol), ethanolamine (cephalin or phosphatidylethanolamine), or serine (phosphatidylserine). Important as structural components of cell membranes and as constituents of lipoproteins.

---

phosphorus, as phosphate it is a major constituent of all living cells. Bones contain most (600–900g) of this essential non-metallic mineral present as phosphate. Present in all natural food, especially those rich in calcium and protein.

Daily UK household supply in 1986 (not allowing for 10 per cent wastage and out-of-home meals) averaged 1,249mg (1,349mg with contributions from alcoholic drinks and confectionery) derived mainly from (per cent) milk and products, 32 (liquid milk, 19); cereals, 23; meat and products, 17. Food additives, e.g., polyphosphates, increase intake by about 10 per cent.

Functions in the form of phosphate as a constituent of bones, teeth, ATP and creatine phosphate (immediately available energy stores), nucleic acids, nucleotides, phospholipids and some proteins. Takes part in many metabolic processes.

Absorbed as free phosphate in the mid-jejunum. Absorption regulated by active vitamin D, and prevented by antacids, which bind phosphates.

Excretion via kidneys regulates plasma levels of phosphate. Regulation controlled by active vitamin D, which reduces excretion, and by the parathyroid hormone, which increases it.

Deficiency unlikely as a result of low dietary intake, but may arise secondarily from diminished intestinal absorption or excessive urinary excretion. Resulting hypophosphataemia (low blood phosphate levels) affects functions of most cells causing abnormalities in the blood cells and liver. Symptoms include muscular weakness and bone pains. Leads to rickets in children and osteomalacia in adults.

Requirement US and EC RDA is 800mg.

Toxicity rare except when kidney failure prevents normal phosphate excretion. Hyperphosphataemia (high blood phosphate level) depresses active vitamin D production, decreasing calcium absorption. Whether the increasing intake of phosphate food additives is contributing to the excess bone loss found in osteoporotic women is not yet clear.

Distribution in foods (in mg per 100g): Cheddar cheese, 520; liver, 360–370; lentils, 240; wholemeal bread, 230; eggs, 220; lean meat, 180–200; cod, 170; yogurt, 140; peas, 100; white bread, 97; milk, 95; winter cabbage, 54; watercress, 52; potatoes, 40.

---

photosynthesis, the synthesis of carbohydrates from carbon dioxide and water by green plants in the presence of light (solar energy).

---

phylloquinone, *see* vitamin K.

---

phytase, enzyme that splits phosphoric acid from phytates.

---

phytate, salt of phytic acid, which is the hexaphosphoric acid of inositol. Calcium-magnesium and potassium-magnesium phytate complexes are found in cereal grains and pulses up to a level of 5 per cent. In the seed and seedling, the enzyme phytase also present makes them readily available sources of phosphorus. Phytase dephosphorylates phytic acid, removing its mineral complexing ability. Phytase is inactive in dry, dormant seeds, but becomes activated by moisture, warmth and the right acidity. Yeast or sourdough fermentation of flour in bread-making activates phytase and lowers phytate levels by one-third to one-half, the loss being rapid when low-extraction (white) flour is used, but slow for high-extraction (wholemeal) products. Unleavened (unfermented) wheat breads have very high phytate levels. Phytase activity in soya bean products appears low.

Nutritionally, phytates are of concern because of their ability to form insoluble complexes with minerals, making them unavailable to the body. Particularly affected are copper and zinc and a synergistic or additive-binding effect can occur when two or more minerals are present together, such as zinc and calcium, copper and zinc. Phytate-binding of calcium and magnesium may or may not assist their absorption and fibre rather than phytate may be responsible for poor calcium absorption from wheat breads. Whether phytate inhibits or has no effect on iron absorption is disputed.

---

phytic acid, present in cereal grains and pulses as phytates.

phytin,   calcium-magnesium complex of phytic acid.

phytomenadione,   *see* vitamin K.

phytosterols,   plant sterols, e.g., beta-sitosterol, stigmasterol, sitostanol, ergosterol, that are poorly absorbed. On irradiation, ergosterol forms ergocalciferol, vitamin D_2. Some, e.g., beta-sitosterol, inhibit absorption of cholesterol.

phytoagglutinins,   *see* lectins.

phytylmenaquinone,   *see* vitamin K.

pica,   desire for extraordinary articles of food. Often seen in iron deficiency and sometimes experienced in pregnancy.

picolinic acid,   metabolite of tryptophan and isomer of niacin. Forms chelates with minerals (e.g., zinc, chromium) and is suggested to improve their absorption.

PKU,   *see* phenylketonuria.

placebo,   an inert substance given as a medicine. Often produces beneficial effects in patients due to their expectation of benefit causing the brain to produce 'endorphins' (the body's own pain relievers). The placebo effect of a treatment is thought not to last more than three weeks. In experimental research on a new medicine or foodstuff, the placebo effect of the treatment is allowed for by giving some patients placebos identical in appearance to the test substance and others the test material itself, neither the patient nor physician knowing which is which — a double-blind trial.

plaque,   raised lesions in arterial walls of sufferers from atherosclerosis; or dental plaque, which is formed of insoluble polymers of glucose and fructose (dextrans and levans) built by enzymes from *Streptococcus mutans*, the bacterium mainly responsible for dental caries, that adhere to the teeth and protect bacteria from the cleansing action of the tongue.

plasma, blood with the cells removed. Transparent, straw-coloured, fluid part of the blood with a volume of about 3.5 l in a 70 kg man. Carries immense numbers of ions, inorganic molecules and organic molecules in transit to various parts of the body or that aid in transport of other substances. Clots on standing because, unlike serum, it contains the blood-clotting factors.

plasmalogens, phospholipids constituting as much as 10 per cent of the phospholipids of brain and muscle. Structurally similar to phosphatidyl-ethanolamine.

platelets, small, granulated cells in the blood. Formed in the bone marrow. Normally about 300,000 per ml. Live a week or so. Collect at site of injury to blood-vessel wall (platelet aggregation) and discharge the contents of their granules (platelet release). Granule contents cause: more platelets to aggregate, forming a plug; the blood vessel to constrict, inhibiting bleeding; and thromboxane A_2 to be formed by the platelets, which promotes further aggregation and vasoconstriction. A blood clot may then form, which stops bleeding but can block the vessel (thrombosis), particularly if the lumen is narrowed by atherosclerosis.

PMS, *see* pre-menstrual syndrome.

PMT, pre-menstrual tension, a symptom of pre-menstrual syndrome (PMS) (*which see*).

poisoning, due to food, *see* food poisoning.

pollen, male fertilizing powder discharged from flower's anthers. Bee pollen is a mixture of bee saliva, plant nectar and pollen. It is collected from hives and sold as a loose powder or in tablet form. Evidence for its health and curative benefits is anecdotal.

Dried bee pollen contains 10–36 per cent (average 20 per cent) protein with a reasonably high essential amino acid content, 10–15 per cent simple sugars as in honey, small quantities of fats, significant amounts of potassium, magnesium, phosphorus, calcium, copper and iron, and some vitamins (thiamin, riboflavin, pantothenic acid, vitamin C, biotin and carotenes). A nutritious food for those able to afford spoonful quantities. Can trigger an allergic attack in those sensitive to pollen.

polymer, many identical small molecules joined together to form one large one, e.g., lignin, starch.

polyneuropathy, disease of the nervous system involving more than one nerve. Nerves of the legs affected more than those of the arms. Usually a dysfunction in both sensory (leading to 'pins and needles', severe nerve pains) and motor (leading to impaired knee and ankle jerks, muscle wasting, etc.) nerve fibres. Causes: deficiency diseases, e.g., beriberi, pellagra, burning feet syndrome, alcoholic neuropathy, vitamin B_6 deficiency; metabolic diseases, e.g., diabetes, uraemia, porphyria; chemical poisoning, e.g., with lead, arsenic, mercury; infective, e.g., diphtheria, leprosy; in association with cancer; prolonged daily supplementation with over 200mg vitamin B_6.

polynucleotidase, enzyme that completes breakdown of nucleic acids to nucleotides. Present in intestinal digestive juices.

polynucleotide, many nucleotides linked to form a chain, e.g., RNA and DNA.

polypeptide, peptide formed from ten or more amino acids. Very large polypeptides are proteins.

polyphenol oxidase, *see* phenolase.

polyphosphates, additives used to process meats and particularly poultry and fish, apparently to improve flavour and texture. They increase the water content of the product.

polysaccharides, complex carbohydrates that, on complete hydrolysis, yield monosaccharides which may be all the same or a mixture of two or more different ones. The monosaccharides are linked in straight or branched chains that vary in length and complexity between and within polysaccharides. Large molecules with high and variable molecular weights. Amorphous, tasteless and often insoluble. Include the available carbohydrates (starches and glycogen) and dietary fibres (e.g., cellulose, mucilages and gums). All dietary fibres, except lignin, are polysaccharides.

---

polyunsaturated/saturated fatty acid ratio, *see* P/S.

---

polyunsaturates, food fats/oils rich in polyunsaturated fatty acids, e.g., sunflower oil, polyunsaturated margarine. *See* fatty acids.

---

pork, pig meat. A chemical present in the flesh of full-grown males gives it an unpleasant 'boar-odour' detectable by 92 per cent of women but only 56 per cent of men. Lean pork provides (per 100g): energy, 147 kcal; (g) water, 71.5; protein, 20.7; fat, 7.1; (mg) iron, 0.9; zinc, 2.4; thiamin, 0.89; riboflavin, 0.25; niacin, 10.0; vitamin B_6, 0.45; (μg) vitamin B_{12}, 3.0.

---

postprandial, following a meal, e.g., postprandial blood sugar rise.

---

potassium, the principal cation (positively charged ion) inside cells. Body cells contain about 136g of this essential mineral, four-fifths of it in the muscles, and body fluids only about 3g. The potassium content of foodstuffs is very variable.

Daily UK household supply in 1986 (not allowing for 10 per cent wastage and out-of-home meals) averaged 2,694mg (2,956mg with contributions from alcoholic drinks and confectionery) derived mainly from: (per cent) vegetables, 33; milk and products, 20; cereals, 13.

Functions in regulating acid base and water balance. Takes part in cell membrane transfer and in nerve and muscle function. Activates certain enzymes.

Absorbed readily.

Excreted mainly via the kidneys, which cannot conserve it nearly as effectively as they can sodium. Output closely follows dietary intake. Except in diarrhoea only a little is lost in the faeces (most of that present in digestive juices being re-absorbed) and negligible amounts in sweat.

Deficiency unlikely as a result of low dietary intake but may arise secondary to therapy with thiazide group diuretics and as a result of breakdown of tissue protein with which it is associated such as occurs in diabetics, in underfeeding and after injury. Symptoms include muscular weakness, paralysis and mental confusion.

Requirement No RDA set, but USA estimated minimum daily requirement is 2,000mg. Some studies suggest that increasing the dietary intake may improve the blood-pressure lowering effects of decreasing dietary sodium.

Toxicity occurs in kidney failure or as a result of shock after injury. Symptoms of the resulting hyperkalaemia (high blood levels of potassium) usually include muscular weakness and mental apathy. If severe, affects heart action.

Distribution in foods (in mg per 100g): dried brewer's yeast, 1,700; dried dates, 750; mushrooms, 470; winter cabbage, 390; lean meats, 350–370; bananas, 350; chicken, apricots and grapes, 320; watercress, 310; tomatoes, 290; yogurt, 240; wholemeal bread, 220; orange juice, 180; milk, 150; eggs, 140; white bread, 100.

---

potato, a starchy root or tuber of *Solanum tuberosum*. Cheap food that, on its own, can support life for a considerable time. Very low in fat. Low in protein, but it is of high biological value. Because eaten in large quantities, it is a useful source of protein, fibre, thiamin and niacin and provides a fifth of the UK daily intake of vitamin C. Fattening reputation undeserved unless cooked in fat or oil. Contains toxic glycosides, e.g., solanine, mainly in skin and outer layers of green, damaged or badly stored tubers.

Old raw potatoes provide (per 100g): energy, 87 kcal; (g) water, 75.8; protein, 2.1; fat, 0.1; carbohydrate, 20.8; total dietary fibre, 2.1; (mg) thiamin, 0.11; riboflavin, 0.04; niacin, 1.7; vitamin C, 30 in fresh-dug maincrop decreasing to 8 after 8–9 months' storage; iron, 0.5; zinc, 0.3; copper, 0.15.

---

potato, sweet, starchy root or tuber of the herbaceous plant *Ipomoea batatas* cultivated in hot climates, e.g., southern USA. The red and yellow varieties provide vitamin A activity.

---

ppb, parts per billion or per thousand million (e.g., μg/kg).

---

ppm, parts per million (e.g., mg/kg).

ppt, parts per trillion or per million million (e.g., ng/kg).

---

pregnancy, a balanced diet is particularly important with special regard to increased protein, calcium and vitamin requirements, readily met by increasing milk intake (skimmed if excessive weight increase is a problem), and ensuring plenty of fresh fruit and vegetables. Iron supplements are usually prescribed by the doctor who should be consulted before any other vitamin or mineral supplements are taken. The safe level of alcohol intake during pregnancy is zero consumption. While vitamin A is required for foetal growth, high intakes can cause malformations in the foetus. Hence, pregnant women should avoid consuming liver, and liver products such as pâté, which can have high levels of vitamin A, and only take supplements of vitamin A (or other vitamins and minerals) on doctor's advice. *See also* neural tube defect.

---

pre-menstrual syndrome (PMS), experienced by many women in the days leading up to menstruation. Symptoms may include depression, irritability, tension (pre-menstrual tension — PMT), breast tenderness, food cravings, headaches and oedema. Sufferers may have an increased dietary requirement for vitamin B_6. Some supplement with a dietary source of gamma-linolenic acid.

---

preservatives, substances intended to prevent food decomposition caused by bacteria, moulds or yeast. Regulations not only specify permitted preservatives but also the foods in which they may be used and the concentrations. Sulphur dioxide and hydroxybenzoates are the most used preservatives and are permitted for fruit and vegetable products, beer, meat products, sauces and spices. Propionic acid is used mainly for bread and flour confectionery. Sodium nitrite and nitrate are used in cured meats including bacon and ham. Sorbic acid can be used to preserve the gelatin in soft capsule shells. *See* additives.

---

pressor amines, substances that raise the blood-pressure — catecholamines.

---

pressure cooking, employs higher temperatures for shorter times than open pan cooking. Relative value nutritionally compared with the latter is variable and depends on the type of food and volume of water used. Leaching rather than heat is the principal cause of nutrient loss. Open pan cooking with minimal water and particularly 'waterless' cooking, appears superior in retaining vitamin C and B vitamins compared with either pressure cooking or open pan cooking employing traditional volumes of water.

procaryotes,   cellular organisms without distinct nuclei, e.g., bacteria.

prolamines,   plant storage proteins insoluble in water but soluble in alcoholic solutions. They contain large amounts of proline and glutamine and have a low content of lysine and other essential amino acids. The high content of prolamine in cereal proteins is largely responsible for their low nutritional value, e.g., maize and sorghum proteins are over 50 per cent prolamine, wheat and barley 40–45 per cent, but rice and oat proteins have only around 10 per cent prolamine and an acceptable lysine content.

proline,   a non-essential amino acid. Prevalent in collagen.

propionic acid,   a three carbon fatty acid. One of the volatile fatty acids formed during colonic fermentation of dietary fibre.

propolis,   a mixture of waxy and resinous substances collected by bees from various trees and used to seal leaks in their hives. Possesses anti-oxidant and anti-bacterial activities. Obtainable in food supplement form.

prostacyclins (PGI),   prostanoids produced by the action of cyclo-oxygenase enzyme on 20 carbon polyunsaturated fatty acids in blood-vessel walls, lung, heart, kidney and stomach.

prostaglandins (PG),   term commonly used for all the prostanoids though chemically it should exclude the thromboxanes. Produced by the action of cyclo-oxygenase enzyme on 20 carbon polyunsaturated fatty acids in many tissues including kidney and brain.

prostanoids, commonly called prostaglandins (though this chemically excludes the thromboxanes). Hormone-like substances produced by the action of the enzyme cyclo-oxygenase on 20 carbon polyunsaturated fatty acids. Series 1 are derived from gamma-linolenic acid, Series 2 from arachidonic acid and Series 3 from eicosapentaenoic acid (EPA). Series 2 and 3 comprise prostaglandins (PG), prostacyclins (PGI) and thromboxanes (TXA) and Series 1 just PGs and TXA. Individual prostanoids are denoted by letters of the alphabet and their series by a number suffix. *See* Figure 2, page 79.

Very potent, short-lived, locally acting substances that control or affect many body processes including blood clotting, blood-pressure, uterine contractions, reproductive cycle, electrolyte excretion, pain, etc.

Particularly interesting nutritionally are those concerned in blood clotting. TXA_2 produced by blood platelets strongly promotes blood clotting, whereas PGI_2, produced by blood-vessel walls, discourages it. TXA_3 has little effect on blood clotting and PGI_3 discourages it. Since their precursors, arachidonic acid for TXA_2 and PGI_2 and EPA for TXA_3 and PGI_3, compete for the same cyclo-oxygenase enzyme, the increased proportion of EPA to linoleic acid (arachidonic acid precursor) in the diet of Greenland Eskimos, who eat large quantities of marine animals whose oils are rich in EPA, is thought to be responsible both for their low incidence of coronary heart disease and their increased tendency to bleed.

---

prosthetic group, the non-protein part of an enzyme (usually formed from a B vitamin) that binds tightly to the protein apoenzyme to form the active or holoenzyme (e.g., flavin mononucleotide and flavin adenine dinucleotide).

---

protamines, small proteins, strongly basic because of their high content of arginine and other basic amino acids. Found in fish roes. Used commercially in production of delayed action insulin.

---

protein, crude, the approximate protein content of a food as used in food tables. Obtained by multiplying its nitrogen content by the nitrogen conversion factor, 6.25.

---

protein efficiency ratio (PER), is the weight gained by young growing animals per g of protein eaten. Maximum value (e.g., with egg protein) is

4.4 and that of casein is 2.5. Proteins with zero values (e.g., gelatin) do not support growth when fed alone.

---

protein quality,   refers to the concentration of essential amino acids in the food protein relative to their concentrations in the proteins to be synthesized in the consumer. It is expressed in various ways, including biological value, chemical score, net protein utilization, protein efficiency ratio.

---

protein-energy malnutrition (PEM),   describes a wide range of the clinical symptoms of starvation seen when lack of food is aggravated by chronic infectious diseases. Continued restriction of both dietary energy and protein as well as other nutrients, produces marasmus, which is characterized by a generalized loss of body tissue. When energy intake is adequate but there is quantitative and qualitative deficiency of dietary protein, symptoms include oedema and the condition is called kwashiorkor. PEM is the most important public-health problem in the underdeveloped world today.

---

protein-energy percentage or ratio,   is the proportion of the total energy in the food or diet supplied by protein expressed as a percentage or ratio, e.g. (as percentage), cod, 91; meats, 51–66; skimmed milk, 41; egg, 31; whole milk, 20; wholemeal bread, 16.

---

proteins,   are large complex molecules that form 10–15 per cent of the energy value of most well-balanced diets. Body proteins are dependent for their formation and maintenance on dietary protein. They contain the elements carbon, hydrogen, oxygen, nitrogen, usually sulphur and some-times phosphorus, present as amino acids linked in very long polypeptide chains. About 20 amino acids are found in proteins and the proportions in which they occur, the sequence in which they are arranged and the overall molecular shape are what give proteins their individuality.

Functions are diverse and include structural and protective roles (e.g., muscle, skin, hair, fur, feather, fish fins and scales), catalytic (enzymes), transport (e.g., of fat, minerals, oxygen), hormonal (e.g., insulin).

Chemically, simple proteins consist only of amino acids. In complex proteins, the polypeptides are combined with other substances such as haem, vitamin derivatives, lipids and carbohydrates.

Animal proteins are of two kinds:

1. fibrous, in which the polypeptide chains are coiled in a spiral or helix and cross-linked — these are generally insoluble and digestible only with difficulty, if at all, e.g., keratin, collagen, fibrin, myosin;
2. globular, in which the polypeptide chains are compactly folded and coiled — these are generally soluble, readily digestible and rich in essential amino acids (EAA).

Plant proteins are mostly glutelins, which are insoluble, e.g., glutenin, hordein, oryzenin; and prolamines, also insoluble and very rich in proline, e.g., gliadin, zein.

Soluble proteins undergo a partially reversible change called denaturation when gently heated (e.g., simmered) or treated with acid (e.g., vinegar) or alcohol (e.g., wine), etc. Further heating (cooking) or drastic treatment causes their coagulation, an irreversible process that makes the protein insoluble.

Digestion and fate   About 92 per cent of the protein in a Western diet is digested and absorbed. Digestion commences in the stomach where the protein polypeptides are broken down into smaller ones called proteoses and peptones by pepsin. In the duodenum, trypsin in the pancreatic juices splits these to smaller peptides that are acted on by peptidases in the intestinal juices and split usually into di- or tri-peptides or amino acids, which are absorbed. Amino acids pass in the blood to the liver and other tissues where they are used:

1. for synthesis of body protein. Dietary amino acids and those from the breakdown of body proteins form about 200g new protein daily in an adult man.
2. as a source of amino groups ($-NH_2$), which are used to convert keto acids derived from carbohydrates and fats into amino acids. Vitamin B_6 is a coenzyme for these reactions, known as transaminations. Excess amino nitrogen is converted by the liver into urea, which is excreted in the urine.
3. as an energy source (after transferring their amino group), being converted to the tissue fuels, glucose (glycogenic amino acids) and/or acetoacetic acid (ketogenic amino acids).
4. as protein reserves, called labile body protein, which is probably physiologically unimportant and amounts to 175–350g in the adult.
5. for synthesis of non-protein derivatives, e.g., porphyrins (haem), purines, pyrimidines, neurotransmitters, hormones, etc.

Plant versus animal proteins   The former appear to have a hypocholesterolaemic effect compared with the latter, possibly because of their higher arginine/lysine ratio.

Requirements   Dietary protein must supply sufficient of the eight amino acids that the body cannot make itself — the essential amino acids (EAA) — plus enough amino nitrogen for the body to synthesize the other nutritionally non-essential ones as required. Animal proteins are generally of higher biological value than plant proteins, which are often low in one or more EAA — the limiting amino acid. In a mixed diet, a deficiency of an EAA in one protein is made up by its abundance in another, such proteins being described as complementary. All these factors are taken into account by the UK RDA, which indicates that the protein requirement will be satisfied if 10 per cent of the total energy intake is provided by protein, assuming the mixed protein of the usual UK diet has a net protein utilization of 75. For the moderately active young man this amounts to 72g daily.

The NACNE report suggests that the present UK intake of protein at 11 per cent of total dietary energy (including alcohol) continues unchanged, and that the greater proportion of vegetable protein developing from other recommendations is appropriate.

Excretion   A moderately active man consuming about 300g carbohydrate, 100g fat and 100g protein daily, must excrete about 16.5g nitrogen per day, of which 95 per cent is eliminated by the kidney and most of the rest in the faeces. In man most nitrogen is excreted as urea.

Deficiency (*see also* protein-energy malnutrition; kwashiorkor):
1. Primary — most adults remain healthy on a wide range of intakes (50–150g daily). On low intakes, hormone balance alters to conserve protein and the liver reduces urea formation, conserving amino nitrogen for amino acid synthesis. Deficiency in children results in cessation and reduction in growth. The effect on organs and tissues is related to their speed of protein turnover, being fastest in the intestinal lining and digestive glands (leading to failure to digest food, diarrhoea, loss of water and electrolytes), then the liver (failure to synthesize proteins, particularly serum albumin leading to oedema; and lipoprotein apoproteins leading to a fatty liver), followed by skeletal muscle (leading to muscle wasting) and red blood cells (leading to anaemia). Collagen and central nervous system protein turnover is slow, so connective and nervous tissues are well maintained.
2. Secondary — may arise if dietary carbohydrate is deficient, causing protein to be used mainly for energy; through loss of protein in the urine or through bleeding; through intestinal disorders leading to failure in protein absorption; through failure of a damaged liver to synthesize proteins; through tissue damage (trauma, e.g., burns, fractures, operations) that leads to temporary general body tissue breakdown.

Toxicity   Intake seldom exceeds 20 per cent of dietary energy, though in some communities it may reach 250–300g daily (e.g., Masai warriors of Central Africa, Australian range-riders), apparently causing no ill-effects.

Distribution in food (in g per 100g and, in brackets, the percentage of the total energy contributed by protein — both figures important as regards the protein value of a food): soya bean flour (low-fat), 45.3 (51); soya bean flour (full-fat), 36.8 (32); Cheddar cheese, 26.0 (26); lentils, 23.8 (31); livers, 20.1–21.1 (45–56); meats, 20.3–20.8 (51–66); chicken meat, 20.5 (67); mackerel, 19.0 (34); chicken meat plus skin, 17.6 (31); cod, 17.4 (91); cottage cheese, 13.6 (57); eggs, 12.3 (33); wholemeal bread, 8.8 (16); white bread, 7.8 (13); rice, 6.5 (7); peas, 5.8 (35); yogurt, 5.0 (38); skimmed milk, 3.4 (41); whole milk, 3.3 (20); watercress, 2.9 (82); winter cabbage, 2.8 (51); potatoes, (old), 2.1 (10); banana, 1.1 (6); orange, 0.8 (9).

Law From 1986, a food may not legally be described as a 'source'/'rich or excellent source of protein' unless a reasonable daily intake of the food provides at least 12g protein and unless at least 12 per cent/20 per cent of the energy value of the food is provided by protein.

---

proteoglycans, proteins covalently attached to oligosaccharides. Differ from glycoproteins in the chemical nature of their oligosaccharides. Include chondroitin sulphate in cartilage, keratan sulphates in the cornea and loose connective tissues, heparin within mast cells, heparan sulphate on cell surfaces.

---

proteose, first cleavage product in the digestion of proteins in the stomach. Intermediate between proteins and peptones.

---

pro-vitamin A, *see* carotenoids.

---

pro-vitamins, naturally occurring substances that the body can convert into vitamins, e.g., carotenes into vitamin A, tryptophan into niacin, cholesterol derivative in the skin into vitamin D.

---

prunes, dried fruit, providing energy (161 kcal per 100g). Laxative effect due to high content of dietary fibre (16.1g per 100g) and of derivatives of hydroxyphenylisatin that stimulate the smooth muscle of the colon.

P/S, the ratio of polyunsaturated fatty acids in the diet (all *cis* isomers) to saturated fatty acids. Expresses the degree of polyunsaturation of dietary fat. Dietary goals aim to raise the ratio from 0.24 in 1982 and 0.35 in 1986 towards 1 by decreasing saturated fat intake (mainly animal source) and replacing some of it with polyunsaturated fat (mainly plant source).

The P/S of butter is 0.05 and of margarines made only from vegetable oils: hard, 0.32; soft, 0.70; and polyunsaturated, 3.15.

PSP, *see* paralytic shellfish poisoning.

---

psychiatric disorders, may be associated with deficiencies of thiamin, niacin or vitamin B_{12}. The success of orthomolecular medicine megadosage with niacin for the treatment of schizophrenia is disputed.

---

psychoactive substances, in foods include: traces of the hallucinatory alkaloids of ergot in bread; sedative and hypnotic substances in lettuce; dilators and decongestants in lemon juice; the hallucinogenic drug myresticin in nutmeg and mace; piperine in pepper, which is stimulative, carminative and diuretic; and capsaicin from the 'hot' capsicum pepper that stimulates saliva flow and increases blood circulation.

---

psyllium, mucilage derived from husk or seed of *Plantago psyllium*. Like ispaghula it is a mixed polysaccharide with xylose the main constituent sugar. Soluble dietary fibre, but unlike most it contains an unfermentable soluble residue that acts as a bulk laxative. Some, sensitized by inhaling it, experience allergic reactions when consuming it.

---

ptomaines, toxic amines produced by loss of carbon dioxide from amino acids due to intestinal bacterial activity, e.g., putrescine from ornithine, cadaverine from lysine, tyramine from tyrosine, histamine from histidine.

PUFA, polyunsaturated fatty acids. *See* fatty acids, polyunsaturated.

---

pulses, or legumes, are seeds of the *Leguminosae* family. Include peas, beans, lentils and dahls. Grown world-wide and contribute to diets of most peoples, particularly in the East.

Important nutritionally because:

1. most provide 20 per cent protein that, though not of high biological value, being low in the sulphur amino acids, is rich in lysine and so complements cereal proteins;

2. good sources of B vitamins except riboflavin;
3. devoid of vitamin C until sprouted when they become rich sources.

Soya beans are exceptionally nutritious.

Fermentation of their soluble dietary fibre may be the cause of much of the flatulence experienced following their ingestion, particularly of haricot beans.

Their starch contains a higher than usual proportion of amylase and is slowly digested. This, together with their content of soluble dietary fibres, helps account for their low glycaemic indices and makes them useful carbohydrate foods for diabetics.

Some contain toxic substances causing illnesses, e.g., lathyrism, favism, and others can be contaminated with moulds producing aflatoxins, e.g., peanuts. Lectins present are usually destroyed on cooking.

Pulses provide (per 100g dry weight): energy, 320–350 kcal; (g) water, 8–15; protein, 17–25 (soya bean, 38); carbohydrate, 55–65 (soya bean, 20); fat, 1–5 (soya bean, 18); total dietary fibre, 2.9–25.4; (mg) calcium, 100–200; iron, 2–8; carotene, 0.012–0.12; vitamin C, 0 (when sprouted, 10–15); thiamin, 0.2–0.6; riboflavin, 0.1–0.3 (soya bean, 0.75); nicotinic acid, 1.5–3.0.

---

purines, include adenine, guanine, hypoxanthine, xanthine and uric acid. In man, all are excreted as uric acid. Foods traditionally regarded as rich in purines and avoided by those prone to gout or uric acid urinary tract stones include liver, kidneys, sweetbreads, sardines, anchovies, fish roes and yeast extracts. Constituents of nucleic acids (*which see*).

---

pylorus, opening of the stomach into the duodenum, encircled by a sphincter muscle.

---

pyridoxal, pyridoxamine and pyridoxine, *see* vitamin B_6.

---

pyrimidines, include cytosine, thymine and uracil. *See* nucleic acids.

---

pyrrhoea alveolaris, a periodontal (gum) disease in which the teeth become loose and fall out.

Q

quercitin,   a bioflavonoid formed from rutin (another bioflavonoid), by the action of intestinal bacteria.

Quetelet's index,   *see* body mass index.

quince,   sour, pear-shaped fruit of *Cydonia* with flesh similar to that of apple. Rich in pectin and so used in making jams and jellies, and gum, both dietary fibres.

Provides (per 100g): 25 kcal; (g) water, 84; protein, 0.3; fat, trace; carbohydrates, 6.3; dietary fibre, 6.4; (mg) potassium, 200; vitamin C, 15.

R

rabbit,   game meat. Provides (per 100g): energy, 124 kcal; (g) water, 74.6; protein, 21.9; fat, 4.0; (mg) iron, 1.0; zinc, 1.4; thiamin, 1.0; riboflavin, 0.19; niacin, 12.5; vitamin B_6, 0.5; (μg) vitamin B_{12}, 10.

radicals, free,   *see* free radicals.

rancidity,   lipid peroxidation of fats and oils causing unpleasant odour and taste. Delayed by excluding oxygen and by presence of an antioxidant like vitamin E.

rape-seed oil,   rape-seed grows well in temperate climates but the oil, unless produced from the new genetic variety, *Canbra*, contains large amounts of erucic acid (*which see*). As percentage of its total fatty acid composition, erucic acid forms, 33, linoleic acid, 15.5 and alpha-linolenic acid, 10.5 per cent.

RDA,　*see* recommended daily amount.

RDI,　recommended daily intake. *See* recommended daily amount.

RE,　*see* retinol equivalent.

---

recommended daily allowance,　*see* recommended daily amount.

---

recommended daily amount, or, allowance (RDA),　of a nutrient is the average amount of the nutrient (e.g., vitamin, mineral) that should be provided per head in a group of people if the needs of practically all members of the group are to be met. In the case of energy, the RDA for a group is identical with the estimate for the average requirement of the group. In the case of a nutrient, the RDA represents a judgement of the average requirement plus 20 per cent as a margin of safety. Besides incorporating safety margins, they also take account of the needs of growth in children; differences in requirements according to sex and age; differences in degree of physical activity and the additional requirements of pregnancy and lactation.

Individual requirements vary. Many individuals in a group eat less than the RDA for that group without any recognizable signs of deficiency — they may have small requirements. Some individuals with large requirements may not satisfy them with the RDA for their group. RDAs are intended to be large enough to reduce to a minimum the risk that some people may not get enough to meet their needs, but not so large that the amounts are impractical or uneconomic.

RDAs differ from country to country depending on the criteria used in assessing them (e.g., tissue saturation with vitamin C, or, sufficient to prevent scurvy). Those for the UK, USA and WHO/FAO are given in Tables 5–8, pages 224–230, and for the EC in Table 10, page 232.

For certain vitamins and minerals with no set RDAs, the USA have published estimated safe and adequate daily dietary intakes — *see* Table 9, page 231.

Use of RDAs

1. Assessment of dietary surveys — provide a yardstick against which the nutrients in the food eaten by different sections of the community or a whole country can be assessed.

2. Planning diets — for institutions such as hospitals, prisons, old-people's homes, boarding schools, armed services, special individual therapeutic diets.

3. Planning food supplies — for underdeveloped countries and famine relief.

4. Nutritional claims and labelling — for pre-packed foods. A statement of the percentage of the RDA of a nutrient present in a serving of the food allows assessment of the food's value as regards its contribution to the daily requirement for that nutrient and allows comparisons between foods.

5. Nutrient density — expresses the nutritional value of a food in terms of its nutrient and energy content each related to RDA.

---

recommended daily intake (RDI),   *see* recommended daily amount.

---

reduction,   the gain of electrons, e.g., ferric iron + 1 electron → ferrous iron. Embraces gain of hydrogen or loss of oxygen.

---

reference person,   a physically average person defined as healthy, aged 25, with a weight of 65kg (10¼ stone) for a man and 55kg (8½ stone) for a woman.

---

religious and ethnic groups,   some practice dietary restrictions, e.g., Hindus, Jews, Muslims, Orientals (*see* macrobiotics), Rastafarians, Seventh-day Adventists (*which see*) and Sikhs. *See* Table 16, page 295.

---

renal,   kidney.

---

renal threshold,   for a substance is the level in the blood above which the kidney's ability to re-absorb it is exceeded and the substance spills over into the urine. For glucose this level is normally 180mg/dl.

Table 5: Recommended daily amounts (RDAs) of food energy and some nutrients for population groups in the UK

Age range (years)	Occupational category	Energy MJ	kcal	Protein g	Thiamin mg	Riboflavin mg	Niacin. equivs. mg	Vitamin C mg	Vitamin A (RE) µg	Vitamin D µg	Calcium mg	Iron mg
BOYS												
under 1		2.2–4.1	530–980	13–24.5	0.3	0.4	5	20	450	7.5	600	6
1		5.0	1200	30	0.5	0.6	7	20	300	10	600	7
2		5.75	1400	35	0.6	0.7	8	20	300	10	600	7
3-4		6.5	1560	39	0.6	0.8	9	20	300	10	600	8
5-6		7.25	1740	43	0.7	0.9	10	20	300	*	600	10
7-8		8.25	1980	49	0.8	1.0	11	20	400	*	600	10
9-11		9.5	2280	57	0.9	1.2	14	25	575	*	700	12
12-14		11.0	2640	66	1.1	1.4	16	25	725	*	700	12
15-17		12.0	2880	72	1.2	1.7	19	30	750	*	600	12
GIRLS												
under 1		2.1–3.8	500–910	12.5–23	0.3	0.4	5	20	450	7.5	600	6
1		4.5	1100	27	0.4	0.6	7	20	300	10	600	7
2		5.5	1300	32	0.5	0.7	8	20	300	10	600	7
3-4		6.25	1500	37	0.6	0.8	9	20	300	10	600	8
5-6		7.0	1680	42	0.7	0.9	10	20	300	*	600	10
7-8		8.0	1900	47	0.8	1.0	11	20	400	*	600	10
9-11		8.5	2050	51	0.8	1.2	14	25	575	*	700	12***
12-14		9.0	2150	53	0.9	1.4	16	25	725	*	700	12***
15-17		9.0	2150	53	0.9	1.7	19	30	750	*	600	12***

Age range (years)	Occupational category	Energy MJ	Energy kcal	Protein g	Thiamin mg	Riboflavin mg	Niacin. equivs. mg	Vitamin C mg	Vitamin A (RE) µg	Vitamin D µg	Calcium mg	Iron mg
MEN												
18-34	Sedentary	10.5	2510	63	1.0	1.6	18	30	750	*	500	10
	Moderately active	12.0	2900	72	1.2	1.6	18	30	750	*	500	10
	Very active	14.0	3350	84	1.3	1.6	18	30	750	*	500	10
35-64	Sedentary	10.0	2400	60	1.0	1.6	18	30	750	*	500	10
	Moderately active	11.5	2750	69	1.1	1.6	18	30	750	*	500	10
	Very active	14.0	3350	84	1.3	1.6	18	30	750	*	500	10
65-74	Assuming a	10.0	2400	60	1.0	1.6	18	30	750	*	500	10
75+	sedentary life	9.0	2150	54	0.9	1.6	18	30	750	*	500	10
WOMEN												
18-54	Most occupations	9.0	2150	54	0.9	1.3	15	30	750	*	500	12***
	Very active	10.5	2500	62	1.0	1.3	15	30	750	*	500	12***
55-74	Assuming a	8.0	1900	47	0.8	1.3	15	30	750	*	500	10
75+	sedentary life	7.0	1680	42	0.7	1.3	15	30	750	*	500	10
Pregnancy		10.0	2400	60	1.0	1.6	18	60	750	10	1200**	13
Lactation		11.5	2750	69	1.1	1.8	21	60	1200	10	1200	15

RE, 1 retinol equivalent (3.33 IU) = 1µg retinol or 6µg beta-carotene or 12µg other biologically active carotenoids.

* Those not sufficiently exposed to sunlight and the house-bound should receive a supplement of 10µg daily.

** For the third trimester only.

*** This intake may not be sufficient for 10 per cent of girls and women with large menstrual losses.

Taken from the DHSS Report on *Health and Social Subjects* No. 15 (1981).

Table 6: Recommended daily amounts (RDAs)* of vitamins and minerals for which claims may be made in foods in UK

Vitamin or mineral	Calculated as	RDA
vitamin A	µg retinol or µg retinol equivalents	750µg
thiamin	mg thiamin	1.2mg
riboflavin	mg riboflavin	1.6mg
niacin	mg nicotinic acid *or* nicotinamide *or* niacin equivalents	18mg
folic acid	µg total folic acid (includes polyglutamates)	300µg
vitamin B_{12}	µg cobalamines	2µg
vitamin C	mg ascorbic acid *or* dehydroascorbic acid	30mg
vitamin D	µg ergocalciferol *or* cholecalciferol	2.5µg
calcium	mg calcium	500mg
iodine	µg iodine	140µg
iron	mg iron	12mg

*The RDAs chosen by MAFF are likely to meet the needs of most people (The Food Labelling Regulations, 1984).

Table 7: Recommended dietary intakes — FAO/WHO

Age range (years)	MJ	kcal	Protein g/kg	Vitamin A (RE) µg	Vitamin D µg	Thiamin mg	Riboflavin mg	Niacin. equivs. mg	Vitamin B_{12} µg	Folate µg	Vitamin C mg	Calcium g	Iron mg
CHILDREN													
0-1	0.47	110/kg	1-3	300	10	0.4	0.6	6.6	0.3	50	20	0.5-0.6	7
1-3	5.7	1360	1.19	240	10	0.5	0.7	8.6	0.9	100	20	0.4-0.5	7
4-6	7.6	1830	1.01	300	10	0.7	0.9	11.2	1.5	100	20	0.5-0.5	7
7-9	9.2	2190	0.88	390	2.5	0.8	1.2	13.9	1.5	100	20	0.4-0.5	7
BOYS													
10-12	10.9	2600	0.81	570	2.5	1.0	1.4	16.5	2.0	100	20	0.6-0.7	7
13-15	12.1	2900	0.72	720	2.5	1.2	1.7	20.4	2.0	200	30	0.6-0.7	12
16-19	13.0	3100	0.60	750	2.5	1.4	2.0	23.8	2.0	200	30	0.5-0.6	6
GIRLS													
10-12	9.8	2350	0.76	720	2.5	1.0	1.4	17.2	2.0	100	20	0.6-0.7	18
13-15	10.5	2500	0.63	720	2.5	1.0	1.4	17.2	2.0	200	30	0.6-0.7	18
16-19	9.6	2300	0.55	750	2.5	1.0	1.3	15.8	2.0	200	30	0.5-0.6	19
MEN	12.6	3000	0.57	750	2.5	1.3	1.8	21.1	2.0	200	30	0.4-0.5	6
WOMEN	9.2	2200	0.52	750	2.5	0.9	1.3	15.2	2.0	200	30	0.4-0.5	19
Pregnancy	+1.5	+350	+9	750	10	0.4/ 1000 kcal	0.55/ 1000 kcal	6.6/ 1000 kcal	3.0	400	50	1.0-1.2	19
Lactation	+2.3	+550	+17	1200	10	0.4/ 1000 kcal	0.55/ 1000 kcal	6.6/ 1000 kcal	2.5	300	50	1.0-1.2	19

RE = retinol equivalent.

Table 8: Recommended daily dietary allowances — USA*

Fat-soluble vitamins

Category Age (years) or condition	Weight[a] (kg)	Weight[a] (lb)	Height[a] (cm)	Height[a] (in)	Protein (g)	Vitamin A (μg RE)[b]	Vitamin D (μg)[c]	Vitamin E (mg α-TE)[d]	Vitamin K (μg)
Infants									
0.0-0.5	6	13	60	24	13	375	7.5	3	5
0.5-1.0	9	20	71	28	14	375	10	4	10
Children									
1-3	13	29	90	35	16	400	10	6	15
4-6	20	44	112	44	24	500	10	7	20
7-10	28	62	132	52	28	700	10	7	30
Males									
11-14	45	99	157	62	45	1,000	10	10	45
15-18	66	145	176	69	59	1,000	10	10	65
19-24	72	160	177	70	58	1,000	10	10	70
25-50	79	174	176	70	63	1,000	5	10	80
51+	77	170	173	68	63	1,000	5	10	80
Females									
11-14	46	101	157	62	46	800	10	8	45
15-18	55	120	163	64	44	800	10	8	55
19-24	58	128	164	65	46	800	10	8	60
25-50	63	138	163	64	50	800	5	8	65
51+	65	143	160	63	50	800	5	8	65
Pregnant						60	800	10	10	65
Lactating									
1st 6 months					65	1,300	10	12	65
2nd 6 months					62	1,200	10	11	65

Water-soluble vitamins

Category Age (years) or condition	Vitamin C (mg)	Thiamin (mg)	Riboflavin (mg)	Niacin $(mgNE)^e$	Vitamin B_6 (mg)	Folate (μg)	Vitamin B_{12} (μg)
Infants							
0.0-0.5	30	0.3	0.4	5	0.3	25	0.3
0.5-1.0	35	0.4	0.5	6	0.6	35	0.5
Children							
1-3	40	0.7	0.8	9	1.0	50	0.7
4-6	45	0.9	1.1	12	1.1	75	1.0
7-10	45	1.0	1.2	13	1.4	100	1.4
Males							
11-14	50	1.3	1.5	17	1.7	150	2.0
15-18	60	1.5	1.8	20	2.0	200	2.0
19-24	60	1.5	1.7	19	2.0	200	2.0
25-50	60	1.5	1.7	19	2.0	200	2.0
51+	60	1.2	1.4	15	2.0	200	2.0
Females							
11-14	50	1.1	1.3	15	1.4	150	2.0
15-18	60	1.1	1.3	15	1.5	180	2.0
19-24	60	1.1	1.3	15	1.6	180	2.0
25-50	60	1.1	1.3	15	1.6	180	2.0
51+	60	1.0	1.2	13	1.6	180	2.0
Pregnant	70	1.5	1.6	17	2.2	400	2.2
Lactating							
1st 6 months	95	1.6	1.8	20	2.1	280	2.6
2nd 6 months	90	1.6	1.7	20	2.1	260	2.6

Minerals

Category Age (years) or condition	Calcium (mg)	Phosphorus (mg)	Magnesium (mg)	Iron (mg)	Zinc (mg)	Iodine (μg)	Selenium (μg)
Infants							
0.0-0.5	400	300	40	6	5	40	10
0.5-1.0	600	500	60	10	5	50	15
Children							
1-3	800	800	80	10	10	70	20
4-6	800	800	120	10	10	90	20
7-10	800	800	170	10	10	120	30
Males							
11-14	1,200	1,200	270	12	15	150	40
15-18	1,200	1,200	400	12	15	150	50
19-24	1,200	1,200	350	10	15	150	70
25-50	800	800	350	10	15	150	70
51+	800	800	350	10	15	150	70
Females							
11-14	1,200	1,200	280	15	12	150	45
15-18	1.200	1,200	300	15	12	150	50
19-24	1,200	1,200	280	15	12	150	55
25-50	800	800	280	15	12	150	55
51+	800	800	280	10	12	150	55
Pregnant	1,200	1,200	320	30	15	175	65
Lactating							
1st 6 months	1,200	1,200	355	15	19	200	75
2nd 6 months	1,200	1,200	340	15	16	200	75

* Food and Nutrition Board, National Academy of Sciences–National Research Council Recommended Dietary Allowances, Revised 1989. Designed for the maintenance of good nutrition of practically all healthy people in the United States. The allowances, expressed as average daily intakes over time, are intended to provide for individual variations among most normal persons as they live in the United States under usual environmental stresses. Diets should be based on a variety of common foods in order to provide other nutrients for which human requirements have been less well defined.

[a] Weights and heights of Reference Adults are actual medians for the U.S. population of the designated age.

[b] Retinol equivalents. 1 retinol equivalent = 1 μg retinol or 6 μg β-carotene.

[c] As cholecalciferol. 10 μg cholecalciferol = 400 IU of vitamin D.

[d] α-Tocopherol equivalents. 1mg d-α tocopherol = 1α-TE.

[e] 1 NE (niacin equivalent) is equal to 1mg of niacin or 60mg of dietary tryptophan.

Table 9: Estimated safe and adequate daily dietary intakes of selected vitamins and minerals*

		Vitamins	
Category	Age (years)	Biotin (µg)	Pantothenic acid (mg)
Infants	0-0.5	10	2
	0.5-1	15	3
Children and	1-3	20	3
adolescents	4-6	25	3-4
	7-10	30	4-5
	11+	30-100	4-7
Adults		30-100	4-7

		Trace Elements[a]				
Category	Age (years)	Copper (mg)	Manganese (mg)	Fluoride (mg)	Chromium (µg)	Molybdenum (µg)
Infants	0-0.5	0.4-0.6	0.3-0.6	0.1-0.5	10-40	15-30
	0.5-1	0.6-0.7	0.6-1.0	0.2-1.0	20-60	20-40
Children and	1-3	0.7-1.0	1.0-1.5	0.5-1.5	20-80	25-50
adolescents	4-6	1.0-1.5	1.5-2.0	1.0-2.5	30-120	30-75
	7-10	1.0-2.0	2.0-3.0	1.5-2.5	50-200	50-150
	11+	1.5-2.5	2.0-5.0	1.5-2.5	50-200	75-250
Adults		1.5-3.0	2.0-5.0	1.5-4.0	50-200	75-250

* Because there is less information on which to base allowances, these figures are not given in the main table of RDA and are provided here in the form of ranges of recommended intakes.

[a] Since the toxic levels for many trace elements may be only several times usual intakes, the upper levels for the trace elements in this table should not be habitually exceeded.

Table 10: EC recommended daily allowances (RDAs) for use in nutrition labelling

vitamin A μg	800
vitamin D μg	5
vitamin E mg	10
vitamin C mg	60
thiamin mg	1.4
riboflavin mg	1.6
niacin mg	18
vitamin B_6 mg	2
folacin μg	200
vitamin B_{12} μg	1
biotin mg	0.15
pantothenic acid mg	6
calcium mg	800
phosphorus mg	800
iron mg	14
magnesium mg	300
zinc mg	15
iodine μg	150

renin, an enzyme released from the kidneys in response to a low blood-pressure or sodium deficiency. Carries out the first stage in the conversion of the protein, angiotensinogen, to the octapeptide, antiotensin II, that raises blood-pressure.

---

rennet, preparation of rennin used in cheese- and junket-making. Made from calf stomach, except for vegetable rennet that is derived from plants.

---

rennin, enzyme in gastric juices that coagulates milk protein (caseinogen) thereby preventing its rapid passage from the stomach before it can be partially digested by pepsin. Probably absent in the adult human being. A preparation of rennin, rennet, is used in cheese making.

---

resistant starch, the component of cooked gelatinized dietary starch that resists digestion by pancreatic amylase (starch digesting enzyme) *in vitro* and probably *in vivo*. It is probably derived from the smaller, amylose portion of starch that is coiled, unbranched and harder to digest than the amylopectin fraction. Measurements of dietary fibre by the Southgate method include resistant starch, but the Englyst method excludes it and measures only non-starch polysaccharides. Resistant starch appears to behave like readily fermentable, soluble dietary fibre in the large bowel, moderately raising faecal bulk mainly by increasing bacterial cell content. The resistant starch content of starchy foods is quite low, (e.g., white bread contains about 0.7 per cent), but it may make a substantial contribution to the apparent total dietary fibre content of staple starchy foods with a fairly low non-starch poly-saccharide content and so cannot be ignored in view of the large amounts of such foods consumed regularly, e.g., resistant starch forms as per cent of total dietary fibre (Southgate method): white bread, 30; freshly boiled potatoes, 33; boiled rice, 79.

respiration, tissue, refers to the consumption of oxygen and production of carbon dioxide by tissues oxidizing foodstuffs for the release of their energy.

respiratory chain, a chain of oxidative enzymes and carriers of hydrogen and electrons concerned with the tissue oxidation of foodstuffs for energy release. Intimately linked with phosphorylation and the production of ATP (oxidative phosphorylation). Components of the chain include derivatives of niacin (NAD), riboflavin (FMN and FAD), iron-containing enzymes (cytochromes) and coenzyme Q.

respiratory quotient (RQ), the ratio of volume of carbon dioxide produced to volume of oxygen used when a substance is oxidized. In man the RQ of carbohydrate is 1.0; protein, 0.8; and fat, 0.7.

restoration, replacement of nutrients lost in processing the food, e.g., addition of thiamin, niacin and iron to white flour to replace partially those lost in the milling of wheat when the bran and germ are discarded.

retinal or retinaldehyde, aldehyde form of retinol (vitamin A, *which see*) that takes part in forming visual pigment.

retinoic acid, a retinoid. Acid form of vitamin A (*which see*).

retinoids, generic term for compounds with vitamin A activity. Includes both naturally occurring ones (e.g., retinol, retinoic acid and retinaldehyde) and synthetic ones. Those other than retinol have some but not all of its vitamin A activity, e.g., retinoic acid does not form visual purple or support reproduction.

---

retinol, *see* vitamin A.

---

retinol equivalent (RE), the unit used to express vitamin A activity.
1 RE = 1μg retinol
or 6μg beta-carotene
or 12μg other biologically active carotenoids.

---

rheumatism, muscular, describes a number of conditions — including fibrositis and lumbago — characterized by pain and stiffness of soft tissues. Reduction of obesity may relieve symptoms.

---

riboflavin, water-soluble vitamin and member of the B complex. Also known as vitamin B_2.

Functions Combines with various proteins to form flavoprotein prosthetic groups, e.g., flavin mononucleotide (FMN), flavin adenine dinucleotide (FAD), that act as hydrogen carriers, essential components of the respiratory chain concerned with the tissue oxidation of food. Essential for growth and maintenance of healthy skin and eyes.

Deficiency surprisingly leads to no major illnesses but produces various non-life-threatening symptoms including fissures at corners of mouth (angular stomatitis) and on lips (cheilosis), tongue changes (glossitis), greasy accumulations (seborrhoea) around nose, eyes and mouth, eye-irritation and light sensitivity (photophobia).

Toxicity None reported, even in megadoses. High intakes cause harmless yellow coloration of the urine.

Requirement UK RDA for men is 1.6mg and women, 1.3mg. EC RDA is 1.6mg and US RDA is 1.7mg. Whether requirement is related to calorie intake, like that of thiamin, is disputed.

In the UK about 41 per cent of the daily intake is provided by milk and milk products, 19 per cent by meat and offal and 15 per cent by bread and cereals.

Stability Destroyed by light, the resulting compound, lumiflavin, causing destruction of vitamin C. Cooking losses are due to its light sensitivity and to leaching into cooking water. Stable to oxygen and acid, and to heat except in alkaline solution.

Distribution in foods (in mg per 100g): yeast extract, 6.0; dried brewer's yeast, 4.0; liver and kidney, 1.8–3.3; soya bean, 0.75 (other pulses, 0.1–0.3); Cheddar cheese and wheat bran, 0.5; eggs, 0.47; yogurt, 0.26; meat, 0.24–0.28; milk, 0.19; rice, white flour, fruits, potatoes, and vegetables, poor sources.

---

ribonuclease, enzyme concerned with digestion of ribonucleic acids (RNA). Present in pancreatic digestive juices.

---

ribonucleic acid (RNA), a nucleic acid (*which see*) directly involved in protein synthesis.

---

ribose, pentose monosaccharide. Found in RNA, ATP, NAD, NADP and flavoproteins. Synthesized by the body. Dietary ribose is little used as energy source.

---

ribosomes, small irregularly shaped particles found in all living cells. Made of protein and ribosomal RNA. A cluster of two or more ribosomes associated with a messenger RNA template is the active unit in protein synthesis in living cells. *See* nucleic acids.

---

rice, a cereal second only to wheat in global importance as a staple food for man. Over 90 per cent of its thiamin content is lost in husking and polishing the grain unless it is parboiled first to fix the B vitamins. Further loss of B vitamins occurs on discarding washing and cooking water in the home. These losses are responsible for the outbreaks of beriberi that occur mainly in Asia where it is the staple food. The protein content, though less in amount, is of higher quality than in any other cereal. Lysine is the limiting amino acid, followed by threonine. Brown rice contains 20–25 per cent more lysine than white. Very low sodium content and hence is the cereal used in the Kempner diet (*which see*).

Polished white (milled)/unpolished brown rice provides (per 100g): energy, 359/354 kcal; (g) protein, 7.0/7.4; fat, 0.6/2.2; (mg) sodium, 6/10; iron, 0.6/2.6; thiamin, 0.06/0.41; riboflavin, 0.03/0.09; niacin, 2.5/6.4.

rickets, a disorder of calcium and phosphorus metabolism generally brought about by vitamin D deficiency usually in infancy and early childhood. Leads to poorly formed, soft bones.

RNA, *see* ribonucleic acid.

roasting, *see* dry heat cooking.

roughage, *see* fibre, dietary.

royal jelly, a milky-white substance produced by worker bees as the sole nourishment of the queen bee. Taken in spoonful quantities, it is a good source of B vitamins, particularly pantothenic acid. Contains about 65 per cent water, 12–35 per cent protein and up to 5 per cent fat. Contains substances with the activity of hormones like insulin, oestrogen and testosterone.

rutin, a bioflavonoid (*which see*).

rye, grain. Makes a tasty, nutritious bread.
Flour (100 per cent extraction) provides (per 100g): energy, 335 kcal; (g) protein, 8.2; fat, 1.9; (mg) calcium, 32; iron, 2.7; thiamin, 0.4; riboflavin, 0.22; niacin, 2.6.

S

saccharin, and its sodium and calcium salts, are permitted intense sweeteners (*which see*). Four hundred times as sweet as the same weight of sucrose. Bitter aftertaste.

saccharose,   sucrose or table sugar.

SAD,   *see* seasonal affective disorder.

---

safflower-seed oil,   high in polyunsaturated fatty acids, linoleic acid accounting for 75 per cent of its total fatty acids and alpha-linolenic acid, 0.5 per cent.

---

sago,   obtained from the pith of the sago palm, *Metroxylon sagu*, widely grown in Far East. Pearl sago is a commercial product of almost pure starch being practically devoid of protein (0.2g per 100g), vitamins and minerals.

---

salicylates,   aspirin-like compounds occurring in foods such as berries and oranges, to which some people are sensitive. *See* food intolerance *and* Feingold diet.

---

saliva,   secreted into the oral cavity by three pairs of glands, it is 99.5 per cent water and very slightly acid (pH 6.8). Acts as lubricant for mastication and swallowing. Contains amylase, which begins the breakdown of starch to maltose, but which is quickly inactivated by stomach acid.

Salmonellae,   bacteria causing infective food poisoning called salmonellosis. After *Campylobacter*, it is the most common cause of food poisoning in the UK. Source of infection usually human or animal excreta. Multiply rapidly on foods at room temperature but not if refrigerated at 4°C. Easily killed by thorough cooking to at least 60°C. Foods commonly affected are meat, especially sliced cooked meat and meat pies, hen and duck eggs, synthetic cream, ice-cream, shellfish. Raw eggs and foods made from them, should be avoided. Vulnerable people such as the elderly, the sick, babies and toddlers and pregnant women should only eat eggs that have been thoroughly cooked until the yolks and whites are solid. Eggs should be stored in the refrigerator and cracked eggs should not be used.

Main symptoms, which appear in 12–36 hours and last one to eight days, are abdominal pain, diarrhoea, vomiting and usually fever. *See* food poisoning.

salt, common salt, sodium chloride. Used to enhance flavour and add savour to food (a condiment), to preserve food and as a cheap emulsifier in food processing.

1g (17 mmol) salt provides 0.4g (17 mmol) sodium.

Daily intake of salt in the UK is 7–12g. About 70 per cent is present in food, much of it added during manufacture and about 30 per cent added at table or in cooking. WHO suggest the required daily intake is 5g.

High salt intakes have been linked with prevalence of hypertension in communities. Hypertension is a risk factor for cardiovascular disease. Many, but not all, studies indicate that lowering salt intake (because it lowers sodium intake) may lower blood-pressure, at least in about 20 per cent of the population who are 'salt-sensitive', particularly those already hypertensive. Since some reduction in an intake of 12g will do no harm to anyone and may do good at least to some, the NACNE report recommends a general reduction in salt intake of 1g daily in the short term, and 3g in the long term, to be achieved both in the home and by food processors and that foods should be labelled with their salt content, particularly useful for those on restricted or low-salt diets.

A restricted salt diet provides about 6g salt or 2.3g sodium daily and can be achieved in the home by not adding salt at table, using the minimum of salt and baking powder in cooking, avoiding sodium-rich foods such as ham, bacon, sausages, kidney, tinned meat and fish, shellfish, smoked or salted fish, soya sauce, cheese and (unless specially made at home) sauces, biscuits, scones and cakes, restricting intake of other sodium-rich foods — (mg sodium/100g): bread, 560; salted butter, 870; salted margarine, 800 (the latter two both available commercially unsalted) — and having small helpings of moderate sodium foods — self-raising flour, 350; cream cheese, 300; fresh fish, 100; fresh meats, chicken and liver, 60–93; eggs, 140; certain vegetables (beetroot, carrots, celery, radish, spinach, turnips, watercress), 60–140; milk, 50; pulses, 30–60; dried fruits, 30; beers and wines, 4–28 — but unlimited intake of such low-sodium foods as vegetables (other than above), 2–13; fresh fruit (other than melon and grapes), 1–30; prunes, 12; rice, 6; dates, 5; sago, 3; plain flour, 2–4; nuts (unsalted), 1–20; lard, 2; vegetable oils and white sugar, 0.

Moderate and strict low-sodium diets provide 3.0 and 1.5g salt (1.2 and 0.6g sodium) respectively. They require medical supervision. The Kempner diet (*which see*) provides 0.1–0.15g sodium daily.

---

salts, compounds formed between acids and bases. Nutritionally, salt usually refers to common salt or sodium chloride.

sarcoma, a tumour arising in connective tissue.

---

satiety, hunger and appetite completely satisfied. *See* appetite.

---

saturates, food fats/oils rich in saturated fatty acids, e.g., butter. *See* fatty acids.

Schizophrenia, psychiatric disorder. Success of orthomolecular medicine's use of niacin for its treatment, is disputed.

---

sclerosis, abnormal hardening or fibrosis of a tissue, e.g., arteriosclerosis, disseminated sclerosis.

---

scurvy, vitamin C deficiency disease resulting from prolonged subsistence on diets practically devoid of fresh fruit and vegetables. Causes disturbances in structure of connective tissue leading to swollen, bleeding gums and haemorrhages into the skin, etc. Most at risk are infants and the elderly. Rebound scurvy is sometimes seen in those who abruptly cease megadosing with vitamin C and in the newborn of megadosing mothers.

---

scutellum, *see* flours, wheat.

---

seasonal affective disorder (SAD), a depression triggered by short hours of daylight in autumn and winter and relieved by longer days of spring and summer. Characterized by changes of mood, sleep and energy levels and by intense cravings for carbohydrate- (sugar-) rich food to bring about mood changes.

---

secretin, hormone that powerfully stimulates water and bicarbonate (alkali) secretion by the pancreas, thereby helping to neutralize the acid chyme entering the duodenum from the stomach; also stimulates secretion of pancreatic enzymes. Secreted by the upper intestinal mucosa in response to ingestion of food and resulting increase in stomach acid. Historically the first substance to be identified as a hormone.

selenium, an essential trace element. A 70kg man contains about 13mg. Intake is highly dependent on local soil content. British soils are quite low so UK intake is low compared with the USA, but high compared with Finland and New Zealand. The average UK diet provides about 60µg daily, or possibly only around 43µg now that UK wheat is being used for flour-making instead of Canadian, with up to half being derived from cereals and cereal products and 40 per cent from meat and fish.

Functions in the form of selenocysteine as an integral component of a glutathione peroxidase, an enzyme with an intracellular antioxidant role protecting membrane lipids and possibly protein and nucleic acids against oxidative damage by the superoxide free radical. Its role is synergistic with and overlaps that of vitamin E, but, whereas the vitamin prevents peroxidation, glutathione peroxidase destroys peroxidation products formed in spite of the vitamin.

Absorption takes place mainly in the duodenum. Probably about 80 per cent of the selenium in food and of organic selenium as selenomethionine in supplements is absorbed and a similar proportion of inorganic selenium in sodium selenite, provided it is added to food as selenite selenium on its own may be absorbed less efficiently.

Selenium in food and in selenomethionine appears to be better utilized, and stays in the body longer than selenium in sodium selenite. However, selenite is better when the diet is low in protein (i.e., in the amino acid methionine), because selenomethionine is then used to substitute for methionine in body protein synthesis instead of for glutathione peroxidase formation.

Excreted into the urine and as the garlicky smelling dimethyl selenide in the breath.

Deficiency has been reported in patients on intravenous feeding who suffered from muscle pains and tenderness. Keshan's disease of the heart muscle and Kaschin-Beck disease, which affects the joints of humans and animals, both prevalent in low-selenium areas of China, are prevented by selenium supplementation.

Low selenium levels have been shown to be associated with a higher incidence of cardiovascular disease and cancer and possibly alter the general immune and inflammatory response increasing the susceptibility to muscular disease.

Requirement USA RDA is 70µg.

Toxicity High. Usually due to industrial exposure. Prolonged dietary intake of 5mg daily in a high-selenium area of China caused selenium intoxication (selenosis) in half the population. First signs are garlicky breath, loss of hair and nails and, in the worst cases, lesions of the skin and nervous system. As little as 1mg of selenium as sodium selenite supplement has caused these symptoms.

Distribution in foods (MAFF 1978) (in μg per 100g): wholemeal flour, 53; bread-making flour, 42; mackerel, 35; pork, 14; Cheddar cheese and egg, 12; cod and polished rice, 10; soya bean flour, 9; white flour and almonds, 4; beef, 3; garlic, 2; human milk, 1–2, lamb and cow's milk, butter, cabbage and oranges, less than 1.

---

semolina,   is made from the inner endosperm of wheat grains and is used for making pasta and milk puddings.

Provides (per 100g): energy, 350 kcal; (g) protein, 10.7; carbohydrate, 77.5.

---

sequestrants,   additives (e.g., calcium, potassium and sodium gluconates) that prevent food deterioration by attaching to traces of oxidation-hastening minerals, such as iron and copper, present in the food.

---

serial numbers of additives,   may be used in the ingredients list on food labels as alternatives to their specific names. They often follow the category name that describes the function the additive performs in the food, e.g., colour, 107; preservative, E202; antioxidants, E300. An E prefix indicates that the number has already been approved for use in the EC.

E100	curcumin
E101	riboflavin (lactoflavin)
101(a)	riboflavin-5'-phosphate
E102	tartrazine
E104	quinoline yellow
E110	sunset yellow FCF (orange yellow S)
E120	cochineal (carmine of cochineal or carminic acid)
E122	carmoisine (azorubine)
E123	amaranth
E124	ponceau 4R (cochineal red A)
E127	erythrosine BS
128	red 2G
E131	patent blue V
E132	indigo carmine (indigotine)
133	brilliant blue FCF
E140	chlorophyll
E141	copper complexes of chlorophyll and chlorophyllins
E142	green S (acid brilliant green BS or lissamine green)
E150	caramel
E151	black PN (brilliant black BN)

E153	carbon black (vegetable carbon)
154	brown FK
155	brown HT (chocolate brown HT)
E160(a)	alpha-carotene, beta-carotene, gamma-carotene
E160(b)	annatto, bixin, norbixin
E160(d)	lycopene
E160(e)	beta-apo-8'-carotenal (C_{30})
E160(f)	ethyl ester of beta-apo-8'-carotenoic acid (C_{30})
E161(a)	flavoxanthin
E161(b)	lutein
E161(c)	cryptoxanthin
E161(d)	rubixanthin
E161(e)	violaxanthin
E161(f)	rhodoxanthin
E161(g)	canthaxanthin
E162	beetroot red (betanin)
E163	anthocyanins
E170	calcium carbonate
E171	titanium dioxide
E172	iron oxides, iron hydroxides
E173	aluminium
E174	silver
E175	gold
E180	pigment rubine (lithol rubine BK)
E200	sorbic acid
E201	sodium sorbate
E202	potassium sorbate
E203	calcium sorbate
E210	benzoic acid
E211	sodium benzoate
E212	potassium benzoate
E213	calcium benzoate
E214	ethyl 4-hydroxybenzoate (ethyl para-hydroxybenzoate)
E215	ethyl 4-hydroxybenzoate, sodium salt (sodium ethyl para-hydroxybenzoate)
E216	propyl 4-hydroxybenzoate (propyl para-hydroxybenzoate)
E217	propyl 4-hydroxybenzoate, sodium salt (sodium propyl para-hydroxybenzoate)
E218	methyl 4-hydroxybenzoate (methyl para-hydroxybenzoate)
E219	methyl 4-hydroxybenzoate, sodium salt (sodium methyl para-hydroxybenzoate)
E220	sulphur dioxide

E221	sodium sulphite
E222	sodium hydrogen sulphite (sodium bisulphite)
E223	sodium metabisulphite
E224	potassium metabisulphite
E226	calcium sulphite
E227	calcium hydrogen sulphite (calcium bisulphite)
E230	biphenyl (diphenyl)
E231	2-hydroxybiphenyl (orthophenylphenol)
E232	sodium biphenyl-2-yl oxide (sodium orthophenylphenate)
E233	2-(thiazol-4-yl) benzimidazole (thiabendazole)
234	nisin
E239	hexamine (hexamethylenetetramine)
E249	potassium nitrite
E250	sodium nitrite
E251	sodium nitrate
E252	potassium nitrate (saltpetre)
E260	acetic acid
E261	potassium acetate
E262	sodium hydrogen diacetate
262	sodium acetate
E263	calcium acetate
E270	lactic acid
E280	propionic acid
E281	sodium propionate
E282	calcium propionate
E283	potassium propionate
E290	carbon dioxide
296	DL-malic acid, L-malic acid
297	fumaric acid
E300	L-ascorbic acid
E301	sodium L-ascorbate
E302	calcium L-ascorbate
E304	6-0-palmitoyl-L-ascorbic acid (ascorbyl palmitate)
E306	extracts of natural origin rich in tocopherols
E307	synthetic alpha-tocopherol
E308	synthetic gamma-tocopherol
E309	synthetic delta-tocopherol
E310	propyl gallate
E311	octyl gallate
E312	dodecyl gallate
E320	butylated hydroxyanisole (BHA)
E321	butylated hydroxytoluene (BHT)

E322	lecithins
E325	sodium lactate
E326	potassium lactate
E327	calcium lactate
E330	citric acid
E331	sodium dihydrogen citrate (monosodium citrate), disodium citrate, trisodium citrate
E332	potassium dihydrogen citrate (monopotassium citrate), tripotassium citrate
E333	monocalcium citrate, dicalcium citrate, tricalcium citrate
E334	L-(+)-tartaric acid
E335	monosodium L-(+)-tartrate, disodium L-(+)-tartrate
E336	monopotassium L-(+)-tartrate (cream of tartar), dipotassium L-(+)-tartrate
E337	potassium sodium L-(+)-tartrate
E338	orthophosphoric acid (phosphoric acid)
E339	sodium dihydrogen orthophosphate, disodium hydrogen orthophosphate, trisodium orthophosphate
E340	potassium dihydrogen orthophosphate, dipotassium hydrogen orthophosphate, tripotassium orthophosphate
E341	calcium tetrahydrogen diorthophosphate, calcium hydrogen orthophosphate, tricalcium diorthophosphate
350	sodium malate, sodium hydrogen malate
351	potassium malate
352	calcium malate, calcium hydrogen malate
353	metatartaric acid
355	adipic acid
363	succinic acid
370	1,4-heptonolactone
375	nicotinic acid
380	triammonium citrate
381	ammonium ferric citrate
385	calcium disodium ethylenediamine-NNN'N' tetra-acetate (calcium disodium EDTA)
E400	alginic acid
E401	sodium alginate
E402	potassium alginate
E403	ammonium alginate
E404	calcium alginate
E405	propane-1,2-diol alginate (propylene glycol alginate)
E406	agar
E407	carrageenan

E410	locust-bean gum (carob gum)
E412	guar gum
E413	tragacanth
E414	gum arabic (acacia)
E415	xanthan gum
416	karaya gum
E420	sorbitol, sorbitol syrup
E421	mannitol
E422	glycerol
432	polyoxyethylene (20) sorbitan monolaurate (polysorbate 20)
433	polyoxyethylene (20) sorbitan mono-oleate (polysorbate 80)
434	polyoxyethylene (20) sorbitan monopalmitate (polysorbate 40)
435	polyoxyethylene (20) sorbitan monostearate (polysorbate 60)
436	polyoxyethylene (20) sorbitan tristearate (polysorbate 65)
E440(a)	pectin
E440(b)	amidated pectin
442	ammonium phosphatides
E450(a)	disodium dihydrogen diphosphate, trisodium diphosphate, tetrasodium diphosphate, tetrapotassium diphosphate
E450(b)	pentasodium triphosphate, pentapotassium triphosphate
E450(c)	sodium polyphosphates, potassium polyphosphates
E460	microcrystalline cellulose, alpha-cellulose (powdered cellulose)
E461	methylcellulose
E463	hydroxypropylcellulose
E464	hydroxypropylmethylcellulose
E465	ethylmethylcellulose
E466	carboxymethylcellulose, sodium salt (CMC)
E470	sodium, potassium and calcium salts of fatty acids
E471	mono- and di-glycerides of fatty acids
E472(a)	acetic acid esters of mono- and di-glycerides of fatty acids
E472(b)	lactic acid esters of mono- and di-glycerides of fatty acids (lactoglycerides)
E472(c)	citric acid esters of mono- and di-glycerides of fatty acids (citroglycerides)
E472(e)	mono- and diacetyltartaric acid esters of mono- and di-glycerides of fatty acids
E473	sucrose esters of fatty acids
E474	sucroglycerides
E475	polyglycerol esters of fatty acids
476	polyglycerol esters of polycondensed fatty acids of castor oil (polyglycerol polyricinoleate)

E477	propane-1, 2-diol esters of fatty acids
E481	sodium stearoyl-2-lactylate
E482	calcium stearoyl-2-lactylate
E483	stearyl tartrate
491	sorbitan monostearate
492	sorbitan tristearate
493	sorbitan monolaurate
494	sorbitan mono-oleate
495	sorbitan monopalmitate
500	sodium carbonate, sodium hydrogen carbonate (bicarbonate of soda), sodium sesquicarbonate
501	potassium carbonate, potassium hydrogen carbonate
503	ammonium carbonate, ammonium hydrogen carbonate
504	magnesium carbonate
507	hydrochloric acid
508	potassium chloride
509	calcium chloride
510	ammonium chloride
513	sulphuric acid
514	sodium sulphate
515	potassium sulphate
516	calcium sulphate
518	magnesium sulphate
524	sodium hydroxide
525	potassium hydroxide
526	calcium hydroxide
527	ammonium hydroxide
528	magnesium hydroxide
529	calcium oxide
530	magnesium oxide
535	sodium ferrocyanide (sodium hexacyanoferrate (II))
536	potassium ferrocyanide (potassium hexacyanoferrate (II))
540	dicalcium diphosphate
541	sodium aluminium phosphate
542	edible bone phosphate
544	calcium polyphosphates
545	ammonium polyphosphates
551	silicon dioxide (silica)
552	calcium silicate
553(a)	magnesium silicate synthetic, magnesium trisilicate
553(b)	talc (French chalk)
554	aluminium sodium silicate

556	aluminium calcium silicate
558	bentonite
559	kaolin
570	stearic acid
572	magnesium stearate
575	D-glucono-1, 5-lactone (glucono delta-lactone)
576	sodium gluconate
577	potassium gluconate
578	calcium gluconate
620	L-glutamic acid
621	sodium hydrogen L-glutamate (monosodium glutamate or MSG)
622	potassium hydrogen L-glutamate (monopotassium glutamate)
623	calcium dihydrogen di-L-glutamate (calcium glutamate)
627	guanosine 5'-(disodium phosphate) (sodium guanylate)
631	inosine 5'-(disodium phosphate) (sodium inosinate)
635	sodium 5'-ribonucleotide
636	maltol
637	ethyl maltol
900	dimethylpolysiloxane
901	beeswax
903	carnauba wax
904	shellac
905	mineral hydrocarbons
907	refined microcrystalline wax
920	L-cysteine hydrochloride
924	potassium bromate
925	chlorine
926	chlorine dioxide
927	azodicarbonamide (azoformamide)

Further numbers will be added from time to time.

---

serine, a non-essential amino acid containing a hydroxyl (-OH) group in its side chain.

---

serotonin, a neurotransmitter and vasoconstrictor derived from tryptophan. Present in many tissues especially the intestinal mucosa and blood platelets. Its release from the latter helps to stop bleeding by constricting the blood-vessel. In the brain it appears to play a role in sleep. Does not cross the blood–brain barrier. Present in some fruit and nuts.

serum,   fluid left when the blood has clotted.

---

sesame seeds,   seeds of the tropical and sub-tropical plant, *Sesamum indicum.* Small and varied in colour, cream, tan, brown and black. Hulled seeds are white and waxy looking. Used: for extraction of their oil to make a cream or tahini used in sauces, spreads, dips and salad dressings; and in sweetmeats, stews and to decorate bread, rolls and biscuits before baking.

Provide (per 100g): energy, 588 kcal; (g) protein, 26.4; fat, 54.8; (mg) thiamin, 0.72; riboflavin, 0.09; niacin, 12.6; sodium, 40; potassium, 407; calcium, 131; magnesium, 347; iron, 7.8.

Seventh-day Adventists,   many, but not all, are vegan or lacto-ovo-vegetarian. They neither smoke nor drink alcohol. Average life-expectancy is six years longer in men and three and a half in women than in the rest of the population. Apart from smoking- and drink-related diseases they die from the same diseases as the rest of the population but at a later age, indicating that diet plays a role in their longevity.

---

shellfish,   includes crustaceans, such as lobsters, crayfish, crabs, prawns and shrimps, and molluscs, such as oysters and mussels. All are rich in protein and low in fat with 40–50 per cent of their fatty acids omega 3 polyunsaturated and 9–27 per cent saturated. The total sterol content of molluscs is relatively high but (except for squid) most is not cholesterol, whereas in crustacea cholesterol is the main sterol. Oysters are the richest food source of zinc.

Some people are allergic to shellfish protein. Often gathered from seashores near output of sewage, so care must be taken that they are not infected by bacteria (e.g., *Salmonella*), particularly if eaten raw like oysters. Mussels occasionally cause neurotoxic poisoning. Paralytic shellfish poisoning (PSP) is caused by the concentration in shellfish of toxin from a particular kind of naturally occurring algae. Mussels and other filter feeders are usually associated with PSP rather than crabs and lobsters.

Crustacea (shelled, boiled crab, lobster, prawns and shrimps) provide (per 100g): energy, 107–127 kcal; (g) water, 62.5–72.5; protein, 20.1–23.8; fat, from 1.8 for prawns, up to 5.2 for crab; (mg) cholesterol, from 71 for crab up to 157 for shrimp; zinc, from 1.6 up to 5.5 for crab.

Molluscs (shelled, raw mussels/oysters) provide (per 100g): energy, 66/51 kcal; (g) water, 79.0/85.7; protein, 12.1/10.8; fat, 1.9/0.9; (mg) cholesterol, 36/47; zinc, 1.6/45.0.

siderosis, deposits of excess iron as haemosiderin in the liver, pancreas, skin and joints. If sufficient to disrupt cell and organ function, causes haemochromatosis.

---

silicon, may be an essential trace element for man and may be an integral component of cartilage and connective tissue.

---

single bonds, describes the saturated bonds between atoms found for example in saturated fatty acids.

---

singlet oxygen, a highly reactive form of oxygen consisting of single atoms instead of pairs of atoms (molecules) as in oxygen gas. Not a free radical, though has similar properties.

---

skatole, and indole are putrefaction products of tryptophan particularly responsible for the odour of faeces.

---

sinistrin, storage form of carbohydrate found in garlic. Like inulin, it is a polysaccharide of fructose.

---

sitostanol and sitosterol (beta), little absorbed plant sterols that inhibit absorption of cholesterol. Animal studies show sitostanol is more effective and even less absorbed than sitosterol and both may act by reducing the solubility of cholesterol during digestion.

---

slimming, *see* weight reduction.

---

slow reacting substances (SRS), *see* leukotrienes.

---

slow-reacting substances of anaphylaxis (SRS-A), leukotrienes (*which see*) generated as the result of an allergic reaction.

S-methylmethionine,   *see* vitamin U.

---

smoking,   is a risk factor for coronary heart disease and many cancers. Smokers have an increased risk of osteoporosis since their bone mass is lower than that of non-smokers.

Compared with non-smokers, smokers have the same energy intakes and are less physically active, but have less body fat and so weigh less. Nicotine and the act of puffing itself, cause an immediate transient increase in resting metabolic rate (i.e., the amount of energy required to keep the body 'ticking over' rises), which may explain these findings and also the weight gain after smoking cessation. A UK survey found smokers are less likely to eat breakfast, more likely to consume fried foods frequently and less likely to eat brown bread or fruit frequently. The effects of smoking on taste and appetite may be responsible for these differences. Smoking adversely affects preferences for vitamin C-rich foods. There is an inverse association between smoking and serum vitamin C levels that cannot be explained just by their lower dietary intake of the vitamin. It has been estimated that about 130mg of additional dietary vitamin C daily would be required to raise serum levels to those of non-smokers.

---

snacks,   *see* foods, snack.

SOD,   *see* superoxide dismutase enzymes.

---

sodium,   the major cation (positively charged ion) of extracellular body fluids like blood plasma. The body contains about 92g of this essential mineral of which just over half is in the body fluids, about 35g is in bone and less than 11g is in the cells. It is taken in mainly as common salt (sodium chloride), either naturally present in food or added during processing, including home cooking and at table. The average UK daily salt intake is estimated as up to 12g (corresponding to 4.7g sodium) of which 4g is added in home cooking and at table.

Functions associated with the anions chloride and bicarbonate in regulation of acid base balance. Important in body fluid balance, protecting against excessive water loss. Regulates nerve and muscle function.

Absorbed readily.

Excreted mainly via the urine, output reflecting dietary intake. Kidneys can efficiently conserve sodium, a regulatory mechanism controlled by the hormone aldosterone. Except in diarrhoea, only a little is lost in the faeces (most of that present in digestive juices being reabsorbed) and that lost in sweat is negligible unless there is active sweating when more may be lost in this way than in urine and, unless intake is increased, sodium depletion follows.

Deficiency not found as a result of dietary insufficiency, but may occur secondary to injury and dehydration due to illness or heat exhaustion. Water depletion usually accompanies sodium depletion so blood volume and blood-pressure are low, the mouth is dry and though thirst may be absent there is mental apathy and sometimes loss of appetite and vomiting. In pure sodium deficiency, muscular cramps occur. Sodium depletion without water depletion follows when thirst provoked by heavy sweating is quenched by water to which no salt has been added and is called water intoxication. In addition to anorexia, weakness and mental apathy, there may be muscular twitchings, convulsions and even coma.

Requirement No RDA set, but the US estimated safe minimum daily dietary intake of sodium is 500mg corresponding to 1.3g salt.

Toxicity Excess in the body causes body fluids to increase in volume possibly resulting in oedema. For effect on blood-pressure, and for restricted and low-sodium diets, *see* salt.

Distribution in foods (in g per 100g): salt, 39.3; Camembert and Danish blue cheeses, 1.41–1.42; Cheddar cheese, 0.61; wholemeal and white bread, 0.54; cottage cheese, 0.45; green pepper, 0.21; eggs and celery, 0.14; spinach (boiled), 0.12; carrots, 0.09; meat and chicken, 0.06–0.09; yogurt and cod, 0.08; milk, 0.05; spring greens (boiled) and winter cabbage, 0.01.

---

sodium chloride, *see* salt.

---

solanine, toxic substance in green potatoes that causes gastrointestinal upset.

---

sorbitol, a permitted bulk sweetener, 60 per cent as sweet as sucrose. A six carbon sugar alcohol. Less cariogenic than sucrose. That absorbed is converted to fructose, the rest being fermented in the colon sometimes causing abdominal pain.

---

sorghum, a variety of millet (*which see*).

soya bean, a pulse. Seed of *Glycine max*. Contains about twice as much protein and four to five times as much fat as other pulses. Though methionine is still the limiting amino acid, there is sufficient for its protein to be of good biological value and exceptional among plant proteins.

Contains anti-nutrients: trypsin inhibitors and lipoxygenase enzymes that are destroyed in cooking and indigestible oligosaccharide carbohydrates, leading to flatus because they are fermented in the colon.

Uses As the basis of many sauces and pastes in Chinese cooking; its oil for margarine, and the residual cake as protein source for cattle, pigs and poultry; as an ingredient in many processed human foods, e.g., sausages, biscuits, breakfast foods; for producing textured vegetable proteins and other meat substitutes; as an important constituent of some infant foods and milk substitutes.

---

soya-bean oil, rich in polyunsaturated fatty acids, linoleic acid forming 52 per cent of its total fatty acids and alpha-linolenic acid 7.4 per cent.

---

soya fibre, soya polysaccharide (a fibre-rich product) provides (g per 100g): total dietary fibre, 60 (of which crude fibre is 30); available carbohydrate, 15; crude protein, 12; water, 6; mineral, 5; fat, 2.

---

soya sauce, fermented from soya beans and wheat. Oriental food.

Dark, thick soya sauce provides (American values, per 100g): energy, 64 kcal; (g) water, 68; protein, 9; fat, 0; carbohydrates, 8; (mg) calcium, 19; iron, 2.7; sodium, 5,720; potassium, 358.

---

specific dynamic action, *see* thermogenic effect of food.

---

sphingomyelin, a phospholipid containing the amino alcohol, sphingosine. Found in large quantities in brain and nervous tissue.

---

sphingosine, an amino alcohol found in glycolipids and sphingomyelin.

---

spices, parts of plants, usually the seeds, fruit or flower parts, barks or roots, rich in volatile and essential oils and hydrocarbons that may have a weak action on the nervous system and many in large amounts have toxic actions, e.g., myristin in nutmeg, mace and dill. In large amounts nutmeg can cause stuper and delirium and in smaller amounts may cause vomiting and colic. Used to flavour foods.

---

spina bifida, *see* neural tube defect.

---

spirit, proof, at 51°F contains 57.07 per cent alcohol by volume or 48.24 per cent by weight. Whisky and gin sold in the UK is usually 70 per cent proof, i.e., alcoholic strength about 40 per cent by volume.

---

spirometer, apparatus used in indirect calorimetry. Measures oxygen consumption.

---

spirulina, a blue-green alga found in fresh water, alkaline lakes, S. maxima growing in Mexico, and S. platensis in Thailand and California. Used as food by natives and available dried as food supplements in UK. The dried alga in spoonful quantities is a nutritious food consisting of about 65 per cent high-quality protein with an NPU of 57 per cent, which means that about 37 per cent of the powder is usable protein. However, recently its protein value has been described as less than half of dairy products. It is rich in beta-carotene, and provides B vitamins particularly thiamin and ribo-flavin. It is unusual among plants in containing vitamin B_{12}-type compounds, though many of these appear not to have vitamin B_{12} activity. It is a source of minerals including calcium, magnesium, iron and potassium.

---

sprouting of seeds, practice of allowing bean or pea (legume) seeds to sprout before consumption. Increases vitamin content per gram dry weight, though not necessarily per gram wet weight (as eaten) since sprouts contain 90 per cent water and seeds 6–10 per cent. Changes given on wet weight basis and on dry weight basis in brackets assuming seeds contain 10 per cent water: vitamin C increased up to 10-fold (increased up to 90-fold); thiamin decreased to a quarter (increased up to 2½-fold); riboflavin unchanged (increased up to 9-fold); niacin and vitamin E varies with variety of bean or pea.

sprue, tropical,   a tropical, gastrointestinal disease. Cause unknown but associated with under- and mal-nutrition. Symptoms include sore mouth (glossitis, stomatitis) and fatty diarrhoea. Uncommon today.

---

stabilizers,   *see* emulsifiers; additives.

---

standidization,   of a nutrient refers to additions made to compensate for natural or seasonal variation in the level of the nutrient in the food.

Staphylococci,   bacteria (usually *S. aureus*) that cause toxic food poisoning by releasing toxins (exotoxins) into food before it is eaten. Source of infection is via the hands. Potentially pathogenic though widespread on the skin and present in the nose and throat of 30 per cent of healthy people.

  Staphylococci themselves are quite easily killed by heating food but their exotoxins require boiling for half an hour or heating to 60°C for an hour, to destroy them completely. More resistant to salt than most bacteria, so usually responsible for food poisoning by ham or bacon. Foods commonly affected are pies, meat (especially sliced), gravies, synthetic cream, ice-cream. Main symptoms, which appear in 2–6 hours and last 6–24 hours, are vomiting, abdominal pain and diarrhoea.

---

starch,   the storage form of carbohydrate in most plants. A mixture of two forms of glucose polysaccharide — amylose (usually 15–20 per cent), a coiled unbranched chain that is harder to digest than the other form, amylopectin (usually 80–85 per cent), a highly branched chain. Digested mainly by pancreatic amylase.

  The most important food source of carbohydrate. Found in cereals, potatoes, pulses and other vegetables. Pulses have a higher content of amylose than cereals and root vegetables, which may be partly responsible for the less acute and lower maximum blood sugar rise following their consumption (lower glycaemic index).

---

starch blockers,   inhibitors of the alpha-amylase enzyme that digests starch. Found in kidney beans. *See* weight reduction.

---

starch, resistant,   *see* resistant starch.

starvation, partial or complete absence of food. Occurs during famines; when disease of the digestive tract prevents absorption; when an infection or metabolic disturbance reduces appetite or interferes with metabolism of nutrients; in treatment for severe obesity; and in anorexia nervosa. There is wasting of tissues, loss of body fat with consequent loose skin, atrophy of skeletal muscles, heart, small intestine and all tissues, except the brain, and oedema. Up to 25 per cent of the weight of the healthy non-obese body can be lost without immediate danger to life. Some have survived losses up to 50 per cent. The normal person doing no exercise survives 45–50 days drawing on carbohydrate and fat reserves and tissue proteins for energy. Fatty acids are mobilized from adipose tissues and either used directly by tissues for energy production or, after partial oxidation in the liver, to ketone bodies. Red blood cells and the brain cannot use fatty acids for energy production and carbohydrate stores (about 200g) are quickly used up, so the glucose they need for energy is obtained by gluconeogenesis from fat and amino acids. However, unlike red cells, the brain can adapt to obtain up to 50 per cent of its energy needs from ketone bodies, which can cross the blood–brain barrier.

A supply of 100g carbohydrate daily prevents the onset of ketosis and reduces breakdown of tissue protein.

The intellect remains clear during starvation but personality disorders arise. Terminal stages are usually accompanied by diarrhoea. Treatment by refeeding is simple provided intestinal atrophy is not severe, when small frequent meals of bland foods are required.

---

statistical probability, is an evaluation of experimental results that indicates how likely they are to be real and not simply due to chance. A probability value (P) of 0.05, 0.01 or 0.001 means that only one time in 20, 100, or 1,000 respectively, would the result have been obtained by chance. The lower the P value, the more statistically significant the result, i.e., the more likely it is to be a true finding. The highest P value regarded as indicating results are statistically significant is 0.05. Statistical evaluation of results of nutritional and other studies using material subject to natural variation is particularly important.

---

steaming, cooking using steam from boiling water. Smaller loss of soluble nutrients by leaching than in boiling, because contact between food and water is less. However, longer cooking time is required, so loss of heat-sensitive nutrients such as thiamin and vitamin C, is greater.

stearic acid,   a saturated 18 carbon fatty acid widely distributed in nature. Forms up to 25 per cent of beef fatty acids.

---

stearidonic acid,   a polyunsaturated fatty acid of the omega 3 family with 18 carbons and four unsaturated bonds (C18.4 n-3). Found in blackcurrant seed oil. An intermediate in the body's conversion of alpha-linolenic acid to EPA.

---

steatorrhoea,   fatty stool. Occurs through failure in secretion of bile salts and/or pancreatic juices required for digestion and absorption of dietary fat or in the malabsorption syndrome. Low-fat diet helps. Milk fat usually best tolerated. *See also* triglycerides, medium-chain.

---

steely hair syndrome,   *see* Menke's disease.

---

sterculia gum,   *see* karaya gum.

---

sterilization,   total destruction of all bacteria and spores. Lengthens shelf-life indefinitely, but the prolonged heat treatment usually required spoils the food's texture, colour, flavour and nutritional value.

---

steroids,   lipids with a cylic nucleus of four linked rings. Include the sex and adrenal cortical hormones, cholesterol, bile acids, vitamins D_2 and D_3 and phytosterols (plant sterols).

---

sterols,   steroid alcohols. Include cholesterol found in all animal tissues, coprosterol in faeces and the phytosterols (plant sterols), e.g., beta-sitosterol, many of which inhibit absorption of cholesterol.

---

stigmasterol,   a phytosterol (plant sterol) that is poorly absorbed and interferes with absorption of cholesterol.

---

stomach,   cavity into which food passes from the oesophagus. Wall is muscular, lined by mucosal epithelium and contains secretory glands (the chief cells and parietal cells) that secrete gastric juices, which contain hydrochloric acid and enzymes that initiate protein digestion. The food is thoroughly mixed and passes as a thick fluid called chyme into the duodenum via the pylorus, which is controlled by a sphincter muscle.

---

stomatitis, inflammation of the mouth. Angular stomatitis, fissuring in corners of the mouth, is a symptom of riboflavin, vitamin B_6 or iron deficiency. In the UK, usually indicates ill-fitting dentures.

---

stones, kidney or urinary, occur in kidney and bladder, predominantly in hot climates as sweating contributes to concentrating the urine encouraging their formation. Most contain calcium, often as a mixture of its salts such as phosphates, carbonate or oxalate. About 10 per cent are composed only of uric acid, usually arising as a result of uricaemia and such patients are at risk of gout. About 25 per cent are pure calcium oxalate, and dietary restriction of oxalate-rich foods is sometimes advocated, as well as cessation of any megadosing with vitamin C, which is metabolized to oxalate. Stones of cystine do occur. High liquid consumption dilutes the urine and discourages their formation.

---

stout, *see* beer.

---

stroke, cerebrovascular disease. May result from a blood clot and/or atherosclerosis cutting off the blood supply to an area of the brain, or as a result of a haemorrhage in the brain.

The most important risk factor for stroke is probably high blood-pressure, which is increased by obesity and by high alcohol intake and may be influenced by the intake of common salt. For other risk factors, *see* cardiovascular disease.

---

substance P, a peptide found in the intestinal walls etc. A neurotransmitter.

---

substrate, the substance on which an enzyme acts. Or the medium on which micro-organisms are grown.

sucralose, intense sweetener made from sucrose in which three of its hydroxyl groups are substituted by chlorine. Cannot be hydrolysed by the body and so calorie free. Six hundred times the sweetness of sucrose. Not yet permitted for use in the EC.

---

sucrase, enzyme that splits sucrose into fructose and glucose. Present in intestinal digestive juices.

---

sucrose, commonly called 'sugar'. The chemical name for cane, beet or maple sugar. Also found naturally in many fruits (e.g., pineapple, 7.8g per 100g) and vegetables (e.g., in g per 100g: peas, 2.4; onions, 1.8; carrots, 1.4; potato, cauliflower and white cabbage, 0.1). A disaccharide of glucose and fructose, intermediate in sweetness between its constituent monosaccharides. Digested by the enzyme, sucrase, in the small intestine into glucose and fructose for absorption. Glucose is used for maintaining the blood sugar level, or as a source of immediate energy, while fructose is converted into glucose in the liver where it contributes to the blood glucose or is largely stored as glycogen. Though it provides a quickly digested source of energy, nutritionists advise reducing present annual levels of consumption of 38kg per head to 34kg within five years and 20kg within 15 years and propose that only half of this should come from snacks such as confectionery and soft drinks. This is mainly because it is cariogenic. Also its rapid digestion and absorption produces peaks and troughs in blood glucose levels and in levels of insulin secreted by the pancreas to enable the glucose component to be taken up by the tissues, and because the energy sucrose provides is unaccompanied by other nutrients or dietary fibre. High intakes may contribute to obesity by sparing the use of dietary and body fat as fuel. Raw brown sugars contain traces of other sugars, minerals, B vitamins and colouring matter and so taste better than refined white sugar, but, nutritionally, are little different.

White/demerara sugar provides (in mg per 100g): potassium, 2/89; sodium, trace/6; calcium, 2/53; magnesium, trace/15; iron, trace/0.9; thiamin, riboflavin and niacin, 0/trace.

---

sugar, common term for cane or beet, sugar which is sucrose, but strictly covers any sweet, soluble carbohydrate and includes glucose, fructose, lactose, etc.

sugar alcohols, include mannitol, sorbitol and xylitol. Chemically closely related to carbohydrates. Used as bulk sweeteners.

sugar, blood, *see* blood sugar.

sugar craving, *see* carbohydrate craving.

sugar, mushroom, trehalose.

sugar, non-reducing, sugars that do not have a free carbonyl group ($>C=0$) in their molecule, e.g., sucrose, trehalose.

sugar, reducing, sugars that have a free carbonyl group ($>C=0$) in their molecule, e.g., glucose, fructose, galactose, lactose, maltose, but not sucrose or trehalose.

sulphur, an element present in most proteins and therefore essential for life. Most of the body's sulphur is present as the amino acids methionine and cysteine. Two vitamins, thiamin and biotin and the amino acid taurine, contain sulphur. The body cannot make methionine or cysteine or the vitamins that all have to be supplied as such in the diet. Several enzyme systems, including those using acetyl CoA and glutathione, depend for their activity on free sulphydryl (-SH) groups. Sulphur in the urine is mostly present as sulphate, and inorganic sulphate is also present in the diet.

sunflower seeds, provide (per 100g): energy, 564 kcal; (g) protein, 21; carbohydrate, 18; fat, 49; fibre, 14; (mg) iron, 6.7; calcium, 116.4; zinc, 4.9; sodium, 3.5; potassium, 688; thiamin, 2.3; vitamin E, 52.9.

sunflower-seed oil, rich in polyunsaturated fatty acids, linoleic acid forming 52.0 per cent of its total fatty acids and alpha-linolenic acid, 0.3 per cent.

superoxide dismutase (SOD), enzymes containing either copper and zinc, or manganese, that catalyse the reduction of the charged superoxide free radical anion (O_2^-) to hydrogen peroxide, preventing it starting a free radical chain reaction. Measured in McCord-Fridovich units (which are not IU). $1\mu g$ elemental bovine erythrocyte SOD is equivalent to 16 McCord-Fridovich units.

---

superoxide radical anion, a highly reactive form of oxygen — an electrically charged free radical (O_2^-), substrate for the SOD enzymes. *See* free radicals.

---

supplementary value, or complementary value of proteins, is their ability to make good each other's limiting amino acid. Particularly important in vegetarian diets as most plant proteins have a markedly limiting amino acid. Cereals are low in lysine but contain adequate sulphur amino acids such as methionine and hence complement pulses, which are low in methionine but contain adequate lysine. Many traditional vegetable food combinations contain the complementary proteins of cereals and pulses, e.g., baked beans on toast, tortillas and beans, bread and peanut butter.

---

supplements, food, *see* food supplements.

---

sustained release, describes a food which because it is slowly digested is absorbed over a long time, e.g., lente carbohydrate foods.

Food supplements so described are formulated to release their nutrients over several hours, simulating the slow digestion of a food.

---

sweetbreads, pancreas or thymus. Offal. Lamb's pancreas provides (per 100g): energy, 131 kcal; (g) water, 75.5; protein, 15.3; fat, 7.8; (mg) iron, 1.7; zinc, 1.9; thiamin, 0.03; riboflavin, 0.25; niacin, 7.0; vitamin C, 13; (μg) vitamin B_{12}, 6.

---

sweeteners, bulk, provide bulk, sweetness and calories. Those permitted for use in the UK are hydrogenated glucose syrups, isomalt, mannitol, xylitol, sorbitol and sorbitol syrup. Suitable for use in certain types of confectionery and baked goods as a replacement for sugar, and as sweetening in foods suitable for non-obese diabetics. Appear to be considerably less cariogenic than sugars.

---

sweeteners, intense, provide sweetness without bulk or significant calories. Those permitted for use in the UK and EC are acesulfame potassium, aspartame, saccharin and its sodium and calcium salts and neohesperidin — all synthetic or 'artificial' sweeteners, and thaumatin, a natural protein. Particularly suitable for use in drinks. Non-cariogenic. Each sweetener is to be restricted for use in particular food categories and only up to prescribed maximum levels.

---

sweeteners, permitted, food sweeteners other than carbohydrates permitted for use in the UK. Comprise bulk and intense sweeteners. *See also* additives.

---

synapse (synapsis), the point of communication between two adjacent neurons or nerve cells.

---

syndrome, group of symptoms and/or signs that, when they occur together, are typical of a particular disease, e.g., pre-menstrual syndrome.

---

synergists, enhance the effect of each other so that the combined effect is greater than that of either on its own. The antioxidant effects of vitamin E and selenium in the body are synergistic.

---

syrups, highly concentrated solutions of sugar that are unable to crystallize out owing to presence of small quantities of other substances. Include molasses, treacles and golden syrups, by-products in the manufacture of crystalline cane sugar. Consist of carbohydrate and 20–30 per cent water and, in molasses and treacle, significant amounts of calcium and iron that are partly derived from the vessels used in their processing. Molasses has a laxative effect.

Maple syrup is a natural syrup obtained from the sap of maple trees in Canada and New England. It is 80 per cent carbohydrate and 20 per cent water.

T

tannins, simple or compound polyphenols found in plants, e.g., tea. Astringent to the mouth. Weak protein precipitants used to clarify beer and wines. Anti-nutrients, e.g., inhibit iron absorption.

tapeworms, of pig (*Taenia solium*) and beef (*T. saginata*) form cysts in their mucsles. If infected meat is eaten undercooked, the cysts develop into adult worms in the human gut. They produce eggs in segments passed in the faeces. Normally these are eaten by pigs or cattle, but man may infect himself. The eggs develop in the gut into larvae that penetrate into the muscles or other tissues completing the worm's life cycle in the animals, but causing cysticercosis in man.

tapioca, commercially available in the UK as a preparation of cassava from which most of the protein has been removed leaving almost pure starch.
  Provides (per 100g): energy, 359 kcal; (g) protein, 0.4; carbohydrate, 95.0.

taramasalata, spread or dip made from fish roe. Provides (per 100g): energy, 446 kcal; (g) protein, 3.2; carbohydrate, 4.1; fat, 46.4; (mg) sodium, 650; copper, 5.8; (μg) vitamin B_{12}, 2.9.

taste, sensations excited in the taste-buds in the tongue by contact with saltiness, sweetness, bitterness or acidity. What is commonly called the 'taste of a food' is actually the *perception* of its flavour — a combination of perception of its taste by the tongue and its odour by cells in the nasal cavity.

taurine, an unusual amino acid in that its amino and acid groups are on adjacent and not the same carbon atom and the acid group is a sulphur one. Occurs free in cells of most mammals, particularly in heart muscle and nerve tissue, and is not incorporated into proteins. Absent from plants. Dietary requirement in man unknown, but essential in the diet of some animals like cats that cannot synthesize it, making them obligate carnivores. Man synthesizes it from methionine and cysteine. Levels are lower in vegans who consume none preformed in their diet. It is now added to most infant formulas.

Conjugates (joins) with bile acids in the liver for excretion into the bile. Damps down or balances nerve cell excitation. Present in eye retina and is essential for sight. An antiarrhythmic agent and may also be an anti-atherogenic and antihypertensive agent.

tea, a beverage produced by infusing the fermented and dried leaves of certain shrubs grown in India and elsewhere. Accounted for 65 per cent of the liquid intake, other than water, in the UK though consumption dropped 20 per cent between 1980 and 1989. Itself energy free, but six cups daily with whole milk and sugar could provide 239 kcal, which is 7–10 per cent of the average daily energy requirement.

A 170ml cup contains an average of 56mg caffeine and small amounts of the other methylxanthines, theophylline (1mg) and theobromine (2–2.5mg). In moderate amounts it is consequently a mild stimulant to the nervous system and mild diuretic.

Contains tannins related to bioflavonoids, which may have beneficial properties but also appear to cause indigestion in some people and inhibit non-haem iron absorption. A rich source of oxalates.

Important dietary source of manganese in the UK and also provides fluoride and some zinc, magnesium and potassium.

teeth, structures used for mastication. Subject to dental caries and periodontal disease. Their absence or replacement by poorly fitting dentures can contribute to malnutrition in the elderly.

teratogen, that which disrupts fetal growth and causes malformation in the young, e.g., megadoses of vitamin A; probably folic acid deficiency at or shortly after conception; alcohol.

tetany, a twitching, particularly of the face, hands and feet due to nerves being over-susceptible to stimuli as a result of a deficiency of calcium ions. Sometimes occurs in severe rickets and in malabsorption syndrome.

textured vegetable proteins (TVP), *see* extrusion cooking and meat substitutes.

thaumatin, a permitted intense sweetener. A protein derived from the fruit of the West African plant, *Thaumatococcus daniellii*. Perception of its sweetness is delayed and lasts much longer than the sweet taste of sucrose. Suitable for chewing-gum. At levels below which it sweetens, it is a flavour enhancer. So little is required that its calorie contribution is negligible. *See* intense sweeteners.

---

theobromine, a methylxanthine (*which see*).

---

theophylline, a methylxanthine (*which see*).

---

thermic effect, *see* thermogenic effect of food.

---

thermogenesis, the release of energy as heat. Necessary in warm-blooded animals to maintain body temperature. Normal metabolism generates much of this heat but the body also generates extra heat by 'shivering thermogenesis' and by 'dietary induced thermogenesis' (not the same as the thermogenic effect of food), which is due to stimulation of heat generation in specialized brown fat (*which see*) stores and may be a means of 'burning off excess calories'.

---

thermogenic effect of food, thermogenesis due to metabolism incurred in handling food within the body. Varies with the type of food eaten. Also known as specific dynamic action or thermic effect of food.

---

thiamin, water-soluble vitamin and member of the B complex. Also known as vitamin B_1, and formerly as thiamine and aneurine.

Functions biochemically as the coenzyme thiamin pyrophosphate, which takes part in the release of energy from carbohydrates.

Essential for growth, normal appetite, digestion and healthy nervous system.

Deficiency leads to beriberi. Carbohydrate metabolism is impaired. Early symptoms include mental changes resembling anxiety states with irritability, easy exhaustion and anorexia. Particularly at risk are those on high alcohol intakes or on carbohydrate-rich/low-thiamin diets, e.g., raw polished rice, unfortified white bread, sugars and jams.

Toxicity None, even in megadoses, possibly because only 5mg is the maximum quantity of an oral dose that can be absorbed.

Requirement related to carbohydrate intake or, for practical purposes, to calorie intake at 0.4mg thiamin per 1,000 kcal. Hence UK RDA for moderately active men is 1.2mg and women, 0.9mg. The EC RDA is 1.4mg; US RDA is 1.5mg.

The UK daily supply comes from (per cent): cereals, 48 (bread and flour, 29); vegetables, 10; meat, fish and eggs, 16; dairy products, 11.

Stability Only vitamin C among the vitamins is more unstable. Destroyed by heat in alkaline conditions (e.g., baking powder/soda) and by sulphite preservatives. Lost by leaching into cooking water and in drips from thawing frozen foods unless those liquids are used. Vegetables may lose 25–40 per cent in cooking, meat, 30–50 per cent in roasting or stewing, bread, 15–30 per cent in baking, and a mixed diet, about 25 per cent in cooking. Some loss in food processing and storage, except if deep-frozen. Destroyed by thiaminase enzyme in raw fish.

Distribution in foods (in mg per 100g): brewer's yeast, 15.6; yeast extract, 3.1; pork, 0.89; wheat bran, 0.65; white/brown rice, 0.06/0.41; pulses, 0.2–0.6; liver, 0.21–0.36; fresh fruit and vegetables, 0.02–0.20; egg and mackerel, 0.09; cod, 0.08; beef, 0.07; milk, 0.04; butter and oils, 0.

In the UK and many other countries, white flour and bread are required to be enriched with thiamin.

---

thickeners, additives added to foods to give them uniform texture and the desired consistency, e.g., pectins, vegetable gums and gelatins in ice-cream.

---

thirst, a physiological regulatory mechanism of the body's water balance. Sensation probably produced by a rise in the sodium concentration of blood. Explains why dehydration due to excessive sweating may not cause thirst, as water loss is accompanied by sodium (salt) loss.

---

threonine, an essential amino acid containing a hydroxyl group (-OH) in its side chain. Seldom, if ever, limiting in foods.

---

thrombin, enzyme in blood that converts fibrinogen to fibrin for clot formation.

thrombosis,   blockage of a blood-vessel by a blood clot or thrombus.

---

thromboxanes (TXA),   prostanoids produced by the action of cyclo-oxygenase enzyme on 20 carbon polyunsaturated fatty acids, mainly in blood platelets. *See* prostanoids.

---

thrombus,   clot of blood within a blood-vessel.

---

thymine,   a pyrimidine found in DNA (*see* nucleic acids).

---

thyroid hormones,   synthesized by the thyroid gland from tyrosine and iodine. Stimulate oxidative reactions and generally regulate metabolic rates in the body. *See* iodide/iodine.

---

thyrotoxicosis,   over-production of thyroid hormone due to too high a dietary intake of iodine or over-production of the thyroid-stimulating hormone, thyrotropin.

---

thyroxine,   a thyroid hormone.

---

timnodonic acid,   *see* eicosapentaenoic acid.

---

tin,   may be an essential element for man. A 70kg man contains about 17mg. Less than 1mg daily appears to be consumed as a constituent of food itself. Much more may be added by the use of tin cans and tin foil in packaging, presenting a potential hazard to man. However, most inorganic tin is excreted in the faeces and, apart from rare reports of gastrointestinal symptoms, there is no good evidence of human toxicity from this source. The toxic dose of tin is 4.8–7.1mg per kg of body weight.

---

toasting,   *see* dry heat cooking.

tocopherol, *see* vitamin E.

---

tocotrienol, possesses some vitamin E activity and occurs with it in nature.

---

tofu, soya-bean curd. Oriental product. Provides (g per 100g): protein, 5–8; fat, 3–4; carbohydrate, 2–4; water, 84–90.

---

tongue, a mobile, muscular organ in the mouth concerned with speech, mastication, swallowing and taste perception. Its disorders such as glossitis may be symptoms of nutritional deficiencies.

As an offal meat, lamb tongue provides (per 100g): energy, 193 kcal; (g) protein, 15.2; fat, 14.6; (mg) thiamin, 0.17; riboflavin, 0.49; niacin, 8.2; vitamin B_6, 0.17; vitamin C, 7; sodium, 420; iron, 2.3; copper, 0.46; zinc, 2.7.

---

toxin, a poison produced by bacteria and fungi.

TPN, total parenteral nutrition. *See* nutrition, parenteral.

---

trace elements or minerals, essential minerals required in less than 100mg amounts daily.

---

tragacanth, dried gummy exudate from the shrub, *Astragalus gummifer.* A mixed polysaccharide gum (dietary fibre), used as disintegrating agent and binder in tablets and as emulsifying agent in foods and sweets.

***trans* fatty acids,** *see* fatty acids, *trans.*

---

transamination, is the transfer of amino groups from amino acids to particular compounds (alpha-keto acids) for the formation of other amino acids. A reversible process catalysed by transaminases.

transferrin, a plasma globulin protein that transports iron and other minerals such as chromium, manganese and zinc in the blood.

---

transit time, time taken for food to pass through the gut. Decreased by dietary fibres such as coarse wheat bran and by ispaghula and psyllium. Provided there is sufficient time for food to be properly digested and absorbed, the quicker it passes through the gut the less time there is for toxic substances (e.g., carcinogens) to be in contact with the gut walls.

---

trehalase, enzyme in small intestine that splits trehalose to glucose molecules.

---

trehalose, mushroom sugar. Found in fungi and yeasts. Disaccharide of glucose in which the glucose molecules are unusually joined. Digested by trehalase.

---

trends in food consumption in the UK 1980–89, include:
Liquid milk — a decline in overall purchases, but a continuing increase in sales of low-fat milk, which, in 1989, accounted for over 30 per cent of total milk sales from negligible in 1980.
Butter and margarine consumption declined and purchases of low-fat spreads increased. Butter consumption fell by over 50 per cent in the decade. Energy from fat fell from 42.6 to 41.9 per cent of total food energy and the polyunsaturated/saturated fatty acid (P/S) ratio rose from 0.24 to 0.37.
Fruit and vegetables Purchases of fresh and frozen produce increased and that of tinned and dried, declined. Fruit juice sales increased and, by 1989, accounted for 20 per cent of all expenditure on fruit.
Egg purchases fell by 40 per cent over the decade.
Tea, coffee and sugar Coffee consumption declined but not as markedly as tea, which dropped by 20 per cent over the decade. Sugar intake also fell.
Meat and poultry Consumption combined fairly steady with poultry tending to rise at the expense of meat. Purchase of meat products (usually high in fat) rose steadily. Fish and fish product consumption increased.

---

triacylglycerols, the more correct chemical name for triglycerides (*which see*).

trial, double blind, method of investigation in which half the subjects are given the test substance (drug, vitamin, etc.) and the rest receive a placebo (dummy pill) that looks and tastes the same as the test substance. Neither the subjects nor the investigators know who is receiving the test substance until the trial is completed.

---

triglycerides, lipids that are esters of the alcohol, glycerol, with three fatty acids. When solid at room temperature they are known chemically as 'fats' (butter is mostly 'fat') and when liquid as 'oils' (e.g., olive oil, cod-liver oil). Triglycerides containing predominantly saturated fatty acids are usually fats, while those with predominantly unsaturated/polyunsaturated fatty acids are usually oils. Glycerol forms about 5 to 10 per cent by weight of most triglycerides.

Commercially, oils are turned into fats or 'hardened' by (partially) saturating their fatty acids by hydrogenation, as in the production of many margarines.

High levels of triglycerides in the blood are a risk factor for coronary heart disease. High intakes of fish oils, rich in omega 3 polyunsaturated fatty acids, lowr triglyceride levels. *See* cardiovascular disease.

---

triglycerides, medium-chain (MCT), are derived from coconut oil and contain fatty acids of medium-chain length (eight to ten carbons). Used in dietetics as a valuable source of energy for patients with steatorrhoea since they are digested more easily than other triglycerides and after absorption their fatty acids go direct to the liver in the hepatic-portal vein.

---

trypsin, enzyme concerned with protein digestion. Present in pancreatic digestive juices.

---

tryptophan, an essential amino acid. Absent in gelatin and one of the limiting amino acids in the maize protein, zein.

Spares niacin into which some is converted in the body (60mg tryptophan yielding 1mg niacin). Vitamin B_6 is required as coenzyme in the conversion. Helps account for the prevalence of the niacin-deficiency disease, pellagra, in poor communities dependent on maize.

Its putrefaction by intestinal bacteria produces indole and skatole, which are particularly responsible for the odour of faeces.

Precursor of serotonin. *See also* eosinophilia myalgia syndrome.

tuberculosis, bovine, caused by the bacterium *Mycobacterium bovis* that readily infects cattle and is excreted in milk. Ingested by man, it causes enlarged neck lymph nodes and may lead to tuberculosis in any organ and especially bones and joints. Widespread in UK 50 years ago before pasteurization of milk. Disease now almost eradicated in UK cattle. Possible that infected badgers may transmit disease to cattle.

tubers, starchy roots rich in energy but mostly poor in protein, minerals and vitamins. Easily cultivated even in poor soils. Include potatoes, cassava, yams, sweet potatoes and taro.

Provide (per 100g): energy, 50–125 kcal; (g) protein, 1.5–2.5; carbohydrate, 10–25; fat, 0; water, 65–85; (mg) calcium, 10–30; iron, 0.5–2.0; carotene, 0 (except sweet potatoes); vitamin C, 5–25; thiamin, 0.05–0.10; riboflavin, 0.03–0.08; nicotinic acid, 0.5–1.5.

tumour, or neoplasm describes cells in a tissue or organ that proliferate without the normal controls on growth. Malignant tumours (cancer) can spread to adjacent tissues by direct invasion or via the blood or lymph causing a secondary tumour or metastasis to form. Benign tumours are limited to the organ of origin and usually only cause problems of pressure on other organs. Some benign tumours tend to become malignant.

turkey, poultry meat. Usually eaten with the skin, which contains less fat than most poultry skin.

The meat/meat plus skin provide (per 100g): energy, 107/145 kcal; (g) water, 75.5/72.0; protein, 21.9/20.6; fat, 2.2/6.9; (mg) iron, 0.8/0.8; zinc, 1.7/1.6.

tyramine, a toxic amine derived from tyrosine. Present in certain foods (e.g., chocolate, cheese, fish, beans) and in some people is the cause of such foods producing a food-intolerance reaction because it releases histamine from mast cells leading to symptoms like those of an allergic reaction. Also raises blood-pressure by releasing catecholamines, particularly in the presence of drugs that inhibit monoamine oxidase, an enzyme which oxidizes tyramine and catecholamines, when it can result in hypertension, sometimes with fatal results.

tyrosinase, a phenolase enzyme that acts on tyrosine. *See* phenolase.

tyrosine, a non-essential amino acid that can spare essential phenyl-alanine to some extent. Contains an aromatic ring and a hydroxyl (-OH) group in its side chain. Precursor of dopa and hence of the catecholamines and of melanin, the brown pigment in the skin increased by exposure to the sun. Precursor too of the thyroid hormone, thyroxine.

U

ubiquinone, *see* coenzyme Q.

UHT, *see* ultra heat treated.

UK, United Kingdom of Great Britain and Northern Ireland.

ulcer, apthous or mouth, small, superficial, painful ulcers occurring in the mouth, usually in crops. Heal spontaneously. Reason unknown, or may be first sign of coeliac disease, or a reaction to foods/additives.

ulcer, duodenal, peptic ulcer in the duodenum. Three times as common in men as in women.

ulcer, gastric, peptic ulcer in the stomach.

ulcer, peptic, one of commonest diseases in civilized communities. Widely varied incidence, e.g., 6.5 per cent of adult men likely to be affected in London, 15.1 per cent in Aberdeen, Assam and India and 2.5 per cent in the USA.

Describes an ulcer occurring anywhere in the digestive tract exposed to acid gastric juices. Commonest are gastric and duodenal. Probably caused by failure of mucosa to withstand the digestive action of pepsin and hydrochloric acid, possibly due to reduced secretion of protective mucin.

---

ulcerative colitis, a common cause of chronic diarrhoea. Blood and mucus in the stool due to an inflammatory reaction and ulcers in the mucosa of the large bowel, usually the rectum. Cause unknown.

---

ultra heat treated (UHT), sterilization of milk by heating at higher than normal temperatures and for a shorter period of time than in traditional sterilization. Reduces the usual loss of vitamins C, B_{12}, B_6, folate and thiamin. Vitamin profile comparable to that of pasteurized milk but unlike the latter it can be stored for many months. Some alteration of flavour.

---

ultraviolet irradiation, is used to sterilize food surfaces and to convert ergosterol in yeast and fungi and 7-dehydrocholesterol in the skin to vitamins D_2 and D_3 respectively.

---

undernutrition, a general deficiency of food energy, protein and all nutrients.

---

unstirred layer, refers to the aqueous layer next to the intestinal mucosa that contains mucus, etc., and which remains relatively undisturbed by the movement of the main intestinal contents. Digested nutrients must pass through this layer before absorption. Alterations in the thickness of this layer by soluble dietary fibres (e.g., guar gum) have been suggested as the mechanism for their property of slowing down absorption of glucose.

---

uracil, a pyrimidine found in RNA (*see* nucleic acids).

---

uraemia, syndrome produced by kidney failure. Urea and other nitrogenous substances are retained in the blood. When severe, characterized by nausea, vomiting, headache, hiccoughs, weakness, dimness of vision, convulsions and coma.

urea, major nitrogen excretory compound in man and most mammals. Synthesized in the liver via the urea cycle, released into the blood and cleared by the kidney. It constitutes 80–90 per cent of the nitrogen excreted by man on a Western diet.

---

urea cycle, also known after its discoverer as the Krebs urea cycle, is the sequence of events that leads to the formation of urea from ammonia derived from waste nitrogen, mainly from amino acids. Components of the cycle include ornithine, citrulline and arginine. The urea is excreted in the urine.

---

ureotelic, describes animals that excrete waste amino acid nitrogen as urea, e.g., man and other mammals.

---

uric acid, end-product of purine metabolism in man and the higher apes, because, unlike other mammals, they do not possess the enzyme uricase that converts it to allantoin for excretion. Urate crystals in the joints cause gout.
   End-product of all nitrogen metabolism in birds and reptiles.

---

uricase, *see* uric acid.

---

uricotelic, describes animals that excrete waste amino acid nitrogen as uric acid, e.g., reptiles and birds.

---

urine, amber-coloured liquid produced by the kidneys. Main route of excretion from the body of water (about 1,500ml daily), soluble waste products of metabolism and excess water-soluble nutrients. The presence, absence or abnormal levels of constituents are used in the diagnosis of disease.

---

uronates, acid form of sugars. Vegetable dietary fibres are rich sources.

USA, United States of America.

V

valine, a branched chain essential amino acid. Seldom if ever limiting in foods.

vanadium, may be an essential trace element for man. A 70kg man contains about 20mg. Average daily intake is 13µg. Its biological role has yet to be identified. The chief dietary sources in descending order of importance are cereals, fruit and preserves, meat.

veal, calf meat. Provides (per 100g): energy, 109 kcal; (g) water, 74.9; protein, 21.1; fat, 2.7; (mg) iron, 1.2; thiamin, 0.10; riboflavin, 0.25; niacin, 11.5; vitamin B_6, 0.30.

vegans, people who consume no food made or derived from animals and so exclude meat, fish, fowl, eggs, honey, milk and dairy products. Their diet of a combination of cereals with vegetables, plus fruit and nuts provides sufficient essential amino acids and other nutrients except vitamin B_{12}, where a supplement is advised since it is present mainly in foods of animal origin, and possibly zinc because of reduced bioavailability owing to the high phytate content of the diet. Vitamin D deficiency may be a particular problem among coloured immigrant vegans. The iron intake of vegans is higher than that of omnivores but it is in a less bioavailable form (non-haem), the net result being an iron status no worse than that of meat eaters. Most plant proteins are of low quality (except, e.g., soya), being short of one or more essential amino acids. However, when foods from different plant sources are eaten together, deficiency in one (e.g., of lysine in cereals; of methionine and cysteine in vegetables) is compensated for by sufficiency in another. Without dairy products, calcium intake may be low. *See also* fruitarians.

In many respects, vegans are healthier than omnivores, usually having less body fat, lower blood-cholesterol levels, lower blood-pressures, lower blood viscosity, lower levels of one of the blood-clotting factors and appear less prone to coronary heart disease and certain forms of cancer (e.g., breast, uterine, colon, rectum).

vegetables, include leaves (e.g., spinach, cabbage, Brussels sprouts, coriander, parsley, fenugreek, watercress, lettuce); roots (e.g., swedes, parsnips, turnips, onions, radishes); fruits (e.g., aubergines, tomatoes, gourds, marrow); stalks (e.g., celery) and flowers (e.g., cauliflower, globe artichokes). General nutritive properties similar despite their diverse botanical structures. For potatoes and other tubers, *see* potatoes *and* tubers; for legumes *see* pulses.

Poor sources of energy. Because of this and because their bulk is satisfying, they are useful in the prevention and treatment of obesity. Of little value as sources of protein or essential amino acids. All provide dietary fibre. All contain calcium and iron though the presence of phytates and oxalates hinders their absorption. However, the presence of vitamin C in vegetables aids iron absorption. All contain small amounts of vitamin B. Chief nutritive value is as source of beta-carotene, vitamin C and folate.

Green leafy/all other vegetables besides tubers and pulses provide (per 100g as purchased): energy, 10–50/10–50 kcal; (g) water, 75–80/70–90; protein, 1–4/0.5–2.5; carbohydrate, 1–12/2–10; fat, trace/0–0.4; (mg) calcium, 25–500/20–100; iron, 1–25/0.5–4.0; vitamin C, 10–200/5–100; (μg) beta-carotene, 600–6000/0–180; folic acid, 20–100/2–30.

---

vegetarians, people who consume no meat, fish or fowl, nor any of the derivatives of slaughter, e.g., gelatin. Unlike vegans, they consume milk and dairy products (lacto-vegetarians) and some also accept eggs (lacto-ovo-vegetarians), which makes balancing their diets easier. A vitamin B_{12} supplement is sometimes advised, though sufficient is probably obtained from dairy products and milk. Zinc status may be at risk owing to its reduced bioavailability because of the high phytate content of the diet. Iron intake is higher than that of omnivores but it is in a less bioavailable form (non-haem), resulting in an iron status no worse than that of meat eaters. Proteins from egg and dairy sources are high quality, compensating for the poorer quality of proteins from most plant sources.

In many respects, vegetarians are healthier than omnivores, usually having less body fat, lower blood-pressures and a lower incidence of certain forms of cancer. Blood-cholesterol levels of lacto-vegetarians are similar to those of vegans, while those of lacto-ovo-vegetarians are similar to those of omnivores.

---

villus, plural, villi. Microscopic, finger-like projections found in the mucous membrane of the small intestines. *See* intestinal wall.

vitamin A, (retinoids), fat-soluble vitamin. Naturally occurring compounds with vitamin A activity are obtained from animal sources and include retinol, retinoic acid and retinaldehyde. Only retinol has full vitamin A activity, the others fulfilling some, but not all, vitamin A functions. Some carotenoids, notably beta-carotene, that originate from plant sources, are converted to retinol primarily in the intestinal mucosa but also in the liver and other tissues.

Functions Required for vision in dim light (forms visual purple, a pigment in the eye retina), for growth and reproduction, for differentiation and maintenance of normal condition of moist (mucosal) epithelial tissue lining mouth, respiratory and urinary tracts.

Retinoids inhibit carcinogenesis, possibly because they regulate cell differentiation and proliferation. Initial epidemiological surveys indicated an inverse relationship between diets rich in retinol and several types of cancer, but subsequent studies indicated the link was to the carotenoid content. Unlike carotenoids, retinol sensitizes formation of excited oxygen species (free radicals).

Deficiency leads to night blindness, xeropthalmia (drying of tear ducts), keratomalacia (ulceration of the cornea) leading to blindness, stunted growth, increased susceptibility to infections of skin, mucous membranes and respiratory tract.

Toxicity can result from prolonged intakes of retinol of more than ten times the RDA and occasionally even with doses of 5,000IU. It accumulates because it is stored in the liver as retinyl esters (i.e., combined with a fatty acid, usually as retinyl palmitate). For transport round the body, the ester is hydrolysed to free retinol that combines with retinol-binding protein synthesized by the liver. This complex is associated with serum proteins for transport in the blood. Blood levels are necessarily strictly controlled because high levels would cause destruction of red blood cells. High intakes of vitamin A, e.g., in liver and liver products such as pâté or in supplements, by pregnant women, can cause malformations in the foetus and hence must be avoided except on doctor's advice.

Carotenoids are only converted to retinol as required by the body and so do not cause vitamin A toxicity.

Retinol equivalent (RE) The vitamin A activity of all retinoids is expressed in terms of the most active form, retinol:

1 RE = 1μg retinol or 6μg beta-carotene or 12μg other biologically active carotenoids.

1μg retinol = 3.33 IU.

Requirement UK RDA is 750μg (2,500IU). EC and USA RDA is 800μg. Average UK diets provide around 1,300μg, of which about one third comes from carotenoids.

Stable to ordinary cooking but destroyed by high temperatures (frying) and oxygen. Protected from oxidation by vitamin E. Carotene levels in fruit and vegetables reduced by drying and canning. Retinol, and to a lesser extent its esters, are sensitive to atmospheric oxygen, the decomposition being catalysed by metallic ions and both forms are damaged by light. Carotenoids are sensitive to light, oxygen and heat.

Distribution in foods (a) As retinol (in μg per 100g): halibut-liver oil, 60,000; cod-liver oil, 18,000; livers, 9,300–18,100; margarines (required by law to be fortified), 900; butter, 750; egg-yolk, 400; Cheddar cheese, 310; Pacific salmon, 90; herring and mackerel, 45; white fish, 0.

(b) As carotene (in μg per 100g) (divide by 6 to obtain retinol equivalents): red palm oil, 42,000; carrot, 12,000; watercress, 3,000; cantaloup melon, 2,000; apricots, 1,500; tomatoes, 600; butter, 470; winter cabbage, 300; Cheddar cheese, 205; cereals (except maize), potatoes, vegetable oils, 0.

---

vitamin B_1,   *see* thiamin.

---

vitamin B_2,   *see* riboflavin.

---

vitamin B_3,   niacin (*which see*) or sometimes pantothenic acid.

---

vitamin B_4, B_7, B_9, B_{10}, B_{11}, B_{14}, B_{16},   are names given to factors essential for animals but not man, or are names no longer used.

---

vitamin B_5,   pantothenic acid or sometimes niacin.

---

vitamin B_6,   water-soluble vitamin and member of the B complex. Includes pyridoxine (commonest form in vegetable foods), pyridoxamine and pyridoxal (commonest forms in animal foods).

Daily UK household supply in 1986 (not allowing for 10 per cent wastage and excluding out-of-home meals) was 1.73mg (1.91mg with contribution from alcoholic drinks) derived mainly from (per cent): vegetables, 32 (potatoes, 17); cereals and products, 22 (bread, 6); meat and products, 18.

Functions biochemically as pyridoxal phosphate, the coenzyme for many enzymes involved in amino acid metabolism, and so intimately concerned in protein metabolism. Takes part in synthesis of niacin from tryptophan and of longer chain polyunsaturated fatty acids from essential fatty acids.

Required for growth, healthy nervous system, skin and tongue.

Deficiency leads to no specific disease but causes convulsions in infants and skin disorders and peripheral neuritis symptoms in adults. Since intake is mainly from animal-food sources, vegetarians, particularly vegans, may be at risk of deficiency, particularly if menstruating and on the oestrogen contraceptive pill, which increases vitamin B_6 requirement.

Requirement   No UK RDA, but US and EC RDA is 2.0mg.

Daily intake in UK (excluding cooking losses and out-of-home meals) averages 1.36mg, 42 per cent derived from animal products (23 per cent meat, 11 per cent milk), potatoes, over 20 per cent, other vegetables, 15 per cent.

Toxic sometimes in doses over 200mg daily, causing polyneuropathy of the sensory nervous system.

Stability   Relatively stable to cooking processes, but lost by leaching into cooking water and in drips from thawing foods unless these are used, and 25–50 per cent may be lost during cooking of meat and vegetables.

Distribution in foods (in mg per 100g): dried brewer's yeast, 4.2; liver, 0.8–0.4; mackerel, 0.7; avocados and bananas, 0.5; chicken and meat, 0.5–0.3; cod, 0.3; pulses and vegetables, 0.16; eggs, 0.16; wholemeal bread, 0.14; milk, 0.04; fats and oils, 0.

---

vitamin B_{12},   cobalamin. Water-soluble vitamin and member of the B complex. Complex molecule containing cobalt. Includes hydroxocobalamin, the coenzymes adenosylcobalamin and methylcobalamin and, the most stable form, cyanocobalamin. Also known as anti-pernicious anaemia factor, extrinsic factor and, formerly, as animal protein factor. Its absorption requires the presence of intrinsic factor, a glycoprotein normally secreted by the stomach.

Functions biochemically as coenzymes. One, adenosylcobalamin, helps maintain the correct fatty acids in myelin, the fatty sheath around nerves. The other, methylcobalamin, transfers a methyl group from an inactive form of folic acid to homocysteine forming methionine, at the same time helping to regenerate one of the active forms of folic acid that takes part in DNA synthesis, affecting particularly the formation of the nucleus of new red blood cells. Deficiency of either B_{12} or folic acid therefore leads to megaloblastic anaemia, but only deficiency of B_{12} leads to neurological disorders that take longer to become evident. If the cause of megaloblastic anaemia is not correctly diagnosed, its treatment with high doses of folic acid (above 500µg daily) may mask a B_{12} deficiency, allowing neurological disorders to develop unbeknown. A relative deficiency of methionine may be responsible for the neurological disorders.

Vitamin B_{12} is required for red blood cell formation and a healthy nervous system and integrity of the fatty myelin sheath around nerves.

Deficiency leads to megaloblastic anaemia. If it is caused by lack of intrinsic factor, the condition is called pernicious anaemia. Vegans risk a dietary deficiency as it is found only in foods of animal origin, except for Spirulina, but many obtain some from traces in micro-organisms and moulds contaminating their foods. Symptoms include those characteristic of anaemia, a sore tongue and, ultimately, nerve degeneration.

Requirement   UK and US RDA is 2μg. EC RDA is 1μg.

Daily UK household supply in 1986 (not allowing for 10 per cent wastage and excluding out-of-home meals) averaged 6.33μg (6.79μg with contribution from alcoholic drinks) derived mainly from (per cent): meat and products, 45 (offal, 20); milk and products, 24; eggs, 17; fish and products, 11; cereals and products, 3.

Toxicity   None reported, even at megadose levels. Stored in the liver.

Stable to most cooking processes. Former idea that it was destroyed by vitamin C was due to the latter interfering with the estimation of B_{12}.

Distribution in foods (in μg per 100g): liver, 25-110; kidney, 14-55; mackerel, 10; milk, 3; meat, 2-3; eggs, free range/deep litter/battery, 2.9/2.6/1.7 (battery yolk, 4.9); cod, 2; Cheddar cheese, 1.5; cereals, vegetables, pulses, fruits, 0.

---

vitamin B_{15},   *see* pangamic acid. Not a vitamin.

---

vitamin B_{17},   *see* laetrile. Not a vitamin.

---

vitamin B_T,   *see* carnitine. Not a vitamin.

---

vitamin C,   ascorbic acid. Water-soluble vitamin. Used as bread improver.

Functions biochemically as an antioxidant. Required for the hydroxylation of proline to hydroxyproline. This is a step in the synthesis of collagen, the protein of connective tissue and intercellular cementing substances important in maintaining health of bones, teeth, gums, cartilage, capillaries, connective tissue and in the healing of wounds and fractures. Also required for the synthesis of serotonin, noradrenaline and certain steroid hormones; in promoting absorption of iron (non-haem); in maintaining the immune system; in maintaining normal cholesterol levels.

Deficiency leads to scurvy with initial symptoms of lassitude and irritability, followed by those related to defective collagen metabolism such as subcutaneous and other haemorrhages, muscle weakness, soft swollen gums and loosened teeth.

Requirement UK RDA is 30mg — sufficient to prevent scurvy, but many nutritionists think the US and EC RDA of 60mg is closer to requirement for maintaining general good health. Tissue saturation thought to be easily achieved by 200mg daily. In the UK about 50 per cent of the daily intake is provided by vegetables and 39 per cent by fruit.

Toxicity Some reported with prolonged daily intakes of 1g or more. *See* scurvy *and* stones, kidney or urinary.

Stability Least stable of all the vitamins to cooking and food processing, being destroyed by heat, oxygen, alkali and leaching and destruction in cooking water particularly in the presence of copper, iron or nickel. For best retention, cook unsoaked vegetables for minimum time in minimum volume of water.

Distribution in foods (in mg per 100g): acerola, 1,000–2,330; rosehips, 1,250; blackcurrants, 200; parsley, 150; broccoli, 110; green pepper, 100; strawberries and watercress, 60; winter cabbage, 55; oranges, 50; newly-dug main-crop potatoes, 30; peas, 25; liver, 10–23; tomatoes, 20; lettuce, 15; bananas and onions, 10; carrots, 6; milk, 2; fish, trace; meat, 0.

---

vitamin D, fat-soluble vitamin. Includes cholecalciferol (D_3), found in animal tissues and formed by the action of ultraviolet light on 7-dehydro-cholesterol in the skin, and ergocalciferol or calciferol (D_2), produced by irradiation with ultraviolet light of ergosterol in plant sources such as yeast and fungi. Converted in liver into 25-hydroxy-D (calcidiol), the chief form in blood, and then in the kidney into the active (hormone) form, 1,2-dihydroxy-D (calcitriol). Also known as the anti-rachitic vitamin.

Functions Stimulates calcium and phosphate absorption from the small intestine and calcium release and turnover from bone. Since it is produced in one part of the body and functions in another it acts as a hormone.

Deficiency leads to rickets in young children and osteomalacia in adults, both caused by softening of the bones due to lack of calcium phosphate. Possibly 25 per cent of UK children have a daily intake of less than 2.5µg and have hypovitaminosis D. They are at risk of developing rickets.

Possibly contributes to osteoporosis.

Toxicity Most toxic of the vitamins. Prolonged intake of as little as five times the RDA may cause symptoms. Accumulates because stored in the liver.

IU No longer used officially: 1µg = 40 IU.

Requirement UK RDA 10μg (400 IU) for young children and house-bound adults and 2.5μg (100 IU) for other adults. EC and US RDA is 5μg. Food sources are few. In the summer, most vitamin D requirements are met by exposure of the skin to sunlight. Less of the vitamin is formed for a given exposure to sunlight in melanin pigmented (black or brown) skin than in white skin, helping to account for the higher incidence of rickets and osteomalacia in coloured people living in northern latitudes. In winter, the angle of the sunlight to the earth is too low in northern latitudes to cause formation of vitamin D in the skin.

Stable to cooking and most food-processing techniques. Destroyed quite rapidly by light, oxygen and acids.

Distribution in foods (in μg per 100g): cod-liver oil, 210; herring, 22.5; mackerel, 17.5; Pacific salmon, 12.5; egg yolk, 5.0; livers, 0.25–1.13; milk in USA and Canada (fortified), 1.1; butter, 0.76; Cheddar cheese, 0.26; cow's summer milk in UK (unfortified), 0.03; meats, white fish, trace; cereals, vegetables, fruit, 0.

---

vitamin E, fat-soluble vitamin. Also known as the anti-sterility and fertility vitamin because of its effects in animals. Substances with vitamin E activity include the naturally occurring 'd' form of alpha, beta, gamma and delta tocopherol and of alpha tocotrienol and the synthetic 'dl' form of alpha tocopherol. The most potent form, and the only one assigned official IU of biological activity, is d-alpha tocopherol. Relative to it the biological activities of beta, gamma tocopherols and of alpha tocotrienol are about 50, 10 and 30 per cent respectively. Supplied in supplements as d- or dl-alpha tocopherol/tocopheryl acetate/tocopheryl acid succinate. Their currently ascribed relative biological activities are as shown in Table 11:

Table 11: Relative biological activities of different forms of vitamin E supplements

	Biological activity in IU per mg
d-alpha tocopherol	1.49
d-alpha tocopheryl acetate	1.36
d-alpha tocopheryl acid succinate	1.21
dl-alpha tocopherol	1.10
dl-alpha tocopheryl acetate	1.00
dl-alpha tocopheryl acid succinate	0.89

Alpha-tocopherol equivalents Though vitamin E strengths in food supplements are usually given in IU, in the food industry and in medicine they are given as alpha-tocopherol equivalents.

1 alpha-tocopherol equivalent (1α-TE) = 1mg d-alpha tocopherol.

Functions as an antioxidant, protecting polyunsaturated fatty acids (e.g., in cell membranes) from harmful oxidation, neutralizing the effect of harmful free radicals and protecting vitamins A and C from oxidative destruction. However, it can act as a pro-oxidant in the presence of certain metal ions such as ferric iron. Prolongs life of red blood cells. Concerned with normal blood clotting and small blood-vessel health. Acts synergistically with selenium.

Deficiency gives rise to anaemia in the new-born and neurological symptoms in the adult. Deficiency arises mainly from diseases leading to inefficient absorption of fats and may arise from excessive intakes of polyunsaturated fats, mineral oils or oxygen (as in oxygen tents).

Toxicity Little risk below intakes of 600 IU daily. Stored in adipose tissue.

Requirement No UK RDA, but US and EC RDA is 10mg (15 IU). Though requirements increase with increasing polyunsaturated fat consumption, such fats themselves usually contain vitamin E unless denuded of it during processing. Fish oils contain little, and large intakes of the oil must be accompanied by additional vitamin E.

Daily UK household supply in 1986 (not allowing for 10 per cent wastage and excluding out-of-home meals) averaged 8.4mg (12.5 IU) (or 8.5mg with contribution from confectionery), derived mainly from (per cent): oils and fats, 46; vegetables, 13; cereals, 12.

Stability Destroyed by commercial cooking and food processing including deep freezing. Home cooking other than deep frying causes little loss. Destroyed by solvent extraction of vegetable oils but this is avoided by cold-pressing them. Tocopherol form is sensitive to oxygen but esters are stable.

Distribution in foods (mg d-alpha tocopherol per 100g): wheatgerm/sunflower-seed/safflower-seed/maize/soya bean/olive/coconut oils, 133/49/39/11/10/5/0.5; margarines, polyunsaturated/all kinds, 25/8; egg yolk, 4.6; butter, 2.0; parsley, 1.8; broccoli, 1.3; cod, 0.44; herring, 0.2; meats, 0.1–0.15; summer milk, 0.1.

---

vitamin F, incorrect term sometimes used for essential fatty acids.

---

vitamin H, *see* biotin.

vitamin K, fat-soluble vitamin. Also known as the anti-haemorrhagic vitamin. Includes: K_1 (one substance variously known as phylloquinone, phytylmenaquinone, phytonadione) that occurs naturally in foods; K_2 (a group of multiprenyl-menaquinones) formed by bacteria either in the intestines or in fermentations such as putrefying food, with only 75 per cent of the activity of K_1; K_3 (one substance variously known as menadione or menaphthone) produced synthetically that has twice the activity of K_1.

Functions Essential for production of four specific proteins, including prothrombin, concerned in blood clotting.

Deficiency leads to bleeding and haemorrhage. Dietary deficiency not seen except in new-born with sterile intestine. Deficiency induced in subjects with fat malabsorption problems and by destruction of intestinal bacteria by antibiotics.

Toxicity Little reported. Stored in liver.

Requirement None specified and difficult to estimate because of varying intestinal synthesis. USA estimated safe and adequate intake is 70–140 µg.

Stable to most cooking processes but destroyed by light. Some lost in commercial food processing including deep freezing. Relatively stable to heat, decomposed by alkalis, only slowly degraded by atmospheric oxygen.

Distribution in foods Present in fresh leafy green vegetables, e.g., broccoli, lettuce, cabbage and spinach. Ox liver a good source. Most other animal foods, cereals and fruits poor sources.

---

vitamin M, *see* folic acid.

---

vitamin P, bioflavonoids. Not a vitamin.

---

vitamin PP, *see* niacin.

---

vitamin U, S-methylmethionine. An anti-ulcer factor found in various teas. Not a vitamin.

---

vitamins, organic nutrients required in micro amounts for healthy metabolism that must be present in the food because they cannot be synthesized in adequate amounts by the animal or human body. Man requires 13, divided for convenience into two groups, four fat-soluble (A, D, E and K) and nine water-soluble (the B complex — thiamin, riboflavin, niacin, B_6,

B_{12}, folic acid, biotin, pantothenic acid and C).

1. *Fat-soluble vitamins* are present in food fats such as fatty meats, liver, dairy fats, egg yolks, vegetable seed oils and leafy green vegetables. They are digested with fat, require bile and fat for absorption, are transported with fat in the blood and are stored in the liver (A, D and K) and adipose tissue (E). Fat malabsorption disorders can lead to their malabsorption and deficiencies.

They are not excreted in the urine and A and D, particularly, can therefore accumulate in storage tissues to toxic levels. They are excreted in the bile and either reabsorbed via the enterohepatic circulation or excreted in the faeces.

They are relatively stable to normal cooking temperatures but are slowly inactivated by ultraviolet light (sunlight) and by oxidation.

Requirements UK RDAs are: vitamin A, 750μg (2,500 IU); vitamin D, 2.5μg (100 IU). EC and US RDAs are: vitamin A, 800μg; vitamin D, 5.0μg; vitamin E, 10mg (15 IU). US RDA for vitamin K is 80μg.

2. *Water-soluble vitamins* Apart from B_{12}, the B complex are found together in foods such as wholegrain cereals, legumes, leafy green vegetables, meat and dairy products. Vitamin C is found in fresh fruit and vegetables. Vitamin B_{12} is synthesized by micro-organisms, is incorporated into animal tissues and so is present in meat and dairy foods.

They are absorbed in the small intestines, held bound to enzyme and transport proteins and, apart from B_{12} and folic acid, which are stored in the liver, they are excreted in the urine when plasma levels exceed kidney thresholds. Consequently they are less toxic than the fat-soluble ones and, since their storage is minimal, a regular dietary supply is important. The B complex all have coenzyme or prosthetic group functions.

In general, lack of B vitamins affects tissues that are growing or metabolizing rapidly: skin, blood, digestive tract and nervous system. Consequently deficiency symptoms usually include dermatitis, anaemia, digestive difficulties and neurological disorders.

They are somewhat unstable to heat, light and strong acid and alkali solutions, and are leached into cooking water, which should therefore be kept minimal.

Requirement UK RDAs are: thiamin, 1.2mg; riboflavin, 1.6mg; niacin, 18mg; folic acid, 300μg; vitamin B_{12}, 2μg, vitamin C, 30mg.

US RDAs are: thiamin, 1.5mg; riboflavin, 1.7mg; niacin, 19mg; folic acid, 200μg; vitamin B_{12}, 2μg; vitamin C, 60mg; vitamin B_6, 2.0mg. The US estimated safe and adequate intake of biotin is 30–100μg and, of pantothenic acid, 4–7mg.

EC RDAs: thiamin, 1.4mg; riboflavin, 1.6mg; niacin, 18mg; vitamin B_6, 2mg; vitamin B_{12}, 1μg, folacin, 200μg; biotin, 150μg; pantothenic acid, 6mg; vitamin C, 60mg. *See* Tables 5–10 pages 224–231.

Law From 1986, a food may legally be described as a 'source'/'rich or excellent source' of vitamin(s) only if a reasonable daily intake of the food provides at least one-sixth/one-half of the RDA of vitamin A, thiamin, riboflavin, niacin, vitamin B_{12}, folic acid, vitamin C and vitamin D. Unless the claim is made for named vitamin(s), the food must provide two or more of these eight vitamins, which are thought by MAFF to be those most likely to be at risk of being deficient in the diet.

VLDL, *see* lipoproteins, very low density.

vodka, spirit distilled from fermented rye or potatoes. Nearest to pure aqueous alcohol of the alcoholic beverages. Contains very little cogeners (*see* alcohol).

volatile fatty acids, *see* fermentation, colonic.

W

walnuts, nuts providing (per 100g): energy, 525 kcal; (g) protein, 10.6; fat, 51.5; total dietary fibre, 5.2; (mg) potassium, 690.

water, the body of a 65kg man contains about 40l of water, 25l within the cells and 15l in extracellular fluids, e.g., blood. Daily water intake is derived from liquid drunk (about 1l), the water content of food (about 1l) and that yielded by the metabolic oxidation of carbohydrates, proteins and fats (about ¼l). Water balance is maintained by daily loss via the urine (about 1¼l), by evaporation from the skin and lungs (about 1l) and in the faeces (small except in diarrhoea). Essential for life. Vehicle for excretion of soluble waste matter from the body, e.g., urea. Its evaporation from the skin cools the body. Dehydration due to insufficient intake or excessive loss (e.g., in diarrhoea) eventually leads to death. Oedema is the result of water retention.

water, hard, has a higher content of calcium and magnesium and trace elements than soft water, which is more acidic and may dissolve potentially toxic trace elements like lead or cadmium from pipes or rocks. Whether these facts explain the protective effect it appears to have against mortality from cardiovascular disease is not known.

---

water, mineral, natural spring waters containing small quantities of sodium chloride, sodium carbonate and bicarbonate and sometimes iron or hydrogen sulphide. Mineral content seldom more and usually less than 8g per litre. Usually mildly alkaline. Many are naturally aerated with carbon dioxide.

---

water, soft, is more acid and has a lower content of dissolved calcium, magnesium and trace elements than hard water. For relevance to cardio-vascular disease *see* water, hard.

---

watercress, green leafy vegetable providing (per 100g): energy, 14 kcal; (g) protein, 2.9; fat, trace; total dietary fibre, 3.3; water, 91.1; (mg) sodium, 60; potassium, 310; calcium, 220; beta-carotene, 3.0; vitamin C, 60; thiamin, 0.10; riboflavin, 0.10; niacin, 1.8.

---

weight, acceptable, replaces the concept of an 'ideal' weight for an individual. Provided a person's weight falls within the range for their sex and height, it is regarded as acceptable. The values do not include subdivisions for 'frame size'. Nor is there any adjustment for age since people should remain within their range throughout adult life. *See* Table 12.

Table 12: Acceptable weights as recommended by the Fogarty Conference, USA 1979 and the Royal College of Physicians, UK 1983

Height, without shoes		MEN Weight, without clothes						WOMEN Weight, without clothes					
		Acceptable average		Acceptable weight range		Obese		Acceptable average		Acceptable weight range		Obese	
m	in.	kg	lb	kg	lb	kg	lb	kg	lb	kg	lb	kg	lb
1.45	57.1							46.0	101	42-53	92-117	64	141
1.48	58.3							46.5	102	42-54	92-119	65	143
1.50	59.1							47.0	103	43-55	95-121	66	145
1.52	59.8							48.5	107	44-57	97-125	68	150

Table 12 continued

Height without shoes		MEN Weight, without clothes						WOMEN Weight, without clothes					
		Acceptable average		Acceptable weight range		Obese		Acceptable average		Acceptable weight range		Obese	
m	in.	kg	lb	kg	lb	kg	lb	kg	lb	kg	lb	kg	lb
1.54	60.6							49.5	109	44-58	97-128	70	154
1.56	61.4							50.4	111	45-58	99-128	70	154
1.58	62.2	55.8	123	51-64	112-141	77	169	51.3	113	46-59	101-130	71	156
1.60	62.9	57.6	127	52-65	114-143	78	172	52.6	116	48-61	106-134	73	161
1.62	63.4	58.6	129	53-66	117-145	79	174	54.0	119	49-62	108-136	74	163
1.64	64.6	59.6	131	54-67	119-147	80	176	55.4	122	50-64	110-141	77	169
1.66	65.4	60.6	133	55-69	121-152	83	183	56.8	125	51-65	112-143	78	172
1.68	66.1	61.7	136	56-71	123-156	85	187	58.1	128	52-66	114-145	79	174
1.70	66.9	63.5	140	58-73	128-161	88	194	60.0	132	53-67	117-147	80	176
1.72	67.7	65.0	143	59-74	130-163	89	196	61.3	134	55-69	121-152	83	183
1.74	68.5	66.5	146	60-75	132-165	90	198	62.6	138	56-70	123-154	84	185
1.76	69.3	68.0	150	62-67	136-169	92	202	64.0	141	58-72	128-158	86	189
1.78	70.1	69.4	153	64-79	141-174	95	209	65.3	144	59-74	130-163	89	196
1.80	70.9	71.0	156	65-80	143-176	96	211						
1.82	71.7	72.6	159	66-82	145-180	98	216						
1.84	72.4	74.2	163	67-84	147-185	101	222						
1.86	73.2	75.8	167	69-86	152-189	103	227						
1.88	74.0	77.6	171	71-88	156-194	106	233						
1.90	74.8	79.3	174	73-90	161-198	108	238						
1.92	75.6	81.0	178	75-93	165-205	112	246						
BMI*		22.0		20.1-25.0		30.0		20.8		18.7-23.8		28.6	

*Body mass index = weight in kg/height^2 in metres.

weight reduction, or slimming, aims to lose excess body fat, in order to reach an acceptable weight (*see* Table 12, pages 286 and above). Achieved by lowering energy ('calorie') intake to below energy output, thereby mobilizing body fat to make up for the energy deficit. Short-term rapid weight losses with rigorous ('crash') diets depend on losses of body water, glycogen and protein, rather than excess body fat. After the initial rapid weight loss on reducing calorie intake (largely glycogen and water), a loss of ½-1kg per week is desirable for the majority of adults. Body protein, mainly from the muscles, is inevitably lost when slimming, but the diet should aim to minimize this by providing adequate good quality protein. Unfortunately, the body responds to decreased energy intake by decreasing its basic energy requirements (its basal metabolic rate, or, BMR) and, even when calorie consumption is eventually increased to stabilize at the desired weight, this lowered BMR appears to persist. This may help to account for the ease with which weight is regained because the new energy requirement is considerably less than before weight loss, not only because less is needed to move the leaner body about, but less is also required by the body at rest. A permanent adjustment in food choice is needed to achieve and maintain reduced weight, with a change from foods rich in fats (meat, meat products, fried foods) and those rich in sugar, to cereals, bread, vegetables and fruit.

Slimming aids include: (a) very low-calorie diet preparations (also known as protein sparing modified fasts or liquid protein diets). If these are used as a total food substitute, they are dangerous to health, unless they provide a minimum of 400/500kcal per day for women/men and tall women, and 40/50g good-quality protein respectively and the Recommended Daily Allowances of vitamins and minerals. Doctor's advice should be sought before use and their use as the *sole* source of food should not be continued for more than three to four weeks. Prolongation and repetition requires further advice and supervision. This produces effective short-term weight loss, but does not train the person in sensible eating habits and most users regain weight quickly.

(b) bran cereal and skimmed milk. A good cheap variation of (a) and hence with the same provisos regarding medical advice, length of usage and failure to retrain eating habits. The cereal with 1.1/1.8l of skimmed milk for women/men and tall women, plus 60mg iron (as ferrous sulphate), a multivitamin supplement and unlimited calorie-free drinks provide the minimum daily intake of energy, protein and micronutrients, plus bulk (fibre).

(c) fructose preload. This is 50g fructose in 500ml flavoured water, taken 40 minutes before a meal that significantly reduced energy intake (particularly of fat) of normal weight and obese people at the meal compared with a preload of flavoured water with or without aspartame sweetener, even allowing for the 200kcal provided by the fructose. A glucose preload had an intermediate effect.

(d) soluble fibres. These swell when taken with water to give a feeling of fullness, helping to reduce calorie intake at the next meal. They can cause problems in supplement form by swelling in the oesophagus, causing a blockage. The use of guar and locust bean gums for this purpose has ceased since legislation now prohibits their inclusion in food at more than 15 per cent by weight.

(e) starch blockers. Inhibitors of the enzyme amylase that were intended to reduce the digestion of starch so it passes out of the body unabsorbed, but were ineffective.

(f) artificial sweeteners. Some, but not other, studies suggest that the replacement of calorific sweeteners (e.g., sugar) with calorie-free intense sweeteners (e.g., aspartame, saccharin) actually stimulates the appetite, the opposite of the desired effect, because they do not 'satisfy'.

Law   From 1986, a claim that a food is an aid to slimming or weight control, may only be made if the food can contribute to weight control or weight reduction and is accompanied by the words 'can help slimming or weight control only as part of a (calorie/joule/energy) controlled diet'. A food described as having a reduced energy value must not have more than three-quarters of the energy value of a similar non-reduced food. A food (apart from an intense sweetener) claimed to have a low energy value must not provide more than 167 kJ (40 kcal) per 100g of the food and per normal serving of the food. The label of a replacement meal described as suitable to replace part of a daily diet may not offer the product to replace the *whole* diet and must state that the consumer should eat, in addition, at least one daily meal having a high nutritive quality.

Wernicke-Korsakoff syndrome,   form of beriberi affecting the brain. Seen in alcohol abusers on a low thiamin intake.

---

wheatgerm,   the embryo of the wheat grain from which wheatgerm meal and oil are made. Used mainly when added to other foods (e.g., breakfast cereals) as a rich supplement of vitamin E. Low in dietary fibre, high in fat and contains a minimum of 25 per cent crude protein. In spoonful quantities, a good source of energy, essential fatty acids, protein, minerals, vitamins E and B. Some products are defatted to prolong their shelf life, but this also removes much of the vitamin E.

---

whey,   the clear liquid left after the protein of milk has been clotted and most of the fat removed, e.g., after cheese-making.

---

whisk(e)y,   spirit distilled from malted and fermented barley (Irish and Scotch), rye (Canada and USA) or mainly maize (bourbon, USA), usually blended with distilled grain spirit.

Provides (per 100ml): energy, 230 kcal; (g) alcohol, 32.8; carbohydrate, trace.

WHO,   World Health Organization of the United Nations.

wholefoods, retain their full natural nutritive content because nothing edible is removed in their preparation, e.g., wholemeal flour, a peeled orange, but not orange juice. As far as possible, they are additive-free and have been grown with the use of organic, not chemical, fertilizers and are free from pesticides.

---

wind, *see* flatus.

---

wine, alcoholic drink produced by fermentation of grapes by wild yeasts present in the fruit.

Red/rosé (medium)/white (dry)/(medium)/(sweet)/(sparkling) provide (per 100ml): energy, 68/71/66/75/94/76 kcal; (g) alcohol, 9.5/8.7/9.1/8.8/10.2/9.9; carbohydrate 0.3/2.5/0.6/3.4/5.9/1.4.

---

wines, fortified, wines with alcohol added to raise the concentration up to about 15g per 100ml.

Port/sherry (dry)/(medium)/(sweet) provide (per 100ml): 157/116/118/ 136 kcal; (g) alcohol, 15.9/15.7/14.8/15.6; carbohydrates, 12.0/1.4/3.6/6.9.

X

---

xanthan gum, corn-sugar gum. A product of carbohydrate fermentation by the bacterium, *Xanthomonas campestris*. Polysaccharide of glucose, mannose and glucuronic acid. Water-soluble dietary fibre, forming viscous gel. Relatively resistant (compared to, e.g., guar gum) to colonic fermentation.

Used in foods, non-foods and cosmetics as stabilizer and emulsifier and as granulater and binder in tablets.

---

xanthines, purines. Their derivatives, the methylxanthines (*which see*), are important in certain beverages, e.g., tea, coffee.

xenobiotics, substances alien to the body, e.g., drugs, some food additives.

---

xeropthalmia, drying of tear ducts due to vitamin A deficiency.

---

xylitol, a permitted bulk sweetener. As sweet as sucrose. A five-carbon sugar alcohol. Appears to be non-cariogenic itself, but when added to a cariogenic diet it may increase the cariogenicity.

---

xylose, pentose monosaccharide. Found in hemicelluloses (dietary fibres) and in glyco- and muco-proteins.

Y

---

yam, starchy roots or tubers of various species of the climbing tropical plant, *Dioscorea*. Provides (per 100g): energy, 130 kcal; (g) protein, 2; water, 73.0; carbohydrate, 32.4; (mg) vitamin C, 10.

Yang, *see* macrobiotics.

---

yeast, brewer's, derived as a by-product from the brewing of beer and ale. Bitter-tasting. Taken in spoonful quantities mixed with other foods (e.g., breakfast cereals, gravies), it is a rich source of B vitamins, contains 35 per cent crude, fair-quality protein and is rich in chromium, present as glucose tolerance factor, and selenium. High in purines, so unsuitable for sufferers from gout.

---

yeast, torula, a hardy variety cultured as a foodstuff for man and animals. Tasteless. Dried and in spoonful quantites, it is an excellent source of high-quality protein (50–62 per cent crude protein), minerals, B vitamins (including B_{12}), and, if irradiated, of vitamin D (ergocalciferol).

Yin, *see* macrobiotics.

yogurt, deliberately soured or curdled milk produced by adding bacteria (*Lactobacillus acidophilus, L. bulgaricus* and *Streptococcus thermophilus*) that break down the lactose of milk, forming lactic acid. The lactase enzyme present in the bacteria may allow consumption of yogurt by lactase-deficient people.

Low-fat natural yogurt provides (per 100g): energy, 52 kcal; (g) water, 85.7; protein, 5.0; fat, 1.0; lactose, 4.6; (mg) calcium, 180; iron, 0.09; thiamin, 0.05; riboflavin, 0.26; niacin, 1.16.

yuca, *see* cassava.

Z

zein, maize protein. A prolamine. Lacks lysine and tryptophan content is low, so its protein quality is poor.

Sometimes used as a tablet coating.

zinc, the adult body contains about 2.0g of this essential mineral, most being in the bones, 20 per cent in the skin and high concentrations being in the eye and prostate gland. Semen has 100 times the concentration of blood plasma.

Daily UK household supply in 1986 (not allowing for 10 per cent wastage and excluding out-of-home meals) averaged 9.0mg (9.05mg with contributions from alcoholic drinks and confectionery) derived mainly from (per cent): meat, 34; cereals, 23 (bread, 13); milk and products, 19.

Functions Zinc is part of or necessary for over 70 enzymes including those required for synthesis of RNA and DNA and protein. The major zinc protein in saliva, gustin, plays an important role in taste.

Absorption   About 20 per cent of dietary zinc is absorbed. A zinc-binding factor secreted into the intestinal lumen, possibly by the pancreas, promotes zinc absorption.

Phytate and fibre bind zinc, preventing its absorption. Copper, and possibly high levels of inorganic iron as in supplements, interfere with zinc absorption. High calcium and phosphate intake aggravate zinc deficiency.

It can be held in the intestinal cells bound to protein and is transported in the blood bound to protein.

Excreted mainly in the faeces, which contain both unabsorbed or exogenous zinc and endogenous zinc excreted in the bile, in pancreatic and intestinal juices and in sloughed-off intestinal cells. Also excreted in the sweat and urine. Daily body zinc losses amount in women to 1.6mg and in men to 2.2mg with an extra 0.6mg in each seminal emission.

Deficiency due to insufficient dietary intake is seen in those not eating very much meat, particularly if their diet is rich in phytate (e.g., unleavened bread). Malabsorption, increased excretion by the kidneys and increased requirement are other causes of deficiency that may be brought about by drug treatment with corticosteroids and the contraceptive pill, liver and kidney disease and diabetes, pregnancy and alcoholism.

Requirement   No UK RDA. EC and US RDA is 15mg.

Toxicity Prolonged high intakes may lead to copper deficiency, impaired immune response and reduced serum HDL ('good' cholesterol) levels. Medically unsupervised supplementation should not exceed 15mg daily.

Distribution in foods (in mg per 100g): oysters, 45.0; liver, 4.3–7.8; meats, 2.4–4.3; Cheddar cheese, 4.0; lentils, 3.1; haricot beans, 2.8; wholemeal bread, 2.0; eggs, 1.5; chicken, 1.0; white bread, 0.8; cod, 0.4; milk, 0.35.

NUTRITIONAL HEALTH

Table 13: Relation between imperial and metric units

	Imperial		Approximate metric equivalent	
Weight	1 ounce (oz)	28.4	grams (g)	
	3.5 oz	100	g	
	1 pound (lb)	454	g	
	2.2 lb	1	kilogram (kg)	
	8.6 stone	55	kg	
	10.2 stone	65	kg	
	11.0 stone	70	kg	
Volume	1.8 pints (pt)	1	litre (l)	
	1 pt	568	millilitres (ml)	
	1 gallon	4.5	l	
	3.5 fluid oz	100.0	ml	
Length	1 inch (in)	2.54	centimetres (cm)	
	1 foot (ft)	30.5	cm	
	39.4 in	100	cm	
		or 1	metre (m)	
Temperature	32° Fahrenheit (F)	0°	Centigrade (Celcius) (C)	
	212° F	100°	C	
	To convert F° into C°: -32 and then $\times \dfrac{5}{9}$			

Table 14: Atomic weights and symbols of nutritionally important elements

Element	Symbol	Atomic weight	Element	Symbol	Atomic weight
calcium	Ca	40	manganese	Mn	55
carbon	C	12	molybdenum	Mo	96
chlorine	Cl	35.5	nitrogen	N	14
chromium	Cr	52	oxygen	O	16
copper	Cu	63.5	phosphorus	P	31
fluorine	F	19	potassium	K	39
hydrogen	H	1	selenium	Se	79
iodine	I	127	sodium	Na	23
iron	Fe	56	sulphur	S	32
lead	Pb	207	tin	Sn	119
magnesium	Mg	24	zinc	Zn	65.5

NUTRITIONAL HEALTH

Table 15: Quantities and concentrations

1 kilogram (kg)	= 1,000 grams (g)
1g	= 1,000 micrograms (μg, mcg)
1μg	= 1,000 nanograms (ng)
1ng	= 1,000 picograms (pg)

1 litre (l)	= 1,000 millilitres (ml)
	or 100 centilitres (cl)
	or 10 decilitres (dl)
1dl	= 100 ml
1cl	= 10 ml

mg/kg (or μg/g) are parts per million (ppm).
μg/kg (or ng/g) are parts per billion (ppb), or per thousand million.
ng/kg or (pg/g) are parts per trillion (ppt), or per million million.

Table 16: Dietary restrictions practised by religious and ethnic groups

Group	Animal foods eaten	Particular practices	Alcohol
Hindus	Mostly vegetarian. No beef. Fish rarely.	Fasting periods common.	None
Muslims	Halal meat (bled to death in presence of a Muslim who dedicates it to God). No pork. No shell-fish.	Regular fasting including one month Ramadan.	None
Sikhs	Meat from animals killed by one head-blow. No beef.	Generally less rigid than Hindus and Muslims.	None
Jews	Kosher meat (bled to death in Rabbi's presence, then soaked and salted). No pork. Fish with scales and fins.	Meat and dairy foods consumed at separate meals.	Yes
Rastafarians	Vegans who also take milk.	Foods must be organic, I-tal or alive, so no processed foods eaten. No salt added.	None No coffee.

INDEX OF TABLES

INDEX OF FIGURES

BIBLIOGRAPHY

The A to Z of Health Food Terms M. Balfour, J. Allen, (Garnstone Press 1973)

The Bread and Flour Regulations 1984, No. 1304 (HMSO)

McCance & Widdowson's *The Composition of Foods* A. Paul and D. Southgate (HMSO, 4th edition 1978 and First, Second, Third and Fourth Supplements)

'Diet and Cardiovascular Disease' Report by the Committee on Medical Aspects of Food Policy. *Report on Health and Social Subjects No. 28* (DHSS 1984)

The Dietary and Nutritional Survey of British Adults 1990 J. Gregory, K. Foster, H. Tyler, M. Wiseman (HMSO), Commissioned by MAFF and DoH, carried out by the Social Services Division of the Office of Populations Censuses and Surveys in 1986–7.

Eating for Health (DHSS 1979)

The Food Safety Act 1990 (HMSO)

Food Composition and Nutrition Tables 1981/82 (Wissenschaftliche Verlagsgesellschaft mbH, Stuttgart 1981)

The Food Labelling Regulations 1984, No. 1305 (HMSO)

Food Processing and Nutrition A. Bender (Academic Press 1978)

Food Science, a Chemical Approach B. Fox and A. Cameron (Hodder and Stoughton, London, 4th edition 1982)

'Foods which simulate meat' *Report on Health and Social Subjects No. 17* (DHSS 1980)

Harper's Review of Biochemistry D. Martin, P. Mayes, V. Rodwell and D. Granner (Lange Medical Publications, Los Altos, California, USA, 22nd edition 1990)

Human Nutrition and Dietetics S. Davidson, R. Passmore, J. Brock and A. S. Truswell (Churchill Livingstone, Edinburgh, 7th edition 1979)

Look at the Label (MAFF Publication revised 1984)

Manual of Nutrition (MAFF/HMSO, 9th Edition 1985)

The Merck Index (Merck Scharp and Dohme, 9th edition 1976)

NUTRITIONAL HEALTH

Nutrition Reviews: Present Knowledge in Nutrition (Nutrition Foundation, 5th edition 1984)

Nutritional and Safety Aspects of Food Processing Editor S. Tannenbaum (M. Dekker Inc., USA 1979)

A Discussion Paper on 'Proposals for Nutritional Guidelines for Health Education in Britain', prepared for the National Advisory Committee on Nutritional Education by an *ad hoc* working party under the Chairmanship of Professor W. P. T. James, Health Education Council, 1983

'Recommended Daily Amounts of Food Energy and Nutrients for Groups of People in the United Kingdom' *Report on Health and Social Subjects No. 15* (DHSS 1981) (HMSO)

Recommended Dietary Allowances National Research Council (National Academy Press, Washington D.C., 10th edition, 1989)

Review of Medical Physiology W. Ganong (Lange Medical Publications, Los Altos, California, USA, 11th edition 1983)

Science Since 1500 H. Pledge (HMSO 1939)

Sweeteners in Food Regulations 1983, No. 1211 as amended 1988, No. 2112 (HMSO)

'The Use of Very Low Calorie Diets in Obesity' *Report on Health and Social Subjects No. 31* (DHSS 1987)

The Vitamins: Their Role in Medical Practice D. J. Marks (MTP Press 1985)

The following periodicals:
American Journal of Clinical Nutrition
Atherosclerosis
Biological Trace Element Research
British Journal of Cancer
British Journal of Clinical Practice
British Journal of Nutrition
British Medical Journal
Chemist and Druggist
Chemistry and Industry
Clinical Biochemistry
Drug Metabolism Reviews
Food Additives and Contaminents
Food and Chemical Toxicology
Human Toxicology
Journal of the American College of Nutrition
Journal of Food Science
Journal of Laboratory and Clinical Medicine
Journal of the National Cancer Institute

NUTRITIONAL HEALTH

The Lancet
Mineral and Electrolyte Metabolism
New England Journal of Medicine
Nutrition Bulletin
Nutrition Reviews